Post-Conflict Reconstruction

Liverpool Hope University Studies in Ethics Series
Series Editor: Dr David Torevell
Series Deputy Editor: Dr Jacqui Miller

Volume One:
Engaging Religious Education
Editors: Joy Schmack, Matthew Thompson and David Torevell with Camilla Cole

Volume Two:
Reservoirs of Hope: Sustaining Spirituality in School Leaders
Author: Alan Flintham

Volume Three:
Literature and Ethics: From the Green Knight to the Dark Knight
Editors: Steve Brie and William T. Rossiter

Volume Four:
Post-conflict Reconstruction
Editor: Neil Ferguson

Post-Conflict Reconstruction

Edited by

Neil Ferguson

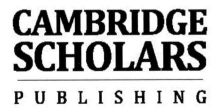

CAMBRIDGE
SCHOLARS

P U B L I S H I N G

Post-Conflict Reconstruction, edited by Neil Ferguson

This book first published 2010

Cambridge Scholars Publishing

12 Back Chapman Street, Newcastle upon Tyne, NE6 2XX, UK

British Library Cataloguing in Publication Data
A catalogue record for this book is available from the British Library

ISBN (10): 1-4438-2578-6, ISBN (13): 978-1-4438-2578-8

CONTENTS

FOREWORD

Explicitly or implicitly, issues of ethics underpin every aspect of life, as
public institutions and private individuals make decisions that will inform
their own welfare and the lives of others. The ethical impulse and its deter-
mination has recently gained considerable intellectual attention, as many
in the academy seek to understand the moral challenges and opportunities
their own subject area presents. This series, which flows naturally from
Liverpool Hope University's unique mission, is distinctive in its multidisciplinary range and encompasses arts and humanities, social sciences,
business and education. Each volume is informed by the latest research and
poses important questions for academics, students and all those who wish
to reflect more deeply on the values inherent within different disciplines.
Bringing together international subject specialists, the series explores the
complexities of ethics, its theoretical analysis and its practical applications
and through the breadth of contributing subjects, demonstrates that understanding ethics is central to contemporary scholarship.

INTRODUCTION

The challenge posed by violence and conflict at all levels of abstraction from intra-individual violence, such as self-harming, to collective inter-group violence aimed at achieving political, social or economic power has been cited by the World Health Organization as the greatest challenge the world will face in this millennium (Krug et al., 2002). The size of the problem created by collective violence in particular is clear in just a few statistics. Approximately 191 million people lost their lives to political violence and warfare in the twentieth century and since the turn of the century it is estimated that approximately four million more have died in armed conflict. Since the end of the Second World War there have been over 190 armed conflicts and every region of the world currently endures armed conflict with 28 conflicts taking place in 24 different countries in 2008 which result in at least 1,000 combat deaths per year. However, the distribution across the regions of the globe is not even, with Africa and Asia being the most affected by war with 11 armed conflicts apiece, or almost 80% of the world's total armed conflicts (*Armed Conflicts Report 2009*).

In addition to these current conflicts raging across the globe many more societies face the challenge of rebuilding post-conflict societies; some 30 conflicts ended in the period from 1999 to 2008 while many more communities endure the violence created by low intensity conflict and terrorism (*Armed Conflicts Report 2009*). This post-conflict recovery does not happen in the immediate aftermath of the hot conflict, indeed it is rare that the signing of the peace accord or the ending of formal hostilities automatically brings a return to normality in these fractured societies. It is more likely that the scarred societies face a period in the twilight between war and peace, a time when the world turns its attention to new problems and seemingly more pressing matters, leaving the country to struggle towards peace and a new social order.

This book is the result of conversations between staff and associates of the Desmond Tutu Centre for War and Peace Studies against the backdrop of the war in Iraq and the unfolding violent aftermath caused by the invasion in 2003. These conversations began by discussing just war theory and how the events in Iraq illustrated the need to reformulate the theory to include *jus post bellum* responsibility alongside establishing the right to go to war and the correct conduct within war. These conversations widened and developed into a discussion about how to right the wrongs of war and begin to repair the damage inflicted by conflict. This damage was not viewed purely in the terms of the cold statistics proffered earlier, or the cost in billions of US dollars it would take to rebuild splintered infrastructure; instead it included the *philosophical*, e.g. reasoning about the nature of war and peace; the *physical*, e.g. the economic, material and physical features of conflict and conflict resolution; the *political*, e.g. the role of local, regional and international actors in reconstructing civil society; the *psychological*, e.g. dealing with the psychological trauma of conflict; and the *sociological*, e.g. restructuring society and building rebuilding social relationships. This volume of the Hope Ethics Series, with its multidisciplinary range of approaches to post-conflict reconstruction, both reflects and further develops these conversations by bringing together members and associates of the Desmond Tutu Centre for War and Peace Studies with other researchers in this area to assemble a cross-disciplinary exploration of current, historical and hypothetical approaches to post-conflict reconstruction and provide some answers to the questions being posed within the Desmond Tutu Centre at Liverpool Hope University.

The main aim of this book is to inquire into the creation of the conditions necessary for the development first of 'negative' peace (dealing with the hot conflict and preventing a return to conflict) and then paving the way to allow the development of 'positive' peace and the removal of structural violence (see Galtung, 1981). The book's contributors deal with the challenges to creating the foundations for positive peace from a variety of perspectives, some of which, such as politics, development studies and even psychology, are normally found in books on peacebuilding and post-conflict reconstruction, but some of the perspectives offered here, such as those from neuroscience, sports studies, the visual arts and psychoanalysis, are atypical. This breadth of perspectives offers innovative insights into the grey space between war and peace, which is home to millions of people across the globe. Many of the contributors take a case study approach and explore this transition from war to peace by examining conflicts and peace building interventions taking place in various countries across the world. To some extent, the range of countries focused on reflects the uneven distribution of the world's conflict and post-conflict zones with the chapters considering post-conflict recovery in Afghanistan, Bosnia, the Congo, Israel, Liberia,

Northern Ireland, Rwanda and Sierra Leone.

In the first chapter **Beverly Metcalfe** examines the role of women in peacebuilding and post-conflict reconstruction. Her chapter draws on a number of case studies with a particular focus on the work of women's NGOs in Afghanistan and Rwanda. Her evaluation of these initiatives demonstrates the considerable and varied role women play in post-conflict reconstruction. Chapter 1 also offers a critique of the dominant views of the role of men and women in conflict which view men as active, territorial and aggressive, while women are perceived as inherently passive, nurturing and peaceable. Metcalfe also explores the impact these views have on women's roles in conflict and peace building.

Chapter 2 demonstrates how sport can be utilized to promote peace and post-conflict recovery through building human relationships. In this chapter **Joel Rookwood** and **Stefan Wassong** evaluate the benefits and limitations of the use of sporting activities to build bridges between fractured communities by comparing and contrasting three different sports programmes (based in the Congo, Israel and Liberia) aimed at building better community relations. Their discussions of these programmes should provide practitioners with some important lessons on how to develop and employ sporting activities as effective tools in post-conflict reconstruction.

Neil Ferguson (Chapter 3) explores the role and impact of Northern Irish integrated school sector and school based cross-community contact initiatives which bring Protestant and Catholic children and adolescents together with the aim of fostering better relationships between these divided communities. The chapter reviews the research examining the impact integrated education has had on attitudes towards members of the other community, increasing cross-community contact, developing friendship ties with children and adolescents across community divides and how these longstanding peace-building interventions can alter the seemingly intractable conflicting ethno-political identities which fuel segregation and sectarianism in post-agreement Northern Ireland.

Ruth Leitch stays with the post-conflict environment of Northern Ireland in Chapter 4 where she summarizes and evaluates an arts based initiative, the Enabling Young Voices Project (EYV), which aims to assess the level and nature of victimhood among young people in post-agreement Northern Ireland. Her chapter examines the impact of the Northern Irish 'Troubles' on children and adolescents, before moving on to discuss both the pedagogical and research facets of the EYV project in depth. Leitch's chapter also employs the first-hand accounts of children and teachers who were involved with the project to illustrate how the conflict and associated community divisions impact on children and the wider community. Leitch's evaluation demonstrates the challenges faced in breaking the silence around issues of trauma and fear which need to be dealt with in order to allow Northern Irish society to move forward towards recovery and reconciliation.

Issues around trauma and post-conflict trauma recovery are further analysed by **Eve Binks** in Chapter 5. Binks provides a detailed exploration of the psychological impact of exposure to political violence. Her chapter illustrates how violence not only harms the intended target, but can have a devastating impact on those who witness it or know the victim, and on the wider community and even future generations. Binks explores psychological trauma, focusing on the psychological consequences of coping with political conflict while evaluating which coping strategies work and those which pose additional harm. Binks then moves on to discuss how to psychologically recover in the post-conflict space and begin to heal the unseen wounds conflict causes.

Frank Wood's (Chapter 6) novel application of observations from neuroscience and brain complexity dynamics to the understanding of how and why post-conflict environments have the propensity to spiral destructively back into conflict are both thought-provoking and original. This chapter examines how the interconnections between parts of the human brain mirror communication processes and relationships between individuals and groups in wider society. Wood develops these neuroscience insights to generate a research agenda and a set of hypotheses which should offer guidance to policy makers, researchers and practitioners in future post-conflict reconstruction activities.

Paddy Greer in Chapter 7 follows on from Frank Wood in offering a further fresh and novel perspective of reconstruction in post-conflict societies. Greer critically examines the role of post-conflict reconstruction in attempting to re-create an anodyne imitation of the pre-conflict environment devoid of meaning and cleansed of the physical signs of conflict and the trauma of war. Greer builds his critique of international post-conflict reconstruction efforts around Lacanian psychoanalytical principles, focusing on the rebuilding of the Stari Most bridge in Mostar, Bosnia. Greer argues that the rebuilt bridge has become a symbol of the absence of peace and potential for future violence in Bosnia instead of the symbol of reconciliation it was envisioned to be by the international community. Chapter 7 concludes by warning that peace building needs empowered citizens, not international efforts which homogenize and disenfranchise.

The final three chapters (8, 9 and 10) all explore the use of Disarmament,

Demobilization and Reintegration (DDR) processes to assist in building peace in post-conflict societies. In Chapter 8, **John Kabia** explores the transitional period after conflict has officially ended and the society is beginning the process of reconstruction by focusing on post-conflict recovery in both Liberia and Sierra Leone. Kabia does this by evaluating the effectiveness of domestic, regional and international peace building efforts taking place in these countries to promote effective DDR and Security Sector Reform (SSR). This chapter concludes that while remarkable progress has been made in building peace and security in both countries, each still faces considerable problems which threaten further recovery and reconstruction.

Neil Ferguson (Chapter 9) further examines the DDR processes which have become a critical aspect of contemporary post-conflict reconstruction activity. Firstly in Chapter 9, Ferguson discusses and defines what DDR entails before exploring the unique case of DDR in Northern Ireland after the signing of the Good Friday (or Belfast) Agreement in 1998. To achieve this Chapter 9 focuses on the decommissioning of paramilitary weapons against the backdrop of security normalization and the release of politically motivated prisoners. Ferguson also discusses the reality of the reintegration of these former combatants into the post-conflict society and their role in both the maintenance and transformation of the conflict in Northern Ireland.

In the final chapter (10) **Ross McGarry** stays with the issues around DDR and focuses on the relatively unexamined area around the homecoming of combat troops who were deployed to fight in conflicts overseas and their reintegration into a non-militarised environment free from political conflict on their return. McGarry does this by focusing on homecoming British soldiers returning from recent military operations in Iraq and Afghanistan. Chapter 10 explores the consequences of being exposed to these conflicts for the returning soldiers and the challenges they face on their initial return to the UK and after their demobilization from the British Army. To add depth to this analysis, McGarry utilizes the first-hand accounts of four ex-soldiers who served in either Iraq or Afghanistan to highlight the problems faced by both the veterans of these conflicts, but also the agencies tasked with their care and support.

As a collection, these chapters offer a glimpse of the multifaceted nature of post-conflict reconstruction and should inspire readers from multidisciplinary backgrounds to widen their conceptions of what is required to rebuild societies after violent conflict, or build bridges in divided communities still under the shadow of political violence. Hopefully in addition to provoking thought and awareness, this book will cause readers to consider developing new approaches or reflect on how to improve current peacebuilding interventions which in turn will be put into practice in post-conflict environments across the globe.

References

Armed Conflicts Report 2009. 2009. Retrieved 9 August 2010 from http://www.ploughshares.ca/libraries/ACRText/ACR-TitlePage.html

Galtung, J. 1981. 'Cultural Violence', *Journal of Peace Research* 27(3): 291–305.

Krug, E. G., et al. 2002. *World Report on Violence and Health*. Geneva. World Health Organization.

CHAPTER ONE

FEMINISM, GENDER AND THE ROLE OF WOMEN'S NGOS IN PEACEBUILDING AND RECONSTRUCTION

BEVERLY DAWN METCALFE AND PAUL BARRY

The UN Security Council Resolution 1325 on *Women Peace and Security*, signed on 31 October 2000, reflected a commitment to women's peace activism. It brought together member states to provide for women and girls in war to ensure full participation of women in humanitarian, conflict resolution, peacebuilding and post-conflict initiatives. This marked a change for global policy interventions regarding women's roles in conflict and reconstruction efforts for civil society, and challenged dominant stereotypes of both men's and women's roles in war and reconstruction. Women's resistance to violence is widely believed to be a resistive force in both local and national movements. This raises concerns about women's and men's essentialism: are men inherently territorial and aggressive and women naturally nurturing and peaceable? Or do the interactions of men and women constitute the social relations of power? This chapter considers some of these issues in relation to women's movements and women's peace organizations in mobilizing to support post-conflict rehabilitation as well as negotiating and participating in peacebuilding alliances, strategies, and networks. The chapter draws on a number of cases, specifically Rwanda and Afghanistan, to illustrate women's activism in fighting for peace, negotiating for peace and reconstructing civil society. As part of the debate the chapter critiques dominant views about women's role in war and conflict. We suggest that essentializing accounts of women as wives, mothers and caretakers discourages their inclusion in political tactical areas, as well as undermining support for other marginalized groups. While we do not want to underplay the significance of women's movements and peace organizations, we stress that all of humanity should recognize that men and women are violated emotionally, economically and politically by war.

While much of the work on conflict resolution focusses on the government or public level, the resolution of contemporary conflict is very much a holistic process that is simultaneously conducted at the private, grassroots level (Metcalfe & Rees, 2010; Metcalfe, 2010). Many of the efforts under way to sustain peace in countries and regions beset by, or emerging from, violent conflict are undertaken by grassroots organizations formed by those whose lives are most directly and significantly affected by the conflict. A substantial proportion of these organizations are formed and staffed by women. These non-governmental organizations (NGOs) are playing an increasingly active role in dispute resolution and post-conflict reconstruction and peacebuilding (Al-Ali, 2003).

In the following chapter we expand gender theorizing in post-conflict scenarios and women's involvement in war. We consider alternative understandings of peace processes and outline gender perspectives of conflict at the interpersonal, meso and macro levels. We argue that women's NGOs' efforts have evolved gradually, but these organizations are now considered key stakeholders by international organizations in post-reconstruction victim support, political campaigning and, significantly, seen as vital by UN agencies in assisting war efforts. We also maintain, however, that in some geographic territories women's access to political advocacy and engagement in post-conflict reconstruction is curtailed by commitment to patriarchal regimes, and reform will not move forward until additional international support is given.

Theorizing Gender in War, Conflict and Reconstruction of Civil Society

The concept of "gender" relates to all the qualities of what it is to be a man or a woman, socially and culturally rather than biologically determined (Davis, Evans & Lorber, 2006). This relates to the way society defines appropriate behaviour and access to power resources for men and women, and in practice has referred to the way women are generally discriminated against and have less access to positions of power than men. In development studies of women in third world states, gender analysis of social systems, state formation and international relations study the broader interconnecting relationships through which women are subordinate in society, in the division of labour in the household and economy, in access to resources (including shelter and education) and responsibilities, attributes and capabilities and, finally, in power and privilege in the economic and political realm (Kabeer, 1994).

Research into gender relations has been particularly influential on the field of development studies (Moser, 1989, 1993; Kabeer, 1994), based on the underlying conceptual rationale that because men and women play different roles in society, they often have different needs. Therefore, when identifying and implementing gender planning needs it is important to disaggregate households and families within communities on the basis of gender (Moser, 1989). Consequently, current debates on war, and the emerging discussion on men, women and violence and war, can be traced to feminist theorizing of patriarchal relations in society (Ridd & Callaway, 1987; Davis, 2006). This rests on essentialist accounts presenting men and women as having different but complementary roles in the home and economic sphere. This holds that men are inherently territorial and aggressive, and that women are inherently nurturing and peaceable. Alternatively, cultural theorists point to the importance of cultural conditioning in shaping a myriad of different gender roles and identities (Ashfar, 2007). We will expand on these perspectives in our discussion of Rwanda and Afghanistan.

In contrast to the development field of gender planning and analysis, there is limited literature on the gendered processes of conflict management and peacebuilding, although it is now growing (Moser, 1989, 1983; Pankhurst, 2008). The limited scholarship has been criticized for failing to recognize that international and national structures of power and patterns of

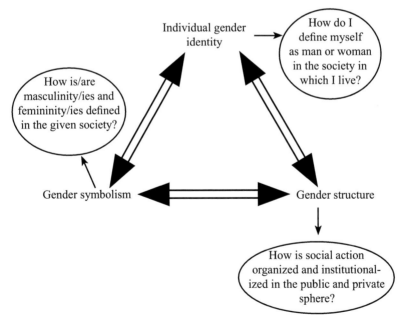

Fig. 1-1. Reimann's Gender Triangle (2002: 5)

resource allocation, which may contribute to conflict, are based on a range of inequalities or differences. Inequality can emanate from a number of different dimensions including regional, social, ethnic, religious and gender identities. Cordula Reimann (2002) illustrates the dynamics of gender relations in the form of a "Gender Triangle" which describes gender in three ways: the individual gender identity (how one defines oneself as a man or woman in society); the symbolism signifier (how masculinity and femininity are defined in a given society); and the structure of gender (how social action is organized and institutionalized in the public and private sphere).

Reimann, in line with many critical theory scholars (Metcalfe, 2010), views gender identity as a transformative concept that can be defined by social norms and notions of fluid masculinities and femininities, which in turn can be based on the distribution of labour in the public and private spheres. Gendered power relations are reconfigured by a myriad of processes – for example an occupation may become feminized if the majority of its practitioners are female, and thus devalued; similarly the dominance of men in political leadership and as heads of international organizations or clans/tribes conveys symbolism and imagery of masculinism with power and authority. Men thus embody and signify authority and power (Metcalfe, 2008b). Reimann, like many gender scholars, highlights the power relations and distribution inherent in everyday working and cultural practices. While the framework is useful in unravelling marginalization and difference, it is important to recognize the intersecting dynamics of other signifiers such as race, ethnicity and class. The role of women in NGOs and peacebuilding activities is thus marked by the variety of ways in which women's competencies, identities and relations are subordinate. In war and conflict these gender relations frame the dynamic of interactions in multiple ways.

The social, political and institutional relations are similarly complex in respect of perspectives on peace. The nature of peace was defined by Johan Galtung (1981) as either "negative" (simply an end to hostilities) or "positive" (a sustainable peace). Galtung's approach to conflict resolution states that for truly positive peace, structures must be found that remove the causes of wars and offer alternatives to war. In a positive peace all major conflicts of interest, as well as violence, should be resolved, and society be based on an active and egalitarian civil society, inclusive democratic political structures and equity between ethnic groups and races. Gender and peacebuilding researchers, notably Pankhurst, insist that gender equality must be included in this list (Pankhurst, 2002, 2003, 2008). If women are not included in this list then this ignores the serious impacts on women of post-conflict situations, and other forms of abuse and mass violence.

In order to achieve the ultimate goal of a 'positive peace', a true understanding of the nature of gendered dynamics of conflict is necessary. Conflicts are multilayered and multidimensional and can exist from the local to international level, and they may move in and out and across these arenas. This has been categorized by Lewer in four broad but interlinked levels (Lewer, 1999: 5):

1. the intrapersonal – individual understanding of the root causes of conflict
2. the micro level or interpersonal – conflict between communities or groups
3. the meso level – conflict involving militant groups, local government, UN agencies, international nongovernmental organizations (INGO) and local NGOs
4. the macro level – conflict at the national and international level.

There is a growing awareness among peace and conflict theorists that top-down diplomatic processes of conflict resolution alone are not effective in leading to diplomatic interaction across and between these levels. Experiences and needs in conflict and peace may vary at each level and therefore require different management interventions. As Metcalfe and Rees (2010) comment, power, politics and conflicts represent a complex network of multidimensional interests. Reimann (2002) believes conflict analysis benefits from a gender perspective which illuminates how men and women are caught up in different ways in struggles over power and resources through the fluidity of dynamic forms of gendered power relations. This incorporates different gender identities, differential access to and control over resources, political decision making and changes in gender ideologies in specific social-cultural and geopolitical contexts.

Re-Evaluating Gender Ideologies in Conflict and Peace

Gendered qualities associated with masculinity and femininity can be possessed by both men and women at different times and are historically and socially constituted. However, they are often treated as oppositional. Masculinity has been associated with objectivity, reason, autonomy, and power and production, while femininity has been equated with subjectivity, emotion, passivity, dependency and reproduction (Metcalfe, 2008b; Reimann 2002; Davis, 2006). The conventional definition of war and peace refers to these by associating aggression, violence and heroism with masculinity, and nurture, pacifism and compassion with femininity (Connell, 2002;

Connell & Messerschmidt, 2005; El-Bushra 2007; Molyneux, 1985).

Research by El-Bushra (2007) and Jones (2008) on gendered understandings of conflict reveals how gender ideologies can be manipulated in conflict which can help to construct a sense of a dominant gender identity or ethno-nationalism. This is apparent through dominant cultural discourses and everyday social practices and interaction. In some societies and cultures, being a "proper man" has become inseparable from the capacity to use force and control weapons. (This applies particularly to African nations, and also Islamic regions such as Iraq and Afghanistan. See Connell, 2002; Jacobs et al, 2000; Pankhurst, 2003.)

Warring parties often appeal to men's masculinity to encourage them to take up arms in defence of a country, ethnic group or political cause. While these dynamics are to some extent globally configured, they also vary across regions, depending on how feminine/masculine characteristics are represented and interpreted. It is fair to argue, nevertheless, that men and masculinity are seen as embodying power and authority "skills" necessary to engage in warring activities (Connell and Messerschmidt, 2005). However, as feminist commentators note, men are the primary losers in war (they dominate casualty rates), and cannot always live up to the masculine ideal (Connell, 2002). Those who refuse to fight have faced ridicule, imprisonment or even death for their lack of "courage". This highlights the importance of addressing men's needs and experiences as well as women's.

A view of femininity that concentrates on its link with motherhood, nurture and non-violence has been referred to as the "maternalist position" (Davis, 2006). "Mothering work" "naturally" rejects war, which increases with women's abilities to resolve conflicts non-violently. These perceptions feature in international development discourse, especially by those agencies that play a role in managing efforts to build peace after conflict. Unesco's Director-General Federico Mayor declared: "Women and life are synonymous terms. A woman gives life – she is the most apt at preserving it" (Reimann, 2002: 22 and UNDP, 2003). This position "ghetttoizes" women by placing them in a category of their own, removing them from the diversity of identities and experiences available to men. Research from Ridd and Callaway (1987) show how an ideology of femininity can also represent the heightened sentiments of societies in conflict. Women's bodies and women as a group have become bearers of a group's culture and identity. For example, Greek Cypriot women were said to embody a symbolic power by maintaining the ideals of chastity and motherhood. This led to the violent targeting of Greek Cypriot women by the invading Turk army as a political attack against the Greek Cypriot identity (Ridd & Callaway, 1987: 22). Bizarrely, more recent political commentary on the Iraq and Afghanistan invasions has used women's fragility and their position in an Islamic state as one of the justifications for US and allied intervention (Al-Ali, 2001; Ashfar, 2007). Appropriating the feminine then is used as an international relations tactic to justify violence (Metcalfe, 2008a, 2010). The realization that women are inextricably linked in war and conflict, irrespective of dominant mother and caring discourses, underplays the harsh realties of war-torn territories. This suggests that a number of dynamics need to be considered. These include the agency of women, the explicit recognition of the geographies of femininities/masculinities, emphasizing the interplay among local, regional and global politics and, finally, gendered notions of embodiment which undo traditional stereotypes of gender performativity.

Women, Men and War

A wealth of literature has assessed the impact of conflicts since the Cold War, as well as other forms of sexual violence. With the growth of informal wars, generally taking place within territory contested by various protagonists, the recognition grew that there were direct and terrible implications for ordinary citizens – men, women and children, amongst whose homes and livelihoods these conflicts were being fought – and that the different impacts on these groups needed to be better understood by humanitarian and aid agencies (Jacobs et al., 2000; Jones, 2008). Scholars acknowledged that disinterested bystanders do in fact contribute directly and indirectly to peace/war through their everyday social practices. Accounts of the impact of conflicts and other forms of mass violence since the Cold War show that the direct physical impacts on women are often extreme. Redin and Sirleaf (2002: 9), for example, describe with sincere compassion the serious physical impacts on women:

> Wombs punctured with guns. Women raped and tortured in front of their children. Rifles forced into vaginas. Pregnant women beaten to induce miscarriages. Foetuses ripped from wombs. Women kidnapped, blindfolded and beaten on the way to school or work. We saw the scars, the pain, the humiliation. We heard accounts of gang rapes, rape camps, and mutilation. Of murder and sexual slavery.

The acts of violence are not just physical, they victimize women and impose psychological, sexual and emotional traumas. War increases women's burden of work while failing to provide additional resources. When

managing postwar livelihoods, there is a breakdown in all services including health, financial and market services and education all of which impact
particularly heavily on women's condition.

However, the view that war threatens women's security, through essentializing sexual identity by fundamentally positioning them as victims of
war during and after wartime, needs reassessment. First, there is evidence to
suggest that women support war; they may even participate in armed combat (Jabri, 2006). The "maternalist position" is immediately put in doubt by
women's continued involvement in violent conflict – Ugandan women's role
as army combatants, for example, and a number of women's suicide campaigns
on behalf of Al-Qaeda. Women do not speak as one voice on issues on war and
peace. They are divided by political identities and allegiances. Significantly,
where women do take on peace initiatives they are often based on a pragmatic
response to desperate situations rather than on an inherently pacifist orientation.
These observations suggest that always seeing women as victims of war is to
deny the complex realities of women's embodied experience, denying them
agency as Connell and Messerschmitt (2005) argue. El-Bushra (2007) speaks
passionately about their "trauma" and "resilience", especially in Africa.
These are not the only reasons, of course. Many women become committed to peace organizations because of a sense of empowerment – resisting,
challenging, negotiating, rediscovering and planning lives after war, after
experiencing the failed politics of violence (El-Bushra, 2007). This phrase
was the common cry of Rwandan women who formed the Pro Femmes
Twesehamwe who gained government support.

Men's experiences of war, however, are also ambiguous. As Connell asserts, men in the history of social, economic and political organizing "have
predominated in the 'spectrum of violence'" (2002: 33). However, this
ambiguity rests on the fact that gender relations and femininities and masculinities are multiple and fluid (Connell and Messerschmidt, 2005). It is
important to note that war is indiscriminate in its capacity to kill, demolish
and destroy livelihoods. It touches existing differences of power and access
to resources, weakening those with already limited powers, whether men,
women or children. Women suffer through the violence and deprivation
imposed on their men, just as men are affronted and emasculated through
the abuse and belittlement of their wives, mothers and daughters. Within the
household, both men and women struggle to provide, assist and emotionally
respond to war experiences. Men, too, experience sexual violence, and it is
important not to ignore aspects of war policy that acknowledge gendered
constraints on men who take part in, or resist war.

The foregoing discussion has highlighted that the gendered international relations of women's organizations terrain is difficult to navigate due to the ingrained belief and value systems concerning women's capacity to engage in peacebuilding and reconstruction efforts, as well as the symbolism and imagery associated with war, violence and masculinity. In order to understand women's roles and experiences of war and reconstruction we need to evaluate the agency of women, the geographies of femininities/ masculinities, and global-local linkages in international power relations that determine and shape conflict, and thus help constitute gendered notions of embodiment. We argued at the beginning of the chapter that the UN 2000 1325 resolution gave impetus to women's organizations. The subsequent advance of women's organizations and their influence on war and peace processes has nevertheless been slow, especially in acknowledging gendered perspectives, and we develop these ideas in the next section.

Moving Forward: the Role of Women and NGOs and Peacebuilding

There has been growing interest in documenting women's NGOs' efforts in responding to war and post-conflict resolutions. Studies of Cambodia, El Salvador and Rwanda are amongst the many studied (see El-Bushra, 2007). Recent research has attempted to document women's peace activism. There are now a considerable number of women's peace activist organizations operating in every continent (El-Bushra, 2007; Pankhurst, 2008). While many operate at grass roots level, others have a national, regional or international profile. Activism is directed towards global issues of war and peace. Unequivocally, involving women and gender expertise in peacebuilding activities is essential for reconstituting political, legal, cultural and socio-economic and social structures so that they can deliver on gender equality goals. Gender equality brings to peacebuilding new degrees of democratic inclusiveness, faster and more durable economic growth and human and social capital recovery. Indeed, peacebuilding may well offer the single greatest opportunity to redress gender inequities and injustices of the past while setting new precedents for the future (Pankhurst, 2008). But these opportunities can be enhanced significantly, or constrained, by how the international community sets its priorities for recovery and uses its resources for peace building.

As the UN Secretary-General's 1998 report stated, "In terms of net transfers, NGOs collectively constitute the second largest source of development assistance" (El-Bushra, 2007: 133). An article in the *New York Times* just before the UN Conference on Environment and Development in 1992 cited development successes by NGOs such as the *Trickle-Up Program*, and stressed their low costs and high impact (UNDP, 2003). Women's NGOs also began to play a role in humanitarian assistance in conjunction with peacekeeping missions. They began to be referred to increasingly in UN resolutions, and some even began to meet informally with members of the UN Security Council to coordinate actions in emergency situations.

Both the number of NGOs and their involvement in national and international policy-making have increased tremendously over the last half century and especially the last several decades. At the time of the foundation of the United Nations in 1945 there were 2865 INGOs; by 1990 that number had increased to 13,591. This compared to 3443 international intergovernmental organizations and roughly 200 nation-states. More significantly, in the 1990s the importance of the NGO role began to be recognized. In human rights, development, environment and even disarmament, NGOs had begun to be recognized for their role in influencing public policy at the UN and on the ground in nation-states (UNIFEM, 2003; Pankhurst, 2002, 2008).

NGOs also matter in intractable conflicts. NGOs play a variety of both positive and negative roles, from conflict resolvers doing Track II diplomacy, to development aid and humanitarian assistance, which can exacerbate or reduce conflict, to human rights advocacy, to election monitoring, to disarmament and to environmental work. Mary Robinson, the UN Commissioner for Human Rights 1997–2002, has stressed the importance of both development aid and conflict resolution organizations being sure, first of all, that they do no harm.

At the 2005 UN World Summit, world leaders reaffirmed the important role of women in conflict prevention, resolution and peacebuilding (UNDP, 2006). They called for the full and effective implementation of the 2000 Security Council Resolution 1325 (referred to in the introduction of this chapter) on Women and Peace and Security. This new resolve for integrated approaches to peacebuilding became a core rationale for the creation of the Peace Building Commission (PBC). In making gender equality the PBC's only thematic mandate, a new doctrinal imperative was created for ensuring systematic attention and resources to the advancement of gender equality within transitional recovery, reintegration and reconstruction efforts.

Indeed, the reality for women in post-conflict situations has grown increasingly difficult as the impact of HIV/AIDS interacts with the effects of poverty, natural disasters and environmental degradation. As the case discussion of Afghanistan shows, the dissolution of strong governance regimes and the criminalization of society endanger NGO efforts. Consequently, today, women in the aftermath of crisis have perilously little protection or access to services, justice, economic security or citizenship. Delivery to meet basic needs and safeguard fundamental rights is unrepentantly lacking. We shall turn to the challenges for the capacity building of women's peace organizations, but now continue with case studies.

Women's Activism, Peace and Reconstruction Efforts

Feminist social science research indicates that women generally are more collaborative than men and thus more inclined toward consensus and compromise (Davis et al, 2006). Women often use their role as mothers to cut across international borders and internal divides. Every effort to bridge divides, even if initially unsuccessful, teaches lessons and establishes connections to help nurture collaboration.

In several instances during the peace talks that led to the Good Friday Agreement in Northern Ireland, male negotiators walked out of sessions, leaving a small number of women like Monica McWilliams and other members of the Northern Ireland Women's Coalition at the table. These women focussed on mutual concerns and shared vision, enabling the dialogue to continue and trust to be rekindled.

During the violence of the first Intifada in the Middle East, Israeli and Palestinian women like Naomi Chazan and Sumaya Farhat-Naser created Jerusalem Link, an umbrella group of women's centres on both sides of the conflict, to convey to the public a joint vision for a just peace. In a time when both communities forbade cross-community meetings, Jerusalem Link activities were permitted because "it's just a group of women talking" (Al-Ali & Pratt, 2009).

Women, then, have played key roles in reconstruction, peacebuilding and managed civil society developments. To demonstrate that feminist critiques of war and conflict should be an ongoing concern for development and security specialists we discuss in detail the cases of Rwanda and Afghanistan, two cases that had very different outcomes for women's status, citizenship and basic human rights.

The Politics of Gender and Reconstruction in Afghanistan

The plight of women in Afghanistan was presented as a humanitarian crisis in the aftermath of 9/11 and the efforts to restore women's rights were explicit in American foreign policy at the time. However, women's oppression and subordination and the poverty and strife of the Afghan population were long established. As Ameena[1] explained, the "tragedy of Afghanistan started with the former Soviet Union which along with its brutalities, paved the way for Islamic regimes" (Ahmed-ghosh, 2006:115). The Russian occupation from 1979 to1989 was characterized by a growing reliance on humanitarian aid and the destruction of the rural economy through counterinsurgency. Rural populations were forced to Afghan cities and refugee camps in Pakistan and Iran. Between 1979 and 1989 an estimated 6 million people fled their homes and became refugees (Emadi, 2008). During this period women's NGOs assisted with a range of welfare and health interventions but faced resistance and an ongoing legitimacy battle with the governing regime. The Islamic state of Afghanistan led by President Rabbani and established in 1992 failed to establish control of the country's territory and the country fell into sectarian warfare. These sectarian struggles were ingrained in everyday culture. Emadi (2008) argues that historically there seemed to be an absence of moral discourse of statehood and governance. In the power struggles that followed, regional warlords acted with impunity and perpetrated forms of extortion that disrupted trade and markets. This period of lawlessness witnessed some of the worst human rights abuses in Afghanistan's history (Emadi, 2008; Kandiyoti, 2007). The Taliban gradually took control of the country and in 1996, after taking Kabul, controlled approximately 90% of the constituencies, backed by foreign oil companies who wanted to secure Afghanistan as a pipeline route. The Taliban led by Mullah Omar promised to restore the rule of law, based on conservative interpretations of Islam influenced primarily by Wahhabi and Pashtun tribal traditions.[2] The Taliban regime recruited by force young Afghan men to enforce laws, and introduced measures to socially control women and gender relations. These included strict dress codes, restricted mobility for women, denying women access to education, reducing the marrying age and enforcing marriages, and removing women from the majority of public roles. Coupled with this there was the further erosion of local livelihoods, criminalization of the economy and an increase in human trafficking which created many advantages for men.

After the fall of the Taliban in 2001 through international intervention, coalition parties formed the Bonn agreement which mapped a framework for state building and reconstruction (Kandiyoti, 2007). Since the fall of the Taliban, many would agree that the political and cultural position of Afghan women has improved substantially. The Afghan constitution states that "the citizens of Afghanistan – whether man or woman – have equal rights and duties before the law". Women have been allowed to return to work, primarily in education and women's health roles. The government no longer forces them to wear the all covering burqa (though many do) and, through quota systems, they have even been appointed to prominent positions in the government. Despite all these changes many challenges still remain. Following Bonn a new constitution was established with a new structure, a lower house (*wolsei jirga*) and an upper house (*meshrano jirga*), where women's political representation was enshrined in law. On the other hand, Article 3 on "Islam and Constitutionality" states that no law can be contrary to the sacred religion of Islam. This declaration of Afghanistan as an Islamic state has been a means of defusing political power struggles in Afghanistan, with its ethically diverse populations, and in institutionalizing male authority. The political tensions between ethnic and political constituencies create a climate for women's struggles which is divisive. Furthermore, women may adopt diverse strategies rather than converge around a common agenda. That said, although women are in parliamentary seats, women are still excluded from the bodies of local governance dispute resolution in tribal *jirgas* and *shuras* which are all-male assemblies.

In her empirical assessment of Afghanistan's parliamentary system Emadi (2008) stresses that the majority of male parliamentarians are against female quotas and see it as a violation of men's rights. Women's capacity to engage in meaningful state building and reconstruction activities and policy planning is continually undermined, as allegiance is first to diverse conservative political parties in respect of ethnic, religious and factional identities (see also Kandiyoti, 2007). And, where decisions have been made by female parliamentarians, culturally the subsequent decisions taken by male members have proved to be final and binding, rendering prior collective decisions by female parliamentarians insignificant and invalid. This means that women's political voice has simply been made quite powerless as they can in effect be overruled by male decisions.

Repression is further evident if one examines cultural and social practices. In rural areas many families still restrict their own mothers', daughters', wives' and sisters' participation in public life. They are still forced into marriages and denied a basic education. Schools for girls have been burned down and little girls have even been poisoned to death for daring to go to school. UNDP indicators for human well-being (latest figures 2007) show that female illiteracy is 89%, that only 30% of the female population has access to education and the life expectancy for women is only 44 (Al-Ali & Pratt, 2009; Metcalfe, 2010), figures that are significantly lower than those of men in Afghanistan. Although national governmental machinery has formulated a development plan and sought to develop women's rights, little progress has been made (Emadi, 2008). Women's agency is intertwined with the National Development Framework which outlines market led and privatization processes for institution and state building. Historically some women's NGOs such as the Revolutionary Association of Women of Afghanistan (RAWA) were treated as enemies of the state and of the ruling parties because they advocated secular economic and political reform, and continuously fought for legitimacy. Much of their work was, therefore, of necessity done through informal means. Other women's organizations currently working in Afghanistan, such as 'Asraf', are very firmly committed to an Islamic state and want to play a role in raising women's health and education standards, and take a non-political stance (Emadi, 2008). This would mean raising education standards but within prescribed limits. The cultural, social and political environment thus make it difficult for women collectively to organize and develop resistance strategies. Kandiyoti (2007) argues that women's NGO efforts need to form broad cross-gender, multi-ethnic and tribal political alliances, and wonders whether this can be achieved under a regime that is pursuing economic liberalization and democratic governance, firmly underpinned by an Islamic conservative philosophy. Emadi (2008) similarly argues that more radical reform is required, urging women to unite. Ahmed-gosh (2006) further argues that a rights-based discourse as currently conceptualized is not appropriate since it is based on the 1948 Declaration of Human Rights which was written for western, secular individualistic societies and does not represent the constitutional framework of Islamic states. She states education is the way forward and that women can be empowered through institutional building efforts that tackle literacy specifically, and that are devised in accordance with Afghan women's social and cultural needs.

Consequently, the legal rights of women continue to represent an area of uncertainty, heighten political instability internally, as well as continue to face severe criticism from the international community. As commentators note, women's oppression and social status in Islamic regimes are often used to legitimize political and international relations defence efforts and tactics. The question arises as to whether this is merely expedient or a genuine concern of focussing on rights and justice. Many women continue to be imprisoned because of family law violations (i.e. refusing to marry husbands chosen by parents). Women's civic participation is largely curtailed and women are not in authority positions in legal and governmental institutions. Differences of view among women parliamentarians have hindered collective unity, and served to subjugate women's interests and concerns.

Further, growing instability and the harassment of female parliamentarians (including threatening phone calls and death threats) by conservatives and fundamentalists make it difficult for women to visit constituencies, and so hinder their public role (Kandiyoti, 2007).

One can thus argue that gender conflict is embedded in all levels of society in Afghanistan, supported by essentialist interpretations of men/women and masculine/ feminine. At the interpersonal levels women's disempowerment permits abuse, forced marriages and limited economic and political freedoms. The micro- and meso-level conflicts are intimately related as they represent multi-layered conflict between tribal communities, and disagreements amongst women's NGOs and their donors. Gender conflict is evident in the different tactics and strategies employed in the international community for reconciliation. Ahmed-gosh powerfully argues that:

> patriarchal institutions in the West will continue to wrestle their differences by using women, their bodies and their lives to play out masculinized power struggles. Women's voices are not heard: women are relegated to the status of symbols for international political battles (2006: 126).

Before rights-based activism can empower women and engender civil society institutions, it is first essential to ensure security and social and economic rights for women.

Rwanda: Empowering Women

The case of Rwanda is dramatically different from that of Afghanistan. After the genocide of 1994, the Minister of Gender and Social affairs in Rwanda, Aloisea Inyumba, represented a powerful leadership figure devising the tactics and strategy of post-conflict reform and peacebuilding. She created programmes to bury the dead, find homes for more than 300,000 orphaned children, and resettle refugees. She also served as Executive Secretary of the National Unity and Reconciliation Commission, which organized national public debates promoting reconciliation between Hutus and Tutsis, and she had been governor of Kigali-Ngali Province (UNIFEM, 2003). However, the history of Rwanda's women's status, their struggles and strife deserves sketching briefly at this point

The first Ministry for Women was established in Rwanda in 1965, but neither this nor the launch of the decade of women in 1975 had a significant impact on addressing women's legal, cultural, social and educational marginalization. The third Global Conference of Women, held in Nairobi in 1985, encouraged Rwandese women to establish the first non-governmental women's organization, *Réseau des Femmes* (RDF). Identifying rural women as a priority, its 29 founders mobilized 330 women across the country. Over the course of time, the RDF gave rise to other groups seeking to address gender imbalances, including voluntary groups that specialized in legal, business, or health issues, and co-operatives. As a result, the political party then in power, the National Revolutionary Movement for Development (MRND), set up the Union of Rwandese Women for Development (URAMA) in 1988. Pressure from URAMA gained women the right to participate in co-operatives and profit-making businesses (Powley, 2003).

Through the early 1990s, Rwandan women had been trying to combat structural problems within society such as food shortages and economic and environmental constraints. Though husbands still controlled resources and owned all the property of the family, women were becoming freer in their everyday movements. Improvements were taking place and women were very active in forming associations and in the informal sector, seeking out income-generating activities. In spite of women's minimal occupancy of political posts and lack of formal education, these groups and associations were beginning to acquire a certain political weight (Jacobs et al, 2000). Even so, social tensions in Rwanda rose during the late 1980s and early 1990s. The harassment of women in pre-genocide Rwanda mirrors the experience of women in other pre-conflict settings. Repression and rape, a gendered expression of the rising extremism, became more commonplace (Powley, 2003). As the threat of civil war loomed in the early 1990s, Hutu extremists sought to circumscribe women's roles radically. Such violence and discrimination were only exacerbated by the outbreak of genocide.

The 1994 genocide perpetrated by Hutu extremists against the Tutsi minority killed an estimated 800,000 people, traumatized survivors and destroyed the country's infrastructure, including the Parliament building. Lasting approximately 100 days, the slaughter led to civil war, with ruling powers eventually being obtained by a former guerrilla army, the RPF, which is still in power today. Between 250,000 and 500,000 women were raped during the 100 days of genocide. Up to 20,000 children were born to women as a result of rape. More than 67% of women who were raped in 1994 during the genocide were infected with HIV and AIDS. In many cases, this resulted from a systematic and planned use of rape by HIV+ men as a weapon of genocide.

During the nine-year period of post-genocide government, from 1994 to 2003, women's representation in parliament reached 25.7%. However, the post-genocide parliamentary elections saw women achieve nearly 50% representation (Powley, 2003). The Rwandan women's movement initially sought to narrow the gaps between men and women across all sectors of society, culminating in gender equality. However, in the aftermath of the genocide, necessity dictated a shift in both the means and the ends, as women were then entrusted with rebuilding their society, structurally and socially. With females comprising 70% of the population at the conclusion of the genocide, women assumed multiple roles as heads of household, community leaders, and financial providers, in order to meet the needs of devastated families and communities. In the years to follow, the aim of the women's movement in Rwanda would evolve from desiring a greater voice and presence in decision-making, within families and the political arena, to legally codifying the achievement of these goals (UNDP, 2006).

Today, Rwanda is governed by the Rwandan Patriotic Front (RPF), an opposition movement-turned-Tutsi political party. The RPF has made a public commitment to unity and reconciliation within the country. Acknowledging the presence, needs and potential role of the predominantly female population, the government has determined that women must be central to the process of governing, reconciling and rebuilding the country. Women who held key positions within the ranks of the RPF have been appointed to strategic posts in the transitional government. Their participation and presence has contributed to progressive gender policies within the administration (Emadi, 2008).

However, even with the implementation of such changes, the largest challenge in modern Rwanda is democratization. In a *United Nations Chronicle* article, author Consuelo Remmert points to the fact that sceptics say that the inclusion of women serves to divert attention from the absence of a more representative government, stressing that ethnic diversity is essential for the establishment of a democratic state in Rwanda. Other challenges to democracy include "Rwanda's prolonged involvement in the Democratic Republic of the Congo's civil war, accusations of human rights abuses at home, the reintegration of accused *genocidaires*, and the challenge of fostering political debate without a return to the extremism of the early 1990s " (UNDP, 2006).

Regarding the issue of inclusivity, Rwanda's government has taken unprecedented steps to increase the participation of women and young people in governance. Joseph Sebarenzi, former Speaker of the Rwandan Parliament now living in exile in the United States, acknowledges that gender representation in Rwanda "is an undeniable fact" and the government should be credited for it, despite its poor record in democracy (UNDP, 2003).

Women's contribution to Rwanda's physical reconstruction, social healing and reconciliation has been recognized and institutionalized by the government. Rwanda's transitional government has established three initiatives to ensure the inclusion of women in decision-making posts: 1) a parallel system of women's councils and women-only elections that ensures a mandate for all election bodies; 2) a triple balloting system that ensures the election of women to a set percentage of seats at both the sector and district levels; and 3) the establishment of the *Ministry for Gender and Women in Development*, as well as gender posts at all levels within Government and ministerial bodies (UNDP, 2003; UNDP, 2006).

Rwanda's new constitution, adopted in May 2003, and the sign up to CEDAW commits the government to representation of women at least 30%. This quota has been met and surpassed, as women now hold nearly 49% of Parliamentary seats, a greater proportion than in any other parliament worldwide. This could at least partially be attributed to the fact that women in government are now perceived by Rwandans as more approachable and trustworthy politicians than their male counterparts (Powley, 2003) in addition to being better at forgiveness, reconciliation and post-conflict peacebuilding.

Even discussions of national security, traditionally a male arena, highlight the public recognition of women's contributions. Women have been instrumental in stabilizing border communities. These women are credited with persuading their husbands and sons living across the border in the Democratic Republic of the Congo to leave rebel groups and return to Rwanda to reintegrate in society. The Rwanda case then represents a significant success for women's engagement and leadership in post-conflict and civil society building efforts.

In conclusion to this section, we note that while the cases of Rwanda and Afghanistan were and are materially different, they represent broader global feminist issues about women's voice in peacebuilding, reconstruction and civil society development. Using Lewer's conflict model, one could argue that gender relations in Rwanda have been completely reconfigured, since institution-building efforts have legitimized women's voice, valued women's contribution, and, most importantly, enabled them to take on roles that had normally been reserved for men. Importantly, transnational dialogue within, and across, communities in Rwanda and across geographical divides assisted peace efforts. How reconstructive efforts rely on grassroots support on the ground. In the following we discuss NGO action to assist aid processes.

The Reality of Women's NGO support?

A recent assessment of the United Nations Development Programme's work in crisis prevention and recovery exposed an comprehensive failure to integrate a gender perspective into the United Nations system's approach to early recovery, transition and reintegration (UNDP, 2003; UNIFEM, 2003;). Justice and security sector reform is the arena in which women's needs are greatest and gaps in response most glaring. Despite increasing violence against women in conflict's aftermath, their protection typically receives less attention than higher profile street crimes, homicides, political corruption, gangs and disarmament, demobilization and reintegration (DDR) initiatives (Braun, 2010). Although recent attention has been given to rape and sexual torture as weapons of war, these very same violations – when committed after a ceasefire (and often by the very same perpetrators) – tend to be recast in peacebuilding processes as private, domestic concerns (Pankhurst, 2003).

Most often, women's security is considered a "human rights" or "women's issue" rather than a security sector imperative. Yet undeniably, in many post-conflict settings, the formal security institutions charged with women's protection, namely the military, civilian police and even peacekeepers, are sometimes among the perpetrators of violence against them and frequently fail to serve as accountability institutions to which women can turn for redress and security (Braun, 2010).

Within and across post-conflict situations, there are sharp inconsistencies in the support provided by the international community to women including variations in effective women's government machinery and women's NGOs efforts. In transitional recovery, women's increased care-burdens and the gender specific impacts of macro-economic, labour and social protection policies are largely unaddressed. For example in Islamic states where conflict exists, such as Iraq and Afghanistan, women's NGOs often have to be registered with the state, and have their activities and membership controlled by the state (as our cases of Afghanistan, an Islamic state, and Rwanda, a democratic one, also revealed). The considerable variance in the standards of basic and emergency health services provided to women in different countries is often associated with the gender ideologies, funding sources and/or political affiliation of the funding partners. This is in part due to the ways in which theories of gender and difference have been formulated, which in practice have tended to marginalize and categorize and not be concerned with including all human populations. Further, the institutional frameworks for development and assistance to women are largely determined by appropriate government agencies to manage women's issues.

In Rwanda, institution-building processes including reconstruction of basic needs and services and democratization involved women and challenged traditional patriarchal relations, and reconfigured gender hierarchies. In contrast, women's status and gender relations in Afghanistan changed little. While women's representation in Afghanistan has a long history, with the Women's Grand Organization formed in 1943 (incorporated into the Ministry of Labour), the Taliban incorporated the Women's Grand Organization with the Women's Association (a Taliban-supported club), and hired men to manage the women's club, instead of women. When the Taliban regime fell in 2001, women's activism went further underground. As our case analysis shows, the creation of the Ministry of Women's Affairs in line with the Bonn Conference agreement had limited impact on women's public role and voice. Women's NGOs were just as marginalized through factions and political rivalries as they had been under Russian occupation and the Taliban. The role of women's NGOs in wars and post-conflict reconstruction is thus complex, involving many multi-layered processes, gendered power relations networks, and a fluid web of political priorities.

Developing Women's Capacity for Managing War and Peacebuilding Efforts

Our case studies suggest that there is a need for international organizations to ensure that women are fully equipped with relevant knowledge and skills to deal with the trauma and violence in post-war conflicts. Women's participation in peace negotiations and post-conflict peace consolidation is increasingly recognized as a vital contribution to long-term recovery and stability. Gender regimes that are premised on patriarchal relations position women as subordinate in both the public and private realm. Women can face profound social resistance when they take on new public roles, and often need support for their efforts to prevent conflict and build peace. Systems to protect women from sexual and gender-based violence range from weak to non-existent; transitional justice mechanisms address crimes against women unevenly, leading to gross patterns of impunity (Braun, 2010). In consequence, women are prevented from making the contribution they would like to post-conflict governance and peace consolidation, their livelihood recovery needs may be put second to the immediate employment and reintegration needs of ex-combatants, and their needs for justice and physical safety are neglected.

One of the most important on-going constraints on women's capacity to engage effectively in conflict mediation and peacebuilding is the experience of sexual and gender-based violence (SGBV) during conflict and its legacy afterwards in terms of elevated levels of gender-based violence, high levels of morbidity, and fear (Jabri, 1996; Pankhurst, 2003; Braun, 2010). The incidence or even the mere threat of sexual and gender-based violence has a profoundly inhibiting effect on women's ability to engage in conflict resolution, peacebuilding and recovery efforts. Very little is known about effective SGBV prevention strategies and support services for survivors are still inadequate.

Moreover, basic security needs are a prerequisite. A UK Department for International Development (DfID) programme aims to create enabling environments for women's effective participation in peace-building and post-conflict recovery by engaging community decision-makers, local police and informal institutions in responding to the needs of women during and after conflict. This programme supports women's community-level efforts to build peace and prevent sexual violence in six countries: Afghanistan, Haiti, Liberia, Rwanda, Timor-Leste and Uganda. The programmes identify and support the practical and effective forms of protection that women in war and armed conflict situations want and believe will enhance their safety. Programming will include building a protective social environment; building women's economic and legal resources for protecting themselves and their families; and supporting women's engagement in conflict resolution and peacebuilding. It is intended that this capacity-building initiative will result in an enhanced engagement by women in local and national peace-building processes, and provide greater empowerment of women to prevent sexual violence and other abuses of their rights.

Another important development tool has been devised by El-Bushra (2003) and is commonly used by women's groups and international organizations. She has documented a *Women's Peace Strategy* that encompasses five areas:

- **Survival and Basic Needs:** Providing food, shelter, medicine and health care to individual families that have been attacked or displaced, caring for vulnerable persons such as pregnant women and orphans during conflict.
- **Peacebuilding and Mediation:** Engaging in peace negotiations, participating in local mediation teams, demonstrating and protesting in favour of peace.
- **Advocacy:** Working with civil society, government in order to promote human rights issues.

- **Women's Inclusion in Decision Making:** Promoting women's
  rights to political participation and security, civic rights education,
  women's leadership and training.
- **Community Engagement:** Carrying out projects to integrate demobilized soldiers, support trauma counselling, peace education, justice
  and reconciliation work.

While these efforts may only touch the tip of the iceberg they are internationally recognized development themes and tools that help shape women's
capacity-building in post-conflict resolution and civil society construction.
We would argue this is an important tactical area for global feminists to
concentrate on and to continue campaigning resolutely for.

Conclusion

This chapter has explored the significance of women's organizations in
managing post-conflict resolution and in organizing strategies to help establish civil society. Clearly women's peace activism is widespread, and
in examining women's role in the field of peace and reconstruction efforts
there are huge risks in failing to understand the dynamics of power relations. For women the main challenge is to avoid essentializing signifiers
which label women as victims and politically neutral carers. The cases of
Rwanda and Afghanistan clearly show the variety of roles that women play.
Women's role in resisting organized violence and genocide has been shaped
by the context specific experiences rather than their peace-oriented natures.
In Rwanda's case it has led to institutional regimes and national machinery
of governance that have reformulated power relations between men and
women and enabled active women's voices to be heard. In contrast, in
Afghanistan institution-building efforts after war and conflict have failed
to remove everyday violence in homes and in rivalries amongst tribes. With
international assistance those women who have attained positions in parliament have faced continuous death threats and lacked opportunities to carve
space in public institutions, or for their voices to be acknowledged. It is
important to acknowledge and understand the individual agency positions
of women/men in particular regimes; the way in which the geography of
masculinities/femininities are constructed and experienced in respect of the
interplay between local and global stakeholders; and finally, within this dynamic, the complexity of power and privilege, and the differential impacts it
has on women and other marginalized groups. This is an avenue for further
research that needs to be continued by feminist development and conflict

scholars. A critical appreciation of agency, the politics of geographic location and insights into embodied subjectivities can provide rich data to help formulate development solutions. The focus on critically unravelling the social and political system and power relations is vital. Multiple forms of power and control co-exist and interact to form complex conflict settings. Devising gender sensitive approaches to plan and manage conflict resolution and peace building incorporates an appreciation that

> only when *women* as the less powerful group attain power and expand their view of how their needs should be satisfied, will *men* as powerful groups and societies be challenged to satisfy their needs and in ways that do not express, coerce or cause structural violence to less powerful groups. (Potapchuk, in Reimann, 2002: 21)

However, as our analyses demonstrate, reconstruction efforts are an ongoing process and there is no one gender development tool that is universally applicable. The case of Afghanistan clearly shows that local women need to unite and engage in rights based awareness and feminist consciousness raising efforts. Further, it seems evident that at every opportunity international organizations should encourage women's organizations active intervention in Afghanistan (Hunt Alternatives Fund, 2010). There is ample evidence, however, that this will continue to be difficult. The lack of security, the criminalized networks and the expansion of the narcotics production trade are affecting social relations and sustaining inequalities, and inhibiting women from collectivizing and organizing (Kandiyoti, 2007). Whatever the outcomes for Afghan women, to further advance feminist critiques of war, peace and conflict resolution we need to stress the interplay of a myriad of differences, framed in a diverse geographic network of different power relations. Thus, rather than view war as the violation of women by men, we should acknowledge that men and women are differently violated by war (El-Bushra, 2007).

Notes

1   Ameena established the Revolutionary Association of Women of Afghanistan (RAWA), with its headquarters in Pakistan, during the Russian occupation. She was assassinated in 1987; feminist organizations believe the KGB were responsible but there is no evidence to confirm this.
2   Wahhabism was founded in the 18th century by Abd al-Wahhab, a Hanbali (Sunni) scholar who advocated sociomoral reconstruction of society based on traditional interpretations of the Qur'an and Hadith.

References

Ahmed-gosh, H. 2006. 'Voices of Afghan women: human rights and economic development,' *International Journal of Feminist Politics*, 8(1): 110–128.

Al-Ali, N. 2003. 'Gender and civil society in the Middle East', *International Journal of Feminist Politics*, 5(2): 213–232.

Al-Ali N., and Pratt, N. 2009. *Women and War in the Middle East: Transnational Perspectives*. London. Zed Books.

Ashfar, H. 2007. 'Women, wars and citizenship, migration and identity: Some illustrations from the Middle East', *Journal of Development Studies*,43(2): 237–244.

Braun, Y.A. (2010), 'Gender, development, and sex work in Lesotho', *Equality, Diversity and Inclusion*, 29(1): 78–96.

Connell, R. W. 2002 'Masculinities, the reduction of violence and the pursuit of peace'. In Cockburn, C., and Zarkov, D. (eds.). *The Postwar Moment: Militaries, Masculinities and International Peacekeeping*. London. Lawrence and Wishart, pp. 33–40.

Connell, R. W. and Messerschmitt, J. W. 2005. 'Hegemonic masculinity: rethinking the concept', *Gender and Society*, 19(6): 829–859.

Davis, K. 2006. 'Feminist politics of location'. In Davis, K., Evans, M., and Lorber, J. *Handbook of Women's and Gender Studies*. London. Sage.

Davis, K., Evans, M. and Lorber, J. (eds). 2006. *Handbook of Women's and Gender Studies*. London. Sage.

El-Bushra, J. 2007. 'Feminism, gender and women's peace activism,' *Development and Change*, 38(1): 131–147.

Emadi, H. 2008. 'The establishment of Afghanistan parliament and the role of women parliamentarians.' *International Journal for Asian Studies* 38/12/2: 5–19.

Galtung, J. 1981. 'Cultural Violence', *Journal of Peace Research*, 27(3): 291–305.

Hutchings, K., Metcalfe, B., and Cooper, B. 2010. 'Exploring Middle Eastern women's perceptions of barriers to, and facilitators of, international management opportunities'. *International Journal of Human Resource Management,* 21(1): 61–83.

Hunt Alternatives Fund. 2010. *The Role of Women in Peace Building*. The Institute for Inclusive Security, www.huntalternatives.org.

Jabri, V. 1996. *Discourses on Violence*. Manchester. Manchester University Press.

Jacobs, S., Jacobson, R. and Marchbank, J. (eds). 2000. *States of Conflict: Gender, Violence and Resistance*. London. Zed Books.

Jones, A. 2008. *Gender Inclusive: Essays on Violence, Men, and Feminist International Relations*. London. Routledge.

Kabeer, V. 1994. *Reversed Realities: Gender Hierarchies in Development Thought*. London. Verso.

Kandiyoti, D. 2007 'Old dilemmas or new challenges? The Politics of Gender and Reconstruction in Afghanistan', *Development and Change*, 38(2): 169–199.

Lewer, N. 1999. 'Non-lethal weapons.' *Forum for Applied Research and Public Policy,* 14(2): 39–45.

Metcalfe, B. D., 2008a, 'Women, management and globalization in the Middle East', *Journal of Business Ethics,* 83(1): 85–100.

Metcalfe, B.D. 2008b. 'A feminist poststructuralist analysis of human resource development: Why bodies, power and reflexivity matter', *Human Resource Development International*, 11(5): 447–465.

Metcalfe, B. D. 2010. 'Reflections on difference: Women, Islamic feminism and development in the Middle East'. In Ozgilbin, M., and Syed, J. (eds). *Diversity Management in Asia*. Cheltenham. Edward Elgar.

Metcalfe, B. D., and Rees, C. J. 2010. 'Gender, globalization and organization: Exploring power, relations and intersections', *Equality, Diversity and Inclusion*, 24(1): 5–22.

Molyneux, M. 1985. 'Mobilisation without emancipation? Women's interests, state and revolution in Nicaragua', *Feminist Studies*, 11(2): 227–254.

Moser, C. 1989. 'Gender planning in the third world: meeting practical and strategic gender needs', *World Development*, 17(11): 1799–1825.

Moser, C. 1993. *Gender Planning and Development: Theory, Practice and Training*. New York/London. Routledge.

Pankhurst, D. 2002 'Making a Difference? The inclusion of gender into international conflict management policies'. In Braig, M., and Wolte, S. (eds). *Common Ground or Mutual Exclusion? Women's Movements and International Relations*. London. Zed Press: 129–135.

Pankhurst, D. 2003. 'Sex wars and other wars: Towards a feminist approach to Peacebuilding', *Development in Practice*, 13(2 & 3): 154–178.

Pankhurst, D. (ed.). 2008. *Gendered Peace: Women's Struggles for Post-War Justice and Reconciliation*. London. Routledge.

Powley, E. 2003. *Strengthening Governance: The Role of Women in Rwanda's Transition*. Washington, DC. Hunt Alternatives Fund.

Redin, E., and Sirleaf, E. J. 2002. *Women, War and Peace: The Independent Experts' Assessment on the Impact of Armed Conflict on Women and Women's Role in Peace Building*. New York. UNIFEM.

Reimann, C. 2002. *"All you need is love" . . . and what about gender? Engendering Burton's needs theory*. Working Paper 10. Bradford. University of Bradford Department of Peace Studies.

Ridd, R., and Callaway, H. (eds). 1987. *Women and Political Conflict: Portraits of Struggle in Times of Crisis*. New York. New York University Press.

UNDP. 2003. *Women in Reconstruction: Rwanda Promotes Women Decision-makers*. Consuelo Remmert, UN Chronicle online edition, http://www.un.org/pubs/chronicle/2003/issue4/0403p25.asp.

UNDP. 2006. *Lessons from Rwanda, the United Nations and the Prevention of Genocide*, http://www.un.org/preventgenocide/rwanda/background.shtml – accessed 4 June 2010.

UNIFEM. 2003. *Report of the Learning Oriented Assessment of Gender Mainstreaming and Women's Empowerment Strategies in Rwanda, 2–12 September*. New York. UNIFEM.

CHAPTER TWO

NGOS: USING SPORT TO PROMOTE PEACE AND INTEGRATION IN FRACTURED SOCIETIES

JOEL ROOKWOOD AND STEPHAN WASSONG

Sport has been used to promote peace and help reconstruct a number of politically tense and fractured societies plagued by conflict. Focussing on the work of three non-governmental organizations (NGOs) which represent variety in terms of focus, magnitude and impact, this chapter examines the definitional and developmental basis of NGOs, and the work conducted by each organization in the context of three specific sports programmes. First, the Congo-based initiative "Peace Games" run by the International Olympic Committee (IOC) in collaboration with the United Nations, which aims to promote a culture of peace and reconciliation. Secondly, the "Football for Peace" (F4P) project, a British Universities programme staged annually in conjunction with the British Council in Israel since 2001. This employs a value-based football coaching programme to facilitate peaceful social inte-gration within Jewish and Arab communities. Thirdly, the "STAR" football scheme established in Liberia by Samaritan's Purse in 2006, which supports the reintegration of child ex-combatants into Liberian society. (The first author has worked on the latter two projects.) Each initiative is explored in terms of its capacity to promote peace and integration in its locality. Concentrating on the role, significance and application of sport, and the organizational and socio-political context of the initiatives and the agencies involved in their implementation, this chapter addresses the suitability and limitations of sport as a medium to facilitate integration and peace promo-tion in fractured communities.

Promoting Peace and Integration

The recent history of civilization contains some compelling evidence of societal transformation, with various forms of development permeating technological, political, socio-developmental and environmental spheres. In some contexts significant advancements in design and invention have facilitated the innovative expansion of modes of communication, medication and transportation. There has also been an increasing consciousness of and response to economic, conservational and humanitarian challenges. However, humans also continue to experience various problems relating for example, to the distribution of global wealth and the patterns of social and political governance, which represent unjust practice in many parts of the world (Barash, 2000). The variety of these examples demonstrates that social development can be considered a multi-disciplinary subject, incorporating geographical, economical, sociological, psychological, anthropological and political concerns, amongst others. Academics focused on offering meaningful contributions to this multifaceted paradigm should consider the significance of relevant overlapping approaches. Scholars should feel compelled to communicate multilaterally with politicians, aid workers, community leaders, students and those representing other relevant groups, to disseminate and share examples of successful and ineffective practice and theory in ways that can encourage, inform and contribute to work in comparable contexts.

In discussing the relative severity of problems facing modern societies, Barash (2000: 3) argues that: "There is reason to believe that our most pressing problem is not hunger, disease, poverty, social inequality, overpopulation, or environmental degradation, but rather violence that human beings commit and threaten to commit against others." Violence assumes many forms including intrapersonal and interpersonal. The former relates to factors such as alcohol and drug abuse, suicide and depression. The latter occurs on an inter-community scale including domestic violence and rape, and on national and transnational levels, such as civil and international wars, terrorism, rebel movements, revolutions and coups. The continuing prevalence of conflict has been noted by various authors reflecting contemporary academic, media, political and humanitarian interests. Katano (2009) states that fifty-seven 'major armed conflicts' have been fought since 1990 (such conflicts are defined as the use of armed force between military forces and/or organized armed groups, with battle-related deaths reaching at least 1000 people in any given year). Although global broadcasters often focus on current inter-state wars (Grossman, 2008), the proportionality of such coverage could be questioned given that most recent conflicts have been intra-national. Katano (2009) states that only four out of these 57 conflicts were fought between states. Civil unrest often stems from rival groups in the same nation seeking autonomy or control over various resources. Conflicts may become international when they involve those representing opposing ideals, identities or movements which extend to or originate in separate countries, crossing both immediate and distant borders. Other examples of the internationalization of wars include the external displacement of populations (often referred to at that point as refugees), the deployment of international resources and the invasion of neighbouring countries (Lederach, 1997).

Engagement in such violence is often characterized and motivated by combinations of hatred, power, greed and pride, together with various allegiances and affiliations to and fear and intolerance of civil, national, ideological, ethnic and religious identities (Rookwood, 2009). The majority of recent armed wars have been fought not on clearly defined battlefields but within and adjacent to communities (Machel, 2001). Such forms of civil conflict often produce severe humanitarian crises as a consequence. Although understanding their extent and cost is problematic given the complexity and dangers associated with undertaking meaningful analysis, most commentators agree that civilian populations are often the primary victims of civil conflict. In addition to human casualties, surviving populations of displaced and non-displaced people are often subjected to psychological scarring, socio-political instability, economic hardships and the prospect of engaging in post-conflict reconstruction amidst damaged architectural infrastructure. Exposure to conflict and impoverished post-war conditions and the experience of fragile relations often serve to reduce community cohesion and other social controls (Wessells, 2009). Also, civilians (particularly youths) who have been subject to such conditions may lack an appropriate reference point for conceptualizing peace and instead be drawn into conflict which they may perceive as their only opportunity to avoid powerlessness (Brett & Specht, 2004). Consequently some have suggested that related research should consider the challenges of conflict in conjunction with rather than in isolation from the possibilities of peace in this regard:

> War or peace; the destruction or the protection of nature; the violation or promotion of human rights and democratic freedoms; poverty or material well being; the lack of moral and spiritual values or their existence and development; and the breakdown or development of human understanding, are not isolated phenomena that can be analyzed and tackled independently of one another. In fact, they are very much interrelated at all levels and need to be approached with that understanding (The Dalai Lama, 1990 Nobel Peace Prize lecture – Piburn, 1997).

Such challenges to the 'peace process' are particularly evident when representative groups such as governments and other agencies demonstrate what is perceived as an unresponsiveness or incapacity to provide services and resources necessary to effectively support post-conflict social development. Due to the experience of similar frustrations and the desire to respond to the need such conflicts produce, a number of organizations (often claiming to be non-aligned, unprejudiced and impartial) devise and implement various forms of programming. These initiatives usually aim to contribute to the advancement of peace, whilst attempting to diminish the reliance of sections of the human race on organized violence. It is important for projects of this nature (and indeed analytical research with a similar scope) to be approached and underpinned by an understanding of the meaning and mechanisms associated with terms such as peace promotion, integration and fractured societies. Such work also necessitates the adoption of a broad value framework. For sociologists and other academics, value-led positions may be viewed as problematic. The relative suitability of various "positive" values implemented in the three projects explored here will be examined later in this chapter; however some fundamental principles can initially be agreed. As Barash (2000: 3) puts it: "Peace, we proclaim, is better than war, just as social justice is better than injustice, environmental integrity is better than destruction."

Returning to definitional issues, in a conflict context, a fractured society can be considered one that is splintered following the exposure to disintegrating processes and experiences. Groups often form opposing identities, and members sense unity amongst peers in organizations that are able to frame a holistic explanation of experience, one which blames antithetical groups and often presents them as an unjust and corrupt enemy that must be fought and defeated (Dolnik & Gunaratna, 2009). Integration, however, is a process or state of social cohesion that facilitates assimilation between individuals in society. A contextualized understanding relates to the social unification of people who represent opposing groups and conflicting identities. In addition, Schirch (2005) argues that integration in fractured societies requires conflicting groups to be able to 're-humanize' their vision of each other as part of a reconciliation process that aims for sustainable co-existence. Regarding peace, although the intricacy of the term renders it subject to varying connotations, in simple terms it can be understood as the absence of war (Wessells, 2009). Peace is considered a primary entitlement, indeed the right to peace is established in the Universal Declaration of Human Rights (1948). Its promotion relates to the public endorsement and effective advancement of the idea of peace, and the mobilization and encouragement of key populations to engage in the programmes, behaviours and structures necessary for peace (Rookwood, 2009). However the notion of the advancement of peace needs to be examined more closely. During the early 1990s the UN Secretary General Boutros Boutros-Ghali (1992) released an 'Agenda for Peace' highlighting four sequential processes of preventive diplomacy, peacemaking, peacekeeping, and peacebuilding. Whilst the chronology of the first three procedures has been accepted and adopted by many researchers and practitioners, Lederach (2005) suggests that the latter notion should be considered relative to a broader time frame (i.e. not merely as a post-conflict construct). He defines peacebuilding as "A comprehensive concept that encompasses, generates, and sustains the full array of processes, approaches, and stages needed to transform conflict toward more sustainable, peaceful relationships ... activities that both preceded and follow peace accords" (1997: 20). Galtung (1998) offers a more succinct contribution, suggesting peacebuilding requires the reconstruction of people and places, the reconciliation of relationships and the resolution of issues and animosities. This research and the initiatives explored here approach the promotion of peace as an attempt to endorse and contribute to the realization of peace. Relevant issues pertaining to the time frame of reconstruction and the sustainability of reconciliation and resolution are considered in this chapter.

NGOs and the Use of Sport for Peace Promotion

> We NGOs ... claim a role in promoting the common good and defending public interest. We are heterogeneous: we come in many shapes and sizes, and we are generally miniscule when compared to governmental or multilateral agencies. Embracing apparently lost causes, we are often rather more committed and militant than efficient in whatever we do, and above all we are an irritant to the establishment, be it the state or the private sector (Grzybowski, 2000: 436).

Forms of social involvement and development range from responding to immediate need to challenging the economic and political structures of society. NGOs, i.e. agencies which are not part of a governmental structure, often assume responsibility for such engagement, and usually focus on the humanitarian or developmental needs of the recipient, or both. Whaites (2000) argues that disasters, famine and civil strife propel humanitarian-based NGOs into the media spotlight, particularly in the context of conflict and post-war reconstruction. Despite claims of neutrality, developmental NGOs are often motivated by ideological or spiritual commitments to social reform (Tandom, 2000). In addition to the perceived heterogeneity and partiality of NGOs, the circumstantial complexity which can hinder their operational capacity has also inspired criticism from some authors:

> Development NGOs are in crisis. They are losing their capacity to engage in critical analysis and propose global solutions: to react to or seize the political initiative; or to situate themselves on the cutting edge of those social and political processes in which new approaches and potential solutions might be found. (Jaimes, 2000: 390)

However this assessment does not consider the approach, proposition, implementation or analysis of local solutions, or their wider significance. The projects examined in this research are framed as local (micro) as opposed to global (macro) initiatives aimed at relationship building, social integration and peace promotion. As Lederach (2005) notes, many developmental NGOs occupy key strategic positions in the formation of cross-sectional relationships, and have achieved positive outcomes for different contexts, populations and individuals, rendering them constructive initiators of change in this respect.

Chester (2004) argues that successful NGO-led interventions can be facilitated through the provision of services and programming which focus on helping specific populations define their problems and find their own solutions to them. Various NGOs have developed collaborative initiatives in order to empower local populations in this way and promote peace and integrative reconciliation by fostering human contact, engagement and bonding (Tidwell, 1998). Traditional cultural activities have been employed, centred on media such as music and expressive art, which reinforce connections with those who share a common cultural heritage (Armstrong, 2004). Educational and sports-based initiatives have also been implemented which are intended as enjoyable social interactions that embody value-based and peace-promoting messages. The employment of sport in this context has been publicly endorsed in various contexts. For example, Nelson Mandela argued that sports such as football are "one of the most unifying activities amongst us" (Kuper, 1994: 138). In addition, at the opening ceremony of the XIIIth Olympic Congress in Copenhagen in 2009 UN Secretary General Ban Ki-moon stated: "Sport can be found anywhere in the world. I have travelled to countries mired in poverty . . . to war-ravaged places where all hope seems lost. Suddenly, a ball appears, made out of plastic bags or newspapers. And we see sport gives life to hopes and dreams" (Rookwood, 2009). Olympic audiences are familiar with such rhetoric. Pierre De Coubertin, the founder of the modern Olympic Games, stressed the power of sport to stimulate peaceful thought and action, arguing that amateur sport can contribute to the development of peaceful internationalism (Wassong, 2006). During the mid-nineteenth-century, English public school educational reformers developed the idea that appropriate forms of sports participation could help develop the character of pupils. The philosophy of "muscular Christianity" involved the use of sport for physical development and to encourage positive social interactions and qualities such as fair play, courage, self-control and unselfishness (Kwauk, 2007). Sporting interaction ranging from exercise and spontaneous recreational play to organized and professionalized forms became perceived as a legitimate medium to affect the character and behaviour of participants. Partly through the example and philosophy of bodies such as the IOC, a similar approach was diffused amongst other high-income countries and was also transferred to colonized populations. As a legacy of the British approach to sporting participation, organization and regulation, sport continues to be used to establish moral boundaries (Sorek, 2005).

There is evidence that involvement in sport can help participants become socially, morally, emotionally, physically and cognitively competent. Positive physiological effects of participation in sport and physical activity have been noted in contemporary society, when combined with the provision of clean air and adequate nutrition. Such sporting interaction can perform a preventive and rehabilitative function in relation to some diseases such as cardio-vascular diseases and decrease the likelihood of unhealthy practices (Rankinen & Bouchard, 2002); and can positively affect self-esteem, self-worth and social integration and help combat discrimination. Sports participation can also attract young people to volunteering, increase measures of altruism and community orientation, and provide opportunities for leadership development (Sugden, 2007). In the context of peace promotion sport has also been found to play an important rehabilitative role for those affected by crisis, discrimination and marginalization (Whitfield, 2006). In addition there is evidence that being labelled an "athlete" reflects positively on youth, and that partaking in sport can alleviate deviant behaviours and promote academic achievement (Bailey, 2005). Furthermore Hedstrom and Gould (2004) claim that the values and ethics promoted in sport can shape the moral character instilled in participants. However, some cautionary and critical perspectives have also been noted in this respect: "Questions remain regarding the values of competitive sport and whether they should be disseminated, what kind of behaviour should be promoted in and through sport, and what criteria should be used for good sport delivery" (Auweele et al., 2006: 15). Such questions are central to the following examination of sport peace projects.

Additionally, Donnelly (1993: 428) states: "We have long held, although with little evidence, that sport participation has the capacity to transform the character of individuals." Ewing et al. (2002) suggest that character relates to moral reasoning, motivational orientation, the ability to understand multiple perspectives, and the affective skill of understanding the experiences of another person or group. However, obtaining evidence of character development is problematic largely because character is difficult to quantify and the effects of sport are hard to measure. Importantly, programmers must develop knowledge of the circumstances under which sport can produce positive outcomes, regardless of whether the intended social outcomes relate to inclusion, development, health, peace promotion or conflict resolution. Partly on the strength of the correlations highlighted here, numerous sport-focussed programmes targeting "high risk" or "marginalized" youth have been established. Many sport projects serving as a co-ordinated and progressive series of activities and experiences have been employed as a platform to facilitate social development in fractured communities in this way to "send a more positive, proactive message to community members, one that puts a new emphasis on community outreach and builds trust, commitment and solidarity" (Hartmann & Depro, 2006: 192). Many of these programmes focus exclusively on positive youth development, aiming to address broader developmental needs as opposed to deficit-based models which focus solely on youth problems. Although it is difficult to develop criteria by which projects should be judged, evaluative analysis should examine the rationale for establishing the initiative, the size and sustainability of the programme, how it addresses barriers, its sensitivity to specific local needs and the availability of appropriate evidence from which conclusions can be drawn.

Sporting Peace Projects

There has been a recent expansion of sports programmes run by sporting organizations and NGOs attempting to intervene in politically sensitive contexts and military conflicts. These are often aimed at contributing to the cessation of hostilities, facilitating reconciliation between opposing groups, and supporting the victims of conflict. As well as various coach development initiatives established in Africa and Asia and education projects staged in the Middle East, interventions also extend to declarations of truce. Key examples include those organized by the IOC and the UN during Olympic events. In 1993 the UN General Assembly adopted the resolution on Olympic truce. This declaration refers to the revival of the ancient "ekecheiria" (truce), in addition to Coubertin's concept of contributing to peace and transnational understanding through the Olympic Games and Olympic movement:

> The goal of the Olympic Movement is to build a better and more peaceful world by educating the youth of the world through sport, practised without discrimination of any kind and in the Olympic spirit, which requires mutual understanding, promoted by friendship, solidarity and fair play … in the interest of contributing to international understanding and the maintenance of peace.

Subsequently, host countries of the Olympic Games have at the IOC's request submitted resolutions on Olympic Peace a year prior to the respective tournament, which can in part be understood as a stimulus to use sport as a vehicle for peace during each Olympiad. As a manifestation of such principles, the IOC have engaged in a number of peace promoting and humanitarian projects.

The first project of this kind was the Peace Games in Congo in August 2006. This was organized by the IOC in collaboration with the United Nations Mission in the Democratic Republic of the Congo (MONUC). Tournaments were staged in basketball and football as well as a variety of distance running events, although the objective of the initiative did not merely involve increasing the athletic ability of young participants but also "to promote a culture of peace and reconciliation [and to offer] the youth of the Democratic Republic of Congo an alternative to violence and hatred" (Wassong, 2008: 323). The Peace Games were staged for the second time in September 2009, the highlight being the "marathon race for peace" in Kinshasa. Three hundred runners took part including MONUC civil personnel and members of the Congolese police and army: "The main objective of the marathon was to show the way followed by the Democratic Republic of Congo towards peace" (Rookwood, 2009). The marathon inspired the organization of other events such as conferences, discussion forums and walks for peace, which helped encourage dialogue focussed on developing peace and respect and overcoming mistrust and violence. Similar projects have been devised in Liberia such as the Sport for Peace programme launched in Liberia in March 2007 as a collaborative effort between the IOC, the UN Mission in Liberia, the Liberian government, the International Olympic Truce Centre, the Liberian National Olympic Committee and several national sporting associations. Football, volleyball and kickball tournaments were staged in order to promote peace. At the launch IOC president Jacques Rogge stated: "This project is an excellent example of how different organisations and institutions can create synergies to achieve a shared objective – the promotion of a peaceful society in Liberia . . . Sport activities promote interaction, tolerance and the spirit of fair-play" (Wassong, 2008: 374).

The IOC sees itself today as a catalyst for collaboration, and the development of many value-based sports programmes has been informed by the philosophy of Olympism. However, in reflecting on Olympic projects staged in developing countries Peacock (2006: 200) argues that many merely represent an "attempt to help the Third World 'catch up,' as it were, to European, or western standards", and contends that unless specific guidelines are followed, such programming could potentially be "doomed to amount to nothing more than a reminder of Western influence in the world" (p. 204). The sustainable significance of such short-term programming and the degree to which promise and practice are aligned through projects of this nature could also be questioned. Additionally, Peacock notes the importance of ensuring that developmental projects are not motivated or funded by misguided priorities, arguing that inspiring the youth and empowering the oppressed requires a collaborative, participatory and open-minded procedure, devising flexible and unprejudiced programmes built on effective partnerships, so that "the religious, ethnic, linguistic, racial, political or economic barriers that often divide communities, even within national boundaries, will begin to fade" (p. 205). The author also argues that for peace projects to be influential there must be a commitment to "people-centred roots. Only an emphasis on the micro-level will bring about changes in both individuals and societies" (p. 205). This is significant for developmental initiatives and provides a guideline to ensure that such programming proves manageable and meaningful.

Switching attention to another political context, the second project, F4P, is a response to the Israel–Palestine conflict, a fractious relationship deeply rooted in history with complex and widespread contemporary manifestations. The modern state of Israel was formed in 1948 under the Zionist movement, which has become the symbol of Judaism and of Jewish national aspirations. Zion is a prophetic and poetic designation, a definitive reference to the existing Israeli capital of Jerusalem which dates to the tenth century BC. However, the existing movement is centred on land formerly (and in some cases currently) recognized internationally as Palestinian (Sugden, 2007). Conflicting claims based on religious and political perspectives on the "rightful ownership" of the land dominate the socio-political dialogue and media representation. These relate to inter-territory issues including the Lebanese wars, the Syrian territory disputes, the attacks directed at and perpetrated by the people of Gaza, the Jewish settlement movement, the demolition of Palestinian homes and the legitimacy of the proposed 'two-state solution'. Given the magnitude of such issues the status of Jewish–Arab relations for those who live side by side in Israel is often overlooked (Liebmann & Rookwood, 2007). Young people are often the primary victims of warfare and in post-war contexts often feel marginalized and excluded from reconstruction activities, as such efforts are often concentrated on adults. F4P is a youth development educational initiative currently managed as a secular organisation underpinned by neutrality, unaffiliated to any religious or political groups. With the widespread passionate interest in football, youth engagement in the sport at a grassroots level has been found to have a positive impact on inter-faith and ethnic cooperation and coexistence in Israel (Ben-Porat, 2006).

Each year 60 staff and students primarily from the University of Brighton, together with up to 500 participants and volunteers from Israel, take part in the project. The model implemented by the NGO F4P involves value-based football coaching to facilitate peaceful integration in Jewish and Arab societies. Coaches are supported practically and linguistically by local figures, and the students follow guidelines provided in a specially produced manual that "emphasises, animates and embodies a series of values that promote play, co-operation, mutual understanding, and aid the cause of conflict prevention and co-existence" (Lambert, 2007: 13). The coaches identify and reinforce specific concrete behaviours attached to the values of neutrality, inclusion, respect, trust and responsibility, so that they may be taken beyond the football field (Stidder, 2007). Regarding neutrality, Lambert (2007: 19) states that "those who participate in F4P – players, coaches, parents, administrators – leave their political views and ideological positions outside . . . such positions are not expressed in and around the F4P experience." Inclusion is instilled through the recognition and welcome involvement of participants irrespective of race, ethnicity, religion, gender or ability. Ramsbotham et al. (2005) argue that respect for adversaries increases the likelihood of sustaining an effort to find peaceful solutions to disputes; and respect is integrated in F4P by encouraging players to recognize the legitimacy and perspective of team mates, opponents, coaches, parents and the rules of the game and those who uphold them. Trust is implemented for example through team-bonding and problem-solving activities during coaching sessions and subsequent social interactions. Sportsmanship is fostered by encouraging players to have faith in the capacities and responsibilities of others, whilst responsibility is also infused during the competitive tournaments in which each project culminates. These festival days provide participants with opportunities to illustrate the tactical, technical and moral lessons they have learned. For example, no referees are supplied and each team has multiple substitutes, with players given the responsibility to adhere to the principles of fair play in respect to the rules of the game and the equitable involvement of all participants. Importantly, teams of mixed ethnicities compete, thus preventing a victory representing a triumph over "the other". Instead teams with multiple identities must cooperate to achieve common objectives.

A similar model was employed on the STAR initiative staged in Liberia by the American NGO Samaritan's Purse, although implemented in a different way. Liberia was severely affected by two civil wars, the first of which commenced in 1989 and the second culminating in 2004. A quarter of million Liberians died during these civil wars, with a further one million displaced. The conflicts were prolonged by the supply of arms from foreign nations and the coercion of youths into combat primarily through abduction (Guannu, 2009). After 2004, with severe competition for the limited resources available and disunity between various factions, many community members struggled to reconstruct lives and identities. Youths who had fought in the conflict often remained feared and were regarded as a continued threat to peace. Within this context reconciliation was considered to necessitate developing social bonds to reduce tensions between child ex-combatants and other community members and to forge or renew the sense of community (Omeje, 2009). The STAR project was established to make a contribution in this regard. The label "star" is noteworthy as it signifies the nation's declaration of independence from the American Colonization Society (Armstrong, 2002), and also serves as an acronym for the value-driven coaching philosophy focussing on self-discipline, truthfulness, appreciation and respect. The project was collaboratively implemented by 16 relatively experienced and skilled British volunteers together with 60 locally-based staff in 2006 and 2007. Football clinics and coach education clinics were staged in the three most populous cities, involving almost 3000 participants.

Discipline was infused by encouraging players to participate according to the regulations and by focussing on concentration and punctuality. Truthfulness was emphasized by referring to cheating and honesty in competitive activities and encouraging the reinforcement of appropriate conduct whilst correcting unsuitable behaviour. Appreciation and respect involved offering both team-mates and opponents a positive reception before, during and after coaching sessions and matches, for example. Football was employed as a non-codified and competitive conflict activity during the various stages of the initiative. For instance, coaches attempted to *cause* conflict situations during sessions to teach participants about positive means of conflict resolution whilst in a safe and controlled environment. However, this relied on the capacity of coaches to provide opportunities for controllable forms of conflict to take place. This was a problem because of their inexperience with this model and approach (suggested by Lambert (2007)). It also proved difficult to provide a consistently 'secure' environment, as the locations selected and the number and behaviour of intrigued onlookers (including UN military personnel) proved difficult to control. In addition, regulatory barriers were consciously overlooked in certain instances, such as the apparatus used and the conditions imposed on player conduct, in order to facilitate teachable moments. In addition tournaments were staged involving mixed teams of child ex-combatants and non-combatants. As part of the coach education programme, local volunteers were trained, each of them being given long-term responsibility for a team that competed in leagues subsequently established and managed by local partners. However, due to organizational and funding issues, some of these leagues were disbanded after the first year. The failure of the project to properly sustain funding of the competitive interactions and train and empower volunteers to adopt long-term ownership and management of the programme is considered representative of the problems commonly experienced with such short-term measures.

Conclusion

There are numerous challenges and limitations associated with sport-for-peace projects; some, although by no means all, have been examined here. For example, the translation system (between English, Arabic and Hebrew in the notable case of F4P) can prove problematic, as some participants grow impatient when values rather than football are discussed, and others demonstrate various forms of resistance to the aspirations of programmes. Overseas trainers can also struggle to identify and communicate key coaching and behavioural indicators without engendering misunderstanding. It is inevitable that participants engage in such initiatives in different ways, some considering them part of a political process, others as "making a difference" and others merely as an opportunity to play football or other sports. It is not possible to represent, reconcile or explain this diversity fully. However, it is important to state that even well intentioned, effectively managed projects may not have the desired impact on every recipient. Indeed, many practitioners cannot even agree on the proposed nature of such outcomes. In addition the socio-political contexts in which programmes operate present numerous difficulties. A notable example concerns the 2006 F4P project which had to be cancelled at the last minute due to Israel's war with Hezbollah (see Sugden, 2007), an experience which underlines the dangers of employing university volunteers and NGO personnel in fractured climates. Furthermore, sustainability is a key challenge to the use of sport in fostering ethno-religious integration and sustaining peaceful interaction. This is particularly notable given the complex and challenging nature of the processes associated with promoting and building peace. The degree of impact longevity is partly informed by the validity of long-term indicators and related conduct which illustrates the extent to which central values are disseminated.

There is little available evidence pertaining to the system of values incorporated into the IOC peace programmes in the Congo. In Israel, the F4P value system may not represent the precise intersection of Jewish and Arabic principles. However, by working with local representatives, the organizers have succeeded in selecting and implementing values that are tested against the realities of a common life and that reflect contemporary society. It is arguable whether the same can be said of the STAR project, as despite providing a more easily memorized structure the values seemed to be imposed on rather than reflective of local culture, largely to fit the acronym (Rookwood, 2008).

In spite of the challenges, however, sports such as football present a potentially valuable tool in developmental and peace building contexts. As Richards (1997: 149) states:

> The shared enthusiasm for soccer is an interesting resource for peacemaking, because it is one of the relatively few widely enjoyed but "neutral" items of cultural common property – unspoilt by war – through which these alienated youngsters might begin to experiment with the direct reconstruction of their social identity ... It offers a neutral space through which combatants and society at large might begin to seek some mutual accommodation in a "shared space" before getting down to the hard tasks of re-forming [specific] social identities and social understandings.

Sport can clearly serve both as a manipulative symbol of discrimination, racism, division, intolerance and misunderstanding, as well as a tool for developing the character of athletes and promoting and building peace and integration in the fractured communities they inhabit. Sporting interactions are social constructs, and can be considered neutral and unaligned – although their function and meaning are dependent on the manner in which they are constructed and experienced. Importantly, however, Richards' argument also underlines the notion that footballing interactions usually lead to rather than being a manifestation of the "hard tasks" represented in peace promotion and integration. The interventions described here should be regarded as initial steps that need to be complemented and substantiated with diverse activities that engender long-term reconciliation. Further understanding needs to be developed pertaining to how sports projects can fit into a larger multifaceted reconciliatory, reconstructive and rehabilitating framework. Peacebuilding must be rooted in and responsive to the subjective realities shaping people's perspectives and needs; and such analysis requires an appreciation of the extent to which they are contextual and culturally sensitive, and the time frame imposed on sport projects relative to the respective peace process. Coakley (2002) suggests that in exemplary programmes participants should feel physically safe, personally valued, socially connected, morally and economically supported, personally and politically empowered, and hopeful about the future. Evidently understanding the extent to which sporting engagement plays a facilitative role within this framework requires further multidisciplinary analysis. It is worth noting that such research is methodologically problematic, as attempts to quantify or definitively state the impact of sport are often limited in scope. Furthermore, development projects cannot be fully understood in isolation from other social factors and reasons for social change, and research approaches that fail both to address this issue and to capture the complexities of the relationship between sport and development are inherently limited and destined to collapse.

There is a growing body of evidence to suggest that character and moral development can be transferred to project participants when sports coaches implement specific teaching strategies to promote a positive change in moral growth (Ewing et al., 2002), which can have a positive impact on the promotion of peace and integration. However, the legacy of such projects needs to be addressed. Subsequent longitudinal research should focus on exploring how the impact of mutual understanding learned through sporting interactions can be translated effectively into the daily life of participants. The long-term benefits of sport participation interventions also need to be examined in this way. The projects staged in the Congo were short-term, grant-funded and seemingly unable to establish sustainability. Similarly the Liberian programme lacked continuity. Programmes of this nature may have short-term halo effects, but the impact is difficult to sustain unless commitment is maintained. Conversely however, F4P is an established, well supported project that allows for a more positive outlook. Sugden (2007: 181) suggests:

> There is convincing evidence that, even in the face of the most challenging socio-cultural and political circumstances, if projects such as this are well thought through, carefully structured and well managed, they do have the capacity to make positive contributions to community relations.

This project is attracting support and requests of involvement locally, whilst inspiring similar ventures in other political contexts. "The idea could go anywhere in the world where there is conflict and division, because people can be brought together through sport" (Whitfield, 2006: xvi).

These projects yield some important lessons regarding the need to facilitate the protection and development of youth participants and volunteer organizers, and avoid the use of externally imposed approaches which marginalize local understandings and practices. Cultural practices play an important role in peace promotion and societal reconciliation, enabling communities to construct meaningful narratives. By orienting them toward peace building, these practices and associated narratives can be framed as opportunities for restructuring collective identities in ways that promote peaceful unity. For inhabitants of fractured communities, reconciliation at the individual level is important, in order for marginalized or hostile members to be re-admitted into the community through the formation of social bonds. In addition however links must be fostered between institutions and infrastructural elements of macrosystems, including provincial or district government, a functioning economy and political system, and inclusive structures of a central government that promote social justice. This is manifested through developments including the reduction of discrimination and oppression, the normalization of non-violent means of conflict resolution, the permeation of representative systems of law and governance, the reconstruction of damaged infrastructure and the equitable redistribution of power and resources. Whilst the variety of these requirements once again demonstrates the multidisciplinary nature of social development and the limitations of individual micro initiatives in isolation, the contribution of programmes that use sport and other modes of social engagement can, when understood within a wider framework, allow for a representative diagnosis of problems and inspire efforts to implement meaningful and sustained solutions.

References

Armstrong, G. (2002). 'Talking up the game: Football and the reconstruction of Liberia, West Africa', *Identitites: Global Studies in Culture and Power,* 9(4): 471–494.

Armstrong, G. (2004). 'Life, death and the biscuit: football and the embodiment of society in Liberia.' In *Football in Africa: Conflict Conciliation and Community,* ed. G. Armstrong and R. Giulianotti. Basingstoke. Palgrave Macmillan.

Auweele, Y., Malcolm, C. and Meulders, B. (2006). *Sport and Development.* Tielt, Belgium. Lannoo Campus.

Bailey, R. (2005). 'Evaluating the relationship between physical education, sport and social inclusion', *Educational Review, 57*(1): 71–90.

Barash, D., ed. (2000). 'Approaches to peace.' In *Approaches to Peace: A Reader in Peace Studies,* pp. 1–4. Oxford. Oxford University Press.

Ben-Porat, A. (2006). 'Split loyalty: Football-cum-nationality in Israel', *Soccer and Society,* 7(2): 262–277.

Boutros-Ghali, B. (1992). *An Agenda for Peace: Preventive Diplomacy, Peacemaking and Peace-keeping.* New York. United Nations.

Brett, R. and Specht, I. (2004). *Young Soldiers: Why they Choose to Fight.* Boulder, CO. Lynne Rienner.

Chester, T. (2004). *Good News to the Poor: Sharing the Gospel through Social Involvement.* Leicester. InterVarsity Press.

Coakley, J. (2002). 'Using sport to control deviance and violence among youth: Let's be critical and cautious.' In *Paradoxes of Youth and Sport,* ed. M. Gatz, M. Messner and S. Ball-Rokeach, pp. 18–35. Albany, NY. State University of New York.

Dolnik, A. and Gunaratna, R. (2009). 'On the nature of religious terrorism.' In *Routledge Handbook of Religion and Politics,* ed. J. Haynes,pp. 343–350. New York. Routledge.

Donnelly, J. (1993). 'Subcultures in sport: resilience and transformation'. In Ingham, A. G. and Loy, J. W. (eds). *Sport in Social Development,* ed. A. G. INgham and J. W. Loy, pp. 119–146. Leeds. Human Kinetics.

Ewing, M., et al. (2002). 'The Role of Sports in Youth Development.' In Gatz, M., Messner, M. and Ball-Rokeach, S. (eds). *Paradoxes of Youth and Sport,* ed.M. Gatz, M. Messner and S. Ball-Rokeach, pp. 31–47. Albany, NY. State University of New York.

Galtung, J. (1998). *Peace by Peaceful Means: Peace and Conflict, Development and Civilization.* New York. Sage.

Grossman, D. (2008). *Writing in the Dark: Essays on Literature and Politics.* London. Bloomsbury.

Grzybowski, C. (2000). 'We NGOs: a controversial way of being and acting.' *Development in Practice,* 10(4): 436–444.

Guannu, J. S. (2009). 'The political history of Liberia and the Civil War.' In Omeje, K. (ed.). *War to Peace Transition,* ed. K. Omeje, pp. 19–40. Lanham, MD. University Press of America.

Hartmann, D. and Depro, B. (2006). 'Rethinking sports-based community crime prevention: A preliminary analysis of the relationship between midnight basketball and urban crime rates', *Journal of Sport and Social Issues,* 30(2): 180–196.

Hedstrom, R. and Gould, D. (2004). *Research in Youth Sports: Critical Issues Status*. East Lansing, MI. Institute for the Study of Youth Sports, Michigan State University.

Jaimes, J. A. (2000). 'NGOs: Fragmented dreams', *Development in Practice*, 10(4): 390–401.

Katano, A. (2009). 'Conflict prevention and peacebuilding.' In *Routledge Handbook of Religion and Politics, ed. J. Haynes, pp. 351–365*. New York. Routledge.

Kuper, S. (1994). *Football Against the Enemy*. London. Orion.

Kwauk, C. (2007). 'Goal! The dream begins: globalizing an immigrant muscular Christianity', *Soccer and Society*, 8(1): 75–89.

Lambert, J. (2007). 'A values-based approach to coaching sport in divided societies. The football for peace coaching manual.' In Sugden, J., and Wallis, J. (eds). *Football for Peace? The Challenges of Using Sport for Co-existence in Israel*, ed. J. Sugden and J. Wallis, pp. 13–34. Oxford. Meyer and Meyer.

Lederach, J. P. (1997). *The Moral Imagination*. New York. Oxford University Press.

Lederach, J. P. (2005). *The Moral Imagination: The Art and Soul of Building Peace*. New York. Oxford University Press.

Liebmann, S. and Rookwood, J. (2007). 'Football for peace? Bringing Jews and Arabs together in Northern Israel,' *Journal of Qualitative Research in Sports Studies*, 1(1): 11–18.

Machel, G. (2001). *The Impact of Armed Conflict on Children*. Cape Town. David Philip.

Omeje, K. (2009). Introduction: Discourses of the Liberian Civil War and the Imperatives of Peacebuilding. In *War to Peace Transition*, ed. K. Omeje, pp. 3-18. Lanham, MD. University Press of America.

Peacock, B. (2006). 'Avoiding Olympic imperialism: shedding trickle-down Olymponomics: in favor of "all sports for all people".' In *Cultural Imperialism in Action – Critiques in the Global Olympic Trust. Eighth International Symposium for Olympic Research*, eds. N. Crowther, R. Barney and M. Heine, pp. 200–209. London, Ontario. International Centre for Olympic Studies.

Piburn, S. (1997). *The Dalai Lama – A Policy of Kindness: Winner of the Noble Peace Prize*. Ithaca, NY. Snow Lion Publications.

Ramsbotham, O., Woodhouse, T. and Miall, H. (2005). *Contemporary Conflict Resolution*. Cambridge. Polity Press.

Rankinen, T. and Bouchard, C. (2002). 'Dose-response issues concerning the relations between regular physical activity and health', *Research Digest: President's Council on Fitness and Sports,* 3(18).

Richards, P. (1997). 'Soccer and violence in war-torn Africa: Soccer and social rehabilitation in Sierra Leone.' In *Entering the Field: New Perspectives on World Football*, ed. G. Armstrong and R. Giuliannotti, pp. 141–158. New York. Berg.

Rookwood, J. (2008). 'Soccer for peace and social development.' *Peace Review* 20(4):, 471–479.

Rookwood, J. (2009). *Social Development in Post-conflict Communities: Building Peace through Sport in Africa and the Middle East*. Saarbrücken. VDM Publishing House.

Schirch, L. (2005). *Ritual and Symbol in Peacebuilding*. New York. Kumarian Press.

Sorek, T. (2005). 'Between football and martyrdom: the bi-focal localism of an Arab-Palestinian town in Israel', *British Journal of Sociology*, 56(4): 635–661.

Stidder, G. (2007). 'Maagan and the German dimension.' In *Football for Peace? The Challenges of Using Sport for Co-existence in Israel,* ed. J. Sugden and J. Wallis, pp. 81–96. Oxford. Meyer and Meyer.

Sugden, J. (2007). 'War stops peace!' In *Football for Peace? The Challenges of Using Sport for Co-existence in Israel,.*ed. J. Sugden and J. Wallis, pp. 172–175. Oxford. Meyer and Meyer.

Tandom, R. (2000). 'Riding high or nosediving: Development NGOs in the new millennium,' *Development in Practice* 10(4): 319–329.

Tidwell, A. C. (1998). *Conflict Resolved: A Critical Assessment of Conflict Resolution.* London. Pinter.

Wassong, S. (2006). 'Olympic education: fundamentals, successes and failures.' In *Cultural Imperialism in Action – Critiques in the Global Olympic Trust. Eighth International Symposium for Olympic Research,* ed. N. Crowther, R. Barney and M. Heine, pp. 220–229. London, Ontario. International Centre for Olympic Studies.

Wassong, S. (2008). 'The Contemporary Legacy of Olympic Peace.' In *Olympismus - Erbe und Verantwortung,* ed. N. Müller and M. Messing, pp. 363–378. Kassel. Agon.

Wessells, M. (2009). 'Community reconciliation and post-conflict reconstruction for peace.' In de Rivera, J. (Ed.). *Handbook on Building Cultures of Peace,* ed. J. de Rivera, pp. 349-362. London. Springer.

Whaites, A. (2000). 'NGOs, disasters and advocacy: caught between the prophet and the shepherd boy,' *Development in Practice*, 10(3): 506–516.

Whitfield, G. (2006). *Amity in the Middle East.* Brighton. The Alpha Press.

CHAPTER THREE

EDUCATION IN A DIVIDED SOCIETY: THE ROLE OF INTERGROUP CONTACT IN PEACE BUILDING IN NORTHERN IRELAND

NEIL FERGUSON

The roots of the conflict in Northern Ireland are tangled and open to conjecture; some cite the Norman Conquest in 1170 as the beginning of Ireland's conflict, and certainly the conflict has its roots in the Reformation and the Plantation of Ulster in the seventeenth century. Indeed, no generation has been spared violence since the Plantation, while the State of Northern Ireland has faced periods of sectarian or political conflict in every decade since its inception in 1921 (Mac Ginty & Darby, 2002). However, the most recent period of sustained conflict which began in the late 1960s and continued until the paramilitary ceasefires of the early 1990s and the signing of the Good Friday (or Belfast) Agreement in 1998 (Purdie, 1990; Mac Ginty et al., 2007) will be the focus of this study. This period of political violence has directly contributed to the deaths of over 3,600 people, mainly innocent civilians (Fay et al., 1998; Mac Ginty et al., 2007) and the injury of an additional 40–50,000.

The Troubles are widely perceived as a primordial ethnic or religious conflict between Protestants and Catholics; however, these religious labels are used as badges of convenience in what is effectively a political struggle between those who wish to see Northern Ireland remain within the United Kingdom and those who desire a reunification of the island of Ireland (Darby, 1983). The majority of Unionists who wish to remain within the UK are also Protestants, while the majority of Nationalists who desire to reunify Ireland are Catholic, so the religious labels reflect these political aspirations, but are by no means exclusive, with up to 28% of Catholics holding pro-union attitudes (see Darby, 1997; Leach & Williams, 1999).

The focus on the conflict as a clash of political aspirations and conflicting identities has led to the social identity approach (Abrams & Hogg, 2004) and particularly its sub-theory of Social Identity Theory (SIT; Tajfel, 1978; Tajfel & Turner, 1979; Tajfel, 1981, Tajfel & Turner, 1986) being extensively applied to the conflict in Northern Ireland (Cairns, Wilson, Gallagher & Trew, 1995; Trew, 1986; Trew & Benson, 1996). SIT views the instigation of inter-group conflict not as a result of a struggle over "real" resources but as the result of merely placing people into different groups or categories. According to SIT, individuals identify with particular groups with which they feel they share a common fate (e.g. Protestants) and make comparisons between their ingroup and other outgroups (e.g. Catholics) to enhance their self-esteem.

This process of social identification and comparison causes an exaggeration of the similarities within categories and the differences between them, which in turn may lead to ingroup favouritism and outgroup hostility. Ingroup identification also leads to depersonalization (Turner, 1982), where the self becomes interchangeable with other group members, so "we" become stereotypical ingroup members and take on the group ideology, culture and values. Therefore SIT has played a key role in understanding the psychological dimensions of ethnic conflict in Northern Ireland (Cairns, 1982; Trew & Benson, 1996; Whyte, 1990).

This conflict has left a divided society, with two separate cultural infrastructures providing separate cultural and sporting organizations, newspapers, preferred histories, political parties and school systems (see Mac Ginty et al., 2007). This paper will focus on the role and impact the education system in Northern Ireland has had on addressing (or maintaining) these community divisions in post-conflict Northern Ireland.

The education system in Northern Ireland reflects the two divided communities, as over 90% of Northern Irish children in elementary and post-elementary education attend either grant maintained schools operated by the Catholic Church or state-controlled schools which are de facto Protestant. This educational apartheid has been viewed as one of the key contributing factors in causing or at least maintaining community division in Northern Ireland (Darby & Dunn, 1987; McEwen & Salters, 1993).

From the mid 1970s parental action groups have made known their dissatisfaction with this segregated system of education and desired to establish integrated schools which aimed to teach approximately equal numbers of Protestant and Catholic school children by a mixed staff of Protestant and Catholic teachers. Due to their efforts the first integrated school (Lagan Valley) was set up in Belfast in 1981 by the All Children Together (ACT) action group. Since 1981 the number of integrated schools has grown in the face of opposition and setbacks and there are currently 61 integrated schools: 20 are integrated post-elementary colleges and 41 are integrated elementary schools with an intake of approximately 19,000 pupils. This integrated school sector is oversubscribed and in 2007 about 700 pupils were turned away (Northern Ireland Council for Integrated Education (NICIE), 2008), while 74% of Northern Irish parents would like more integrated schools to be made available (Gallagher and Smith, 2002). However, it must be remembered that although there has been dramatic growth in the integrated sector it still only caters for approximately 6% of the total Northern Irish school population (McGlynn & Beckerman, 2007). Furthermore, Cairns et al. (1993) discovered that if you ask parents whether they would send their children to a local integrated school, rather than indicating if they felt integrated education was a good idea, parental support fell from approximately 80% to around 15%. Despite objections and uncertainties surrounding integrated schools, the direction of governmental policy and falling student numbers in Northern Ireland implies that more segregated schools will be transformed into integrated schools in the coming years (Community Relations Unit, 2005).

For the other 310,000 plus children who enter the parallel Protestant controlled and Catholic maintained sector there are a number of school-based initiatives which aim to increase cross-community contact, promote greater tolerance and encourage equal opportunities (Gallagher, 2004). The introduction of the Educational Reform (Northern Ireland) Order in 1989 has meant that since 1992 Education for Mutual Understanding (EMU) and Cultural Heritage (CH) have been compulsory cross-curricular themes in both school sectors (EMU had been available as a voluntary programme since 1983). These intervention programmes are addressed by all teachers of all subjects throughout each stage of education.

The rationale for both the development of the integrated education system and the introduction of EMU and CH in segregated schools has at its core Allport's (1954) contact hypothesis, based on bringing together individuals from conflicting groups to construct a situation where ignorance of each side can be replaced by knowledge about each other. This will hopefully result in a decalcification of erroneous perceptions and prejudices (Pettigrew & Tropp, 2000). Allport (1954) suggested four basic conditions to produce optimal contact which have since grown to include the following prerequisites: it must be prolonged, involve some co-operative activity, there must be official support for the integration, the parties should be equal in number and status, there must be one-to-one contact, the contact must be voluntary, involve an opportunity for friendship, provide information to dispel ignorance, highlight similarities and differences and take place in a pleasant surrounding (Cairns, 1996; Pettigrew, 1998).

The Impact of Integrated Education and School Based Intergroup Contact Interventions in Northern Ireland

Research exploring the impact of the integrated sector on fostering better Catholic–Protestant relations has been 'sparse and fragmented' (McGlynn et al., 2004: 165) due to a number of methodological, logistical and ethical problems. In general, research has produced positive findings in terms of an improved quantity and quality of outgroup contact and increased outgroup friendships in comparison to their peers educated in the segregated sector (Davies & Turner, 1984; Irwin, 1991; Hewstone et al., 2006; McClenahan, 1995; McClenahan et al., 1996; Stringer et al., 2000; Stringer & Hunter, 2008).

Stringer et al (2000) compared 1,732 children from integrated and segregated schools and discovered that integrated students reported more social contact with the other community outside school and had more positive views on mixed marriage and integrated education. In a further analysis of this sample and a corresponding sample of 880 parents, employing a LISERL modelling approach which explored a sample of 824 matched parent and child pairs to determine whether in school or out-of-school intergroup contacts moderated the children's group attitudes, while assessing how parental intergroup contacts influence child attitudes (Stringer & Hunter, 2008).

Stringer and Hunter's findings revealed that parental attitudes and levels of outgroup contact influence the choice of school (either integrated or segregated) with more moderate parents with greater intergroup contact being more likely to choose integrated schools. Parents' attitudes also directly influenced child attitudes toward the outgroup, while children attending integrated school reported higher levels of intergroup contact both within and outside school and that this contact (both in and out-of school) moderated attitudes towards the other in both Catholic and Protestant school pupils. These positive findings led Stringer and Hunter to conclude that intergroup contact is a powerful method of challenging negative and extremist attitudes towards outgoup members.

Schubotz & Robinson (2006) compiled a report on the pooled data from three Young Life and Times (YLT) surveys in Northern Ireland from 2003–2005, thus exploring the responses to issues about community relations from a random sample of 5,400 Northern Irish 16-year-olds. Seventy-five per cent of respondents who had taken part in cross-community contact projects had positive or very positive experiences. Over 90% of respondents who attended integrated schools had made friends with the other community, in comparison with 60–69% of their peers in segregated schools. In addition respondents who experienced integrated schooling had significantly more favourable feelings towards the other community, were more inclined to believe their schooling had a positive influence on how they felt about the other community and preferred to live in a mixed neighbourhood, work in a mixed workplace and attend a religiously mixed school. Schubotz and Robinson concluded that integrated schools had a significant impact on how their students view the other community and should be continued to be resourced.

Research findings from studies exploring the positive impact of integrated schools on altering divisive ethno-religious and political identities have been more mixed. As mentioned previously, identity is an important part of the Northern Irish conflict and the partisan identities reflect ingroup tensions (Livingstone & Haslam, 2008), thus an aim of intergroup contact should be to build a common ingroup identity to assist in transforming the conflict (Hewstone & Cairns, 2001). McGlynn et al. (2004) reported that integrated education had important positive impacts on former students (e.g. greater tolerance, feelings of security in mixed environments) but that for the majority (63%) of former integrated students there was no change in their identity through the increased contact they experienced. However, for those who experienced identity transformation they developed a new 'integrated' identity which complemented their existing ethno-religious identities. McClenahan et al. (1996) also found increased cross-community friendships, but no evidence of changes to ethno-religious or political identity.

Recent research by Hayes et al. (2007) explored the long term impact of integrated education on identity and constitutional preferences of Northern Irish adults. They pooled data from the Northern Ireland Life and Times (NILT) surveys from 1998 to 2003, creating a sample of 11,522 adults aged 18+. Their findings indicate that attending an integrated school can have a positive long-term impact on weakening sectarian political outlooks and promoting moderate political beliefs, especially among Protestants. Protestants who had attended integrated schools were also more likely to moderate their political identity and embrace an overarching identity (e.g. Northern Irish) as were their Catholic counterparts. They concluded that intergroup contact is an important and effective tool in reducing prejudice and that the effects of integrated education can have long lasting benefits into adulthood.

Another unseen positive impact of integrated education has been illustrated in recent research. Paolini et al. (2004) suggested that additional benefits may be gained from the 'vicarious' experience of having ingroup friends who have friends in the outgroup. These indirect friendships have a positive impact on intergroup relations, and can be implemented on a larger scale, as each positive direct contact experience has a 'ripple effect' on his or her wider group of friends. These results have important implications for integrated education, mainly because one of the major criticisms levelled at the integrated education sector is that due to the small numbers of students receiving an integrated education in Northern Ireland it is likely to only have a modest impact of segregation and intergroup relations. These findings challenge that criticism and indicate that the direct contact experiences of integrated students may be having a much wider impact via the ripple effect caused by the vicarious experience of having indirect contact with the outgroup. Indeed, Hewstone et al. (2006: 115) concluded that integrated education provides "the greatest potential for implementing peace education" in Northern Ireland.

As noted previously, in addition to integrated schools (which serve less than 10% of Northern Irish children) there are interventions within the segregated education system to improve the quality of knowledge of the other community and increase inter-community contact such EMU, CH and short term cross-community contact schemes. Research evaluating these schemes is limited (Kilpatrick & Leitch, 2004) and superficial (Hewstone et al., 2005). However, reviews of the findings from research with the integrated sector suggest some indications that these interventions are having a positive impact (Trew, 1989; Hewstone et al., 2005).

Through a secondary analysis of Social Attitude data sets from 1989 and 1991 Cairns and Dunn (1995) discovered positive correlations between contact and attitudes towards intergroup mixing and also between contact and positive attitudes towards the other community. In an analysis of contact based interventions Trew (1986) found that interventions allowed Catholics and Protestants to create long lasting friendships with members of the other community and that the contact experiences moderated negative attitudes towards the outgroup.

In a review of the first few years of EMU provision in Northern Irish schools Smith and Robinson (1996) suggested only limited benefits and again remarked on the lack of meaningful contact and discussion of controversial issues. Kilpatrick and Leitch (2004) set out to explore whether EMU or CH had been successful through the use of qualitative interviews, focus groups and classroom observation with students and staff at Protestant controlled, Catholic maintained and integrated elementary and post-elementary schools. The findings illustrate the uneven and superficial nature of much of the EMU, CH and contact based interventions, but they also note that the interventions can lead to positive changes in attitude, increased understanding of the other community and additionally the students viewed sustained long-term contact as an effective way to improve community relations.

Although the majority of studies exploring the impact of the integrated sector and initiatives in segregated schools are positive, it must be noted that these approaches invite a number of criticisms. Many focus on the problems of getting past the culture of avoidance in Northern Ireland in which people stay clear of controversial topics in mixed company (Darby, 1991; Ferguson & Cairns, 1996) thus reducing meaningful contact. Other academics and observers argue that the students at integrated schools are from middle class and mixed residential backgrounds and are not reflective of the children caught up in the conflict, although evidence for this is limited (see Duffy & Evans, 1997; Gallagher et al., 2003).

McGrellis (2004) in interviews with children in both integrated and segregated schools highlights some of the negative findings Kilpatrick and Leitch (2004) discuss, namely that the school interventions gloss over issues in an attempt to reduce in-school tensions. McGrellis also argues that as the contact experience is set apart for the student's community and family, the impact has a limited reach as families and communities place barriers to intergroup contact outside the school gates. Other commentators have questioned the ability and motivation of teachers to deliver contact work and the full curriculum simultaneously, suggesting a large variation in the quality of the contact work (Kilpatrick & Leitch, 2004: Montgomery et al., 2003). The motives of students taking part in cross-community contact are also questioned by McGrellis (2004) and to some extent by Kilpatrick and Leitch (2004), who suggest some take part to learn who the enemy are, so they will be able to spot them in the future and verbally or physically attack them. Worryingly, Schubotz and Robinson (2006) report that 16-year-olds were significantly less optimistic than adults about community relations and were pessimistic about possible improvements in community relations in the future.

Conclusion

In general, research into the impact of integrated and to a lesser degree interventions in segregated schools are having a positive impact on intergroup relations in Northern Ireland, particularly in increasing outgroup friendships and improving attitudes towards mixing and moderating negative attitudes towards the other group. Recent evidence to identity change among those attending integrated schools is promising, but more research supporting these findings is needed in the light of the weight of evidence from earlier studies suggesting this is not taking place.

The research also indicate that the integrated schools and contact programmes in segregated schools are of mixed quality, with many not meeting Allport's (1954) conditions, never mind the conditions developed through SIT research (see Cairns, 1996). The schools and teachers involved need more motivation, training and time to face up to the complexities involved in creating optimal contact which will assist in bringing gains created through building interpersonal friendships into building better intergroup relations.

Northern Ireland has to deal with a long history of intergroup hostility and ethno-political conflict and in doing this the education system has a vital role to play; despite the drawbacks, integrated education and intergroup contact currently offer the best opportunities to develop better relations among Northern Ireland's youth. It is critical that the government continues its support for these initiatives, but also that the educators take note of the research to improve their practice.

References

Abrams, D., and Hogg, M. A. 2004. 'Metatheory: Lessons from Social Identity Research', *Personality & Social Psychology Review*, 8(2): 98–106.
Allport, G. W. 1954. *The Nature of Prejudice*. Reading, MA. Addison-Wesley.
Cairns, E. 1982. 'Intergroup conflict in Northern Ireland,' in H. Tajfel (ed.), *Social Identity and Intergroup Relations*. London. Cambridge University Press: 277–297.
Cairns, E. 1996. *Children and Political Violence*. Oxford. Blackwell.
Cairns, E., et al. 1993. Attitudes towards education in Northern Ireland: A review. In R. Osborne, R. Cormack & A. M. Gallagher (eds.) *After the reforms: Education and policy in Northern Ireland*. Aldershot: Avebury.
Cairns, E., and Dunn, S. 1995. *The Correlates of Adult Cross-community Contact in Northern Ireland: A report to the Central Community Relations Unit*. Coleraine. Centre for the Study of Conflict.
Cairns, E., Wilson, R., Gallagher, T. & Trew, K. (1995). Psychology's contribution to understanding conflict in Northern Ireland. *Peace and Conflict: Journal of Peace Psychology*, *1*, 2, 131-148
Community Relations Unit. *A Shared Future: Policy and Strategic Framework for Good Relations in Northern Ireland*. (2005). Stormont. Community Relations Unit.
Darby, J. 1983. *Northern Ireland: Background to the Conflict*. Belfast. Appletree Press.

Darby, J. 1991. *What's Wrong with Conflict?* Occasional Paper Number Three. Coleraine. Centre for the Study of Conflict.

Darby, J. (1997). *Scorpions in a Bottle: Conflicting Cultures in Northern Ireland.* London: Minority Rights Publications.

Darby, J., and Dunn, S. 1987. 'Segregated schools: The research evidence', in R. D. Osborne et al. (eds). *Education and Policy in Northern Ireland.* Belfast. Policy Research Institute.

Davies, J., and Turner, I. F. 1984. 'Friendship choices in an integrated primary school in Northern Ireland', *British Journal of Social Psychology* 23: 285–286.

Duffy, M. and Evans, G. 1997. 'Class, Community Polarisation and Politics', in L. Dowds et al. (eds), *Social Attitudes in Northern Ireland: The Sixth Report.* Belfast. Appletree Press.

Fay, M. T., et al. 1998. *Northern Ireland's Troubles: The Human Costs.* London. Pluto.

Ferguson, N. and Cairns, E. 1996. 'Political violence and moral maturity in Northern Ireland', *Political Psychology* 17(4): 713–725.

Gallager, A. M., et al. 2003. *Integrated Education in Northern Ireland: Participation, Profile and Performance (Report No 1).* Coleraine. UNESCO Centre, University of Ulster.

Gallagher, T. 2004. 'Education and equality in Northern Ireland', in O. Hargie and D. Dickson (eds), *Researching the Troubles: Social Science Perspectives on the Northern Ireland Conflict.* Edinburgh. Mainstream: 59–84.

Gallagher, T., and Smith, A. 2002. 'Attitudes to Academic Selection, Integrated Education and Diversity within the Curriculum', in M Gray et al. (eds), *Social Attitudes in Northern Ireland: The Eighth Report.* London: Pluto: 120–137.

Hayes, B. C., et al. 2007. 'Integrated education, intergroup relations and political identities in Northern Ireland', *Social Problems* 54(4): 454–482.

Hewstone, M., and Cairns, E. 2001. 'Social Psychology and Intergroup Conflict', in D. Chirot and M. E. P. Seligman (eds). *Ethno-political Warfare: Causes, Consequences and Possible Solutions.* Washington, DC. APA: 319–342.

Hewstone, M., et al. 2005. 'Intergroup Contact in a Divided Society: Challenging Segregation in Northern Ireland', in D. Abrams et al. (eds), *The Social Psychology of Inclusion and Exclusion.* Philadelphia, PA. Psychology Press: 265–292.

Hewstone, M., et al. 2006. 'Intergroup contact, forgiveness, and experience of "The Troubles" in Northern Ireland', *Journal of Social Issues* 62(1): 99–120.

Irwin, C. 1991. *Education and the Development of Social Integration in Divided Societies.* Belfast. Department of Social Anthropology, Queen's University.

Kilpatrick, R., and Leitch, R. 2004. 'Teachers' and pupils' educational experiences and school based responses to the conflict in Northern Ireland', *Journal of Social Issues* 60(3): 563–586.

Leach, C. W., and Williams, W. 1999. 'Group identity and conflicting expectations of the future in Northern Ireland', *Political Psychology*, 20(4): 875–897.

Livingstone, A., and Haslam, S. A. 2008. 'The importance of social identity content in a setting of chronic social conflict: Understanding intergroup relations in Northern Ireland', *British Journal of Social Psychology* 47: 1–21.

McClenahan, C. 1995. *The Impact and Nature of Intergroup Contact in Planned Integrated and Desegregated Schools in Northern Ireland.* Unpublished PhD thesis. Coleraine. University of Ulster.

McClenahan, C., et al. 1996. 'Intergroup friendships: Integrated and desegregated schools in Northern Ireland', *Journal of Social Psychology* 136: 549–558.

McEwen, A., and Salters, J. 1993. 'Integrated education: The views of parents', in R. D. Osborne et al. (eds) *After the Reforms: Education and Policy in Northern Ireland.* Aldershot, UK: Avebury: 161–176.

Mac Ginty, R., and Darby, J. 2002. *Guns and Government: The Management of the Northern Ireland Peace Process.* Basingstoke. Palgrave.

Mac Ginty, R., et al. 2007. 'No War, No Peace: Northern Ireland after the Agreement', *Political Psychology*, 28(1): 1–12.

McGlynn, C., et al. 2004. 'Moving out of conflict: the contribution of integrated schools in Northern Ireland to identity, attitudes, forgiveness and reconciliation', *Journal of Peace Education* 1(2):147–163.

McGlynn, C. & Bekerman, Z. 2007. 'The management of pupil difference in Catholic-Protestant and Palestinian-Jewish integrated education in Northern Ireland and Israel', *Compare* 37(5): 689–705.

McGrellis, S. 2004. *Pushing the Boundaries in Northern Ireland: Young People, Violence and Sectarianism. Families & Social Capital ESRC Research Group Working Paper No. 8.* London. Families & Social Capital ESRC Research Group, London South Bank University.

Montgomery, A., et al. 2003. *Integrated Education in Northern Ireland: Integration in Practice (Report No 2).* Coleraine. UNESCO Centre, University of Ulster.

Northern Ireland Council for Integrated Education. 2008. Retrieved 13 October 2008 from http://www.nicie.org.

Paolini, S., et al. 2004. 'Effects of direct and indirect cross-group friendships on judgements of Catholic and Protestants in Northern Ireland: The mediating role of an anxiety-reduction mechanism', *Personality and Social Psychology Bulletin* 30: 770–786.

Pettigrew, T. F. 1998. 'Intergroup contact theory', *Annual Review of Psychology* 49: 65–85.

Pettigrew, T.F., and Tropp, L.R. 2000. 'Does intergroup contact reduce prejudice?: Recent meta-analytic findings.' In S. Oskamp (ed.), *Reducing Prejudice and Discrimination.* Mahwah, NJ. Lawrence Erlbaum Associates: 93–114.

Purdie, B. 1990. *Politics in the Streets.* Belfast. Blackstaff Press.

Schubotz, D., and Robinson, G. 2006. 'Cross-community integration and mixing: Does it make a difference?', *Research Update* 43: 1–4. Retrieved 13 October 2008 from http://www.ark.ac.uk.

Smith, A., and Robinson, A. 1996. *Education for Mutual Understanding: The Initial Sstatutory Years.* Coleraine. University of Ulster, Centre for the Study of Conflict.

Stringer, M., et al. 2000. *The Impact of Schooling on the Social Attitudes of Children.* Belfast. Integrated Education Fund.

Stringer, M., and Hunter, J. 2008. 'Countering political violence and terrorism in young people through intergroup contacts', in M. D. Ulusoy (ed.) *Political Violence, Organized Crime, Terrorism and Youth.* Amsterdam. IOS Press: 43–51.

Tajfel, H. 1978. *Differentiation between Social Groups: Studies in the Social Psychology of Intergroup Relations.* London. Academic Press.

Tajfel, H. 1981. *Human Groups and Social Categories: Studies in Social Psychology.* Cambridge. Cambridge University Press.

Tajfel, H., and Turner, J. C. 1979. 'An integrative theory of intergroup conflict.' In W. G. Austin and S. Worchel (eds), *The Social Psychology of Intergroup Relations.* Monterey, CA. Brooks/Cole: 33–47.Tajfel, H., and Turner, J. C. 1986. 'The social identity theory of intergroup behaviour.' In S. Worchel and W. A. Austin (eds.), *Psychology of Intergroup Relations.* Chicago. Nelson-Hall: 7–24.

Trew, K. 1986. 'Catholic and Protestant contact in Northern Ireland', in M. Hewstone and R. Brown (eds), *Contact and Conflict in Intergroup Encounters.* Monterey: Brooks/Cole: 33–47.

Trew, K. 1989. 'Evaluating the impact of contact schemes for Catholic and Protestant children', in J. Harbison (ed.), *Growing up in Northern Ireland.* Belfast. Learning Resources Unit, Stranmillis College: 131–159.

Trew, K., and Benson, D. E. 1996. 'Dimensions of social identity in Northern Ireland.' In G. Breakwell and E. Lyons (eds), *Changing European Identities: Social-psychological Analyses of Social Change.* Oxford. Butterworth-Heinemann: 123–143.

Turner, J. C. 1982. 'Towards a cognitive redefinition of the social group.' In H. Tajfel (ed.), *Social Identity and Intergroup Relations.* Cambridge. Cambridge University Press: 15-40.

Whyte, J. H. 1990. *Interpreting Northern Ireland.* Oxford. Clarendon.

CHAPTER FOUR

VOICES FROM THE SHADOWS OF VIOLENCE POST-CONFLICT: USING ARTS-BASED APPROACHES WITH PUPILS AND TEACHERS IN NORTHERN IRELAND

RUTH LEITCH

This chapter summarizes and illustrates aspects of the Enabling Young Voices (EYV) project that was undertaken with teachers and pupils in post-primary schools in a rural area of Northern Ireland, an area which has seen some of the worst effects of the protracted political conflict over the period known as "the Troubles". EYV was designed as a qualitative, in-depth and multi-level research and development project to facilitate pupil voice. Its primary concern was to develop sustainable means to promote creative, pupil-centred educational responses to conflict resolution and peace-building in a society emerging from conflict. The project received government funding from the Office of First Minister and Deputy First Minister, Northern Ireland, under the Victims' Strategy Implementation Fund: Reshape, Rebuild, Achieve (2002). It was a two-year collaborative, inter-agency project, the aim of which was to extend existing research on how young people perceive themselves to have been affected by the Northern Ireland conflict after the ceasefire and to be responsive to these voices through educational developments. The main partners were a university education department, a local education authority (covering education welfare and youth) and a voluntary victims' support organization. In collaboration, the project was designed to (i) respond to an externally driven policy agenda and (ii) centralize a participatory action research framework (PAR). Within this framework, the significant developmental dimension was concerned to pilot effective interventions with young people, teachers and schools in an attempt to improve educational responses to post-conflict issues and, specifically, to create opportunities for young people's voices to be heard on matters of significance to them in this socio-political context.

The Northern Ireland context

Northern Ireland has been and remains a deeply divided (and segregated) society due to the protracted nature of the religious and socio-political divisions. The conflict is most often constructed as a clash of religious identities, although religion is only one dimension of the conflict with the two main protagonists to the conflict characterized (or more often stereotyped) as holding distinct identities: Roman Catholic Irish nationalists who desire Irish unity, and Protestant unionists who wish to remain part of the United Kingdom.

The Northern Ireland conflict spanned more than a generation and is most frequently referred to as "the Troubles". In terms of the human cost, from 1966 until August 1994, with the IRA cessation of violence, there had been a total of 3517[1] deaths and over 40,000 people had been injured.[2] Some 26% of all victims were aged under 22 and 91% of all victims were male (Fay, Smyth & Morrissey, 1997). Since the Good Friday Agreement (1998),[3] a relatively high incidence of post-conflict deaths and violence continue to be recorded (McKittrick et al., 1999; Melaugh, 2007). Recent research on the impact of the Northern Ireland conflict (Muldoon et al., 2006) indicates that, among 2000 individuals surveyed in Northern Ireland, one in ten had been bereaved as a result of the conflict. Political violence had not been distributed evenly across the country, most fatalities occurring in areas of high social deprivation while in more affluent areas violence was minimally experienced (Gallagher, 2004: 633). This differential experience may in part explain the "culture of silence" that persists and is sometimes described as a "safety valve" allowing people in all communities to appear to deny the significance of the impact of this long-term conflict (Leitch, 2000; Smyth, 2004).

Conflict and children

The "culture of silence" extends to conflicting interpretations of the impact on children and young people of growing up in a divided and violent society. Evidence from early research on the psychological impact of the violence was that children and young people were not significantly affected and did in fact appear to cope well within normal anxiety ranges (Lyons, 1971; Harbinson, 1983). The normality and ordinariness of Northern Irish life was referred to as playing a key role in children's stability. Schools were viewed as "safe havens", "oases of calm" or "refuges"; Leitch and

Kilpatrick capture these perceptions among principals and teachers in the results of their 1999 study. This position has, however, been critiqued in more recent times by research highlighting the difficulties associated with the legacy of the protracted conflict on our youth (Gallagher, 2004; Trew, 2004; McAuley, 2004; Muldoon, 2004). In 1996, the United Nations reported a study, under the leadership of expert Graça Machel, which analysed experiences of the impact of armed conflict on children internationally, including Northern Ireland, with a view to raising awareness of such situations and developing an agenda for action. This report recognized that "armed conflict" is a complex term that encompasses a broad range of conflicts from full-scale warfare and genocide (as happened in Rwanda and Cambodia) through to low intensity and episodic conflict. Northern Ireland's most recent "Troubles" are frequently described as "low-intensity urban guerrilla conflict" (Muldoon, 2004: 459). Here, low-intensity conflict has been characterized by multiple forms of conflict and ongoing violence since 1966, including assassinations, bombings, bomb scares, mortar bomb attacks, sectarianism, intimidation, threats, punishment beatings as well as street violence, terrorist acts and violence by the state.

Elsewhere, it has been shown that even when exposure to actual armed violence is limited, the effects on the lives of children and their families have an immense impact (United Nations, 1996: 11). As Lindberg and others (2007: 64) suggest:

> Even children who are not direct targets or victims in national or regional conflicts will be exposed to painful events. They may witness torture and killing, abductions and arrests, and experience disruptions in daily life and school routines.

Many children directly and indirectly affected by violence, even in low-intensity conflicts, will present with psychiatric disorders, most predominantly post-traumatic stress, in the long or short term. Thomas Hammarberg (2007: 1), Council of Europe Commissioner for Human Rights, in an annual lecture in Belfast's Children's Law Centre, spoke of how children in these "troubles"

> experience in many respects the same agony as those in full scale war. During such conflicts that we had here in Northern Ireland or now in Gaza, for instance, children can never feel fully secure – the violence is penetrating their daily lives.

Trauma suffered by families and whole communities may not only result from a single event but rather, as Stewart (2001: 143) indicates, many families in Northern Ireland, particularly those who have lived in localities where on-going political violence is common, experience "continuous, low-intensity trauma". Gibson (2006: 70) compares this type of "on-going stress created by political violence" to the causes of "continuous traumatic stress syndrome" and challenges the current definition of Post Traumatic Stress Disorder (PTSD),[4] which she judges as failing to recognize the experiences of those who are the victims of prolonged, repeated violence, such as political violence. Research evidence in Northern Ireland has suggested that the threats to children during conflict vary markedly, according to gender, age, social, religious or ethnic status and position within the family (Boyden et al., 2002).

Enabling Young Voices project (EYV)

Six years after the political watershed of the Good Friday Agreement, in 2004, the EYV initiative set out to determine whether or not young people now in post-primary education (some of whom have been born just before the period of this "peaceful new beginning") would show differing perspectives on themselves in relation to growing up in Northern Ireland and have a range of differing needs and expectations from those described in previous research studies during the heat of the Northern Ireland conflict (e.g. Leitch & Kilpatrick, 1999; Kilpatrick & Leitch, 2004). EYV was also concerned to explore possibilities to support an "agenda for change", to determine what was achievable in terms of supporting appropriate and effective pupil-centred educational responses in the light of, for example, the introduction of Local and Global Citizenship (LGC) within the revised curriculum for Northern Ireland (CCEA, 2005, 2007).

The Northern Ireland policy agenda, as with many countries emerging from violent conflict, placed a high priority on responding to the perceived needs of those affected most significantly. The Victims' Strategy Implementation Fund provided funding support aimed at 'delivering practical help and services to those who have suffered most over 30 years of violence' (OFMDFM, 2002: 1). Children and young people were identified as an area of specific concern (2002: 15) and education and learning as a priority (2002: 8–9). EYV was designed to respond to this priority but the project team was cognizant, in its research design, of expectations regarding accountability for public funding regarding outcome and impact measures. Thus, within the PAR, a framework of 'illuminative evaluation' (after Parlett

& Hamilton, 1975) was adopted to evidence impact of the initiative rather than any instrumental or experimental approach (e.g. objectives-outcome models). This allowed a comprehensive approach to data collection over the duration of the study, including qualitative (subjective, anecdotal and impressionistic) and quantitative (ratings, measures of changes, differences between groups, schools etc). Nevertheless, ideologically, this approach necessarily involved some "researching on" rather than a "researching with" participants; a subject-object power relationship that the EYV team had no desire to reinforce in an educational context with young people after the conflict: "Young people must not be seen as problems or victims but as key contributors in the planning and implementation of long-term solutions" (United Nations, 1996: 54, para. 242).

With this spirit in mind, the PAR framework[5] aimed to encapsulate the principles and processes necessary (a) for facilitating pupil voice and promoting pupil autonomy, and (b) for teacher transformation and development through practitioner action inquiry (thus also encapsulating teachers' voices). In practitioner action inquiry interventions, members of the EYV project team (comprising a teacher-researcher, an educational welfare officer and a youth worker) provided facilitation, curriculum support, peer support, modelling, information, access to other agencies, materials and methods for reflection and evaluation for the participating teachers (and their pupils). Arts-based methods of inquiry and creative pedagogical approaches were the spine of the PAR and where possible pupils and teachers were actively engaged in collaboration about the project and impact measures.

Art, Pedagogy and Research

Within the PAR framework, the epistemological and instrumental value of integrating art in educational practice with art in educational research was considered crucial to illuminating and breaking through the anticipated culture of silence. Creativity is often a path to reflexivity and, as Barone and Eisner (1997) suggest, the creation of visual art can evoke meanings that elude linguistic description and help people to articulate the unsayable. Thus, arts-based inquiry and pedagogical processes, involving creative expression, were blended to form data collection methods as well as media for helping pupils articulate the contents and meanings of past and present experience associated with growing up and living in Northern Ireland. Combining art in research and art in pedagogy held the potential for shaping and conveying new ideas, insights and perspectives. This mélange is not as strange as it may seem, for, as Kritskaya (2003: 7) indicates, 'Often researchers, who rely on arts-informed approaches to inquiry, deal with the intellectual and emotional tasks similar to those that students grapple with in the classrooms'.

Pedagogy – engaging in "aesthetic experience" (after Dewey, 1989) – is at the heart of artful modes of inquiry and learning through creative expression. Such aesthetic engagement leads to the creation of some new form, whether in image, word or movement; a form which is a means to communication and/or self-expression. In a pedagogical sense, these forms and processes may expand the horizons of an individual's thinking, thus helping them create new understandings, new emotional responses and shaping new skill repertoires or strategies for action. Complementary to the artful engagement is the narrativization of experience. Narrativization, in relation to creative artwork, becomes a form of reflective inquiry – 'the narration of lived experience' (after Bruner, 1990). Here the art piece itself tells the story of experience and, in this manner "art celebrates with intensity the moments in which the past reinforces the present and in which the future is a quickening of what now is" (Dewey, 1934: 17).

Kritskaya (2003), too, sees narration in this context as a potential strategy for educators to liberate memory and allow for a re-articulation of a person's identity where a 'renewed understanding of self becomes possible' (2003: 4) in distinction to others.

Research: Arts-based research is an undefined and contested field within qualitative research (Barone, 2001). In its simplest definition, it is the use of the arts as objects of inquiry as well as modes of investigation (Mc Niff, 1998: 13). In the context of a therapeutic orientation, Huss and Cwikel (2005: 1–16) comment that in the arts-based paradigm, by handing over creativity (the contents of the research) and its interpretation (an explanation of the contents) to the research participant, 'the participant is empowered'. They assert that this intensifies and equalizes the researcher–participant relationship, which, in turn, facilitates the generation of data that is a more exact and explicit cultural representation and one which uses 'emotional as well as cognitive ways of knowing.' Given the pervasive avoidance of talking about the emotional aspects of experience (in this context, the political conflict in Northern Ireland), creative and arts-based methods were viewed as potential means to 'break down the veneer of orderliness, and get back to the (any) underlying turmoil before it was tidied up and made acceptable' (Birtchnell, 2003: 37).

Negotiation of access to participating schools
⇩
Ethical agreement and protocols (principals, parents, young people,
teachers, youth workers, EYV team).
⇩
Baseline data collection with pupils and teachers – focus groups
and mini surveys (awareness, issues and needs analysis)
⇩
Interventions:- (i) Individual schools – supported classroom and
group activities (with pupils and teachers)[6]
(ii) Cross-community engagement between schools
(iii) INSET courses – supporting teacher development through
personal development and action inquiry
(iv) Curriculum and resources development (curricular resource;
directory with/for young people; young persons' website; mini-
conference etc).
⇩
Evaluation of interventions
⇩
Analysis, synthesis and dissemination

Table 4-1. Key steps in the research process

EYV was based in a geographical area that, according to the Cost of the Troubles Study (1999), had experienced the highest number of Troubles-related fatalities outside of Belfast. The area consequently became known locally as 'Murder Triangle'. In addition this area is adjacent to the Irish Republic and residents in these border areas have experienced a high level of both military and paramilitary activity.

A sample of 25 post-primary schools from across this geographical area was invited to participate in the EYV study. Given the 'conspiracy of silence' that permeates Northern Ireland society (Cairns, 1987) and the commonly held view that contemporary schoolchildren, since the conflict, have little or no awareness of the earlier Troubles, the process of negotiating access to schools, pupils and teachers was slow and fraught. Eighteen post-primary schools ultimately agreed to participate.

The sample takes account of differing denominations and school management types in Northern Ireland,[7] as well as geographical location and the uneven distribution of violence even within this area. Over the course of the study, EYV worked directly and indirectly with over 400 young people aged 11 to 18 (45% identified as Catholic; 50% identified as Protestant and 5% identified as other). Fifty-three teachers (45% male, 55% female), representing a percentage profile of identified religious affiliations similar to the pupil sample, agreed to participate across the four main interventions. Additionally, EYV had access to a much wider cohort of teachers and school personnel through awareness-raising and dissemination aspects of the study.[8]

Research methods were chosen to be fit for purpose. Standard qualitative methods of data collection (for level 1 type baseline research and ongoing evaluation) were combined with arts-based methods of inquiry and creative pedagogical approaches (for level 2 type data generation – evidence of learning, insight, transformation and change – within the collaborative developmental aspects of the study). In the latter case, it is not easy (nor necessarily appropriate) to distinguish the research method from the pedagogical processes involved, where the focus was as much on opportunities for personal learning and transformation as for data-gathering. The child-centred research methods and creative processes helped the young people to express their views and feelings on their experiences of growing up in Northern Ireland. Table 4-2 summarizes the differing methods used with pupils and young people across the research and development dimensions of the study.

Ethics and Sensitive Issues

Given the potential sensitivity of focus for the EYV study, the ethical process was carefully considered and, in addition to university ethical scrutiny, an ethical charter was negotiated for all involved, project members being subject to police checks. All post-primary schools invited to participate were fully informed of the project through face to face meetings, prior to agreement. Young people invited to participate were provided with the opportunity to discuss the research process in detail before agreeing to engage. A consent pack was distributed, including an information leaflet, a letter and individual consent forms for parents/guardians and young person consent forms. The consent form was layered so that young people could identify the types of data they were willing to have released for differing research purposes and indicated that they were able to withdraw from the project at any time and that the information would be anonymised. A similar process was set out for teachers participating in EYV.

Without wishing to alarm parents, children or teachers unnecessarily nor

Level 1 methods		Level 2 methods		
Baseline research		Work with young people Individual schools	Work with young people Cross-community	INSET teacher development and Practitioner inquiry
YOUNG PEOPLE	TEACHERS	YOUNG PEOPLE	YOUNG PEOPLE	TEACHERS
Walking (or 3-cornered debates)		Ice-breakers; trust exercises	Icebreakers; trust exercises	Autobiographical timelines
Mini-survey		Discussion; flipchart work	Discussions; flipchart work	Scenarios; recorded discussions
		Collage and storying	Collage and storying	Collage and storying
Focus groups (audio-recorded)		Movement and drama; role-play	Murals and montage	PowerPoint presentations
Incident analysis		Time-line work	Listening exercises	Logs and written reflections
Comments, interviews, recorded reflections, and evaluation sheets etc.		Individually generated activities e.g. interviewing members of the emergency services who had been involved in the Troubles	Individually generated activities e.g. poetry and use of photographs	Multi-media presentations

Table 4-2. Research methods for young people and teachers

put them off participation, the EYV team considered the possibilities that children, or indeed teachers, who participated in the project might unwittingly open themselves up to past experiences of a traumatic nature. The potential for this was disclosed from the outset to allow properly informed consent and was set out in the information pack so that prospective participants could contact EYV project team members to discuss any concerns. In the event, only four parents availed themselves of this facility and only two refused permission for their son or daughter to take part. All participants were made aware of the importance of letting the team members know if they were upset by any of the processes engaged in during EYV and all were made aware of sources of support and helping agencies in the local area and further afield.

Hearing the Voices

Data were handled at two levels. For the baseline, data were reduced through frequency counts and scoring to evaluate the overall impact of the EYV project. This comprised, for example, descriptive statistics of attitudinal change across the main groups of participants before and after the EYV project. Within the PAR, at the qualitative-interpretive level, creative data were analysed thematically, through a form of "connoisseurship" (Eisner, 1985). Thus, verbal, digital and visual data arising from classroom experiences were viewed and reviewed independently by the research team and categorized into themes, using a grounded theory approach, in relation to the aims of the study. Themes were then collated and evidence cross-checked through group examination to interrogate meanings. Since much of the creative data was co-constructed, participants' voices and artistic expressions were also incorporated to "speak for themselves", in order to illustrate the individual and collective expressions of post-conflict experience and any transformative effects deriving from engagement throughout the project. Some of the classroom work and teacher development work is offered below as case illustration.

Illustrations of EYV Research into Practice

It is impossible to report fully the wide range of results and effects resulting from the total EYV study. What is illustrated below, however, is a number of findings from selected aspects of the EYV study, including each of the main strands: Young People; Schools and Teachers; and Curriculum. These will highlight some of the significant ways the data contribute to current debates on such matters as the importance of facilitating young people's voices, identity theory (e.g. "single identity" versus the "social contact" hypotheses), intergenerational impact and trauma and how to promote teacher-centred and pupil-centred educational responses to conflict resolution and peace-building in a society emerging from conflict.

Young People's Voices

Awareness and impact of the political conflict

> Everything has been swept under the carpet and ... you can't speak about it openly, you can't discuss it with some people. (Boy, Year 10)

Despite the perceived "culture of silence", and the prevailing view that schools have been centres of stability in children's lives before and after the conflict (Leitch & Kilpatrick, 1999), the young people surveyed indicated that they were very aware of many aspects of the political conflict, past and present. Twenty-two per cent of the young people felt they had been directly affected with 25% indicating that they had a family member who had died or been injured as a result of the Troubles. This is a high incidence even in compared with recent research where 10% of the adults surveyed across Northern Ireland recorded bereavement of a family member (Muldoon et al., 2006). Only one focus group of young people (Year 9) in a school (in a locality with a low index of conflict-related violence) felt that their educational experiences had not been detrimentally affected in any way by the conflict, indicating that the problems, in their view, belonged to their parents' generation. Others were quite clear that even if they were unscathed, there was an indirect, intergenerational effect. For example:

> We haven't maybe been directly affected but ultimately because of our parents . . . they would have been . . . so it has affected us. We don't maybe have the help at home that we should have and I think that's a factor. (Girl, Year 10: Protestant).

> My dad's younger brother got shot by the Army before I was born and, like, Dad never got over it. This affected the whole house and he still won't mention it but Mum told me that's why he gets depressed and all! (Boy, Year 9: Catholic)

Uncle Liam was beaten with iron bars up our alley and he can't never walk
the same. He used to really scare me when he came to our house in case they
came after him again. (Boy, Year 10: Catholic)

Weingarten (2004) presents a framework for understanding how the
trauma of political violence experienced in one generation can pass to another that did not directly experience it. Within a clinical orientation, she
talks of the importance of family therapists understanding transgenerational
processes and the importance of therapists being safe witnesses to this second-order trauma. Educators, too, need to find ways to increase awareness
of and be sensitive to the impact of transgenerational effects in order to
provide safe means (pastorally and/or through the curriculum) by which to
reduce the worst effects of second-order impact on young people. Given
that the topics "Causes and effects of sectarianism and 'the Troubles'" find
their place in Local and Global Citizenship (LGC) in the revised curriculum
(CCEA, 2005) in NI, there is every possibility that such controversial issues or emotional connections could arise in classrooms through reflective
activities and discussion.

Overall, although the incidence of conflict-related events referred to
was not as great as those identified by young people in the 1999 research,
there were many similarities in the pattern, with a significant number of
young people recalling traumatic events which they associated with – e.g.
shooting incidents when at primary school, threats, intimidation, paramilitary activity, sectarian bullying and attacks on schools. There was a strong
view (72%) that learning specifically about the Troubles and the impact on
people emotionally, socially etc should be addressed in school but there was
also a significant concern about the context in which such matters might be
discussed appropriately and with depth:

If it's the right environment, you can talk about it openly. (Girl, Year 9:
Protestant)

You don't talk about it, you don't ever express your opinion because of what
others may think, you don't ever bring it up. (Boy, Year 10: Catholic)

If you can't talk about your views at home, in case they're different, then
school should be the place. (Boy, Year 8: Protestant)

Through creative and pedagogical processes, young people gradually
began to represent their views on what activities, support and resources they
felt would be helpful in their school to educationally support not only them-

selves but particularly those whom they felt were more directly "victims" of the conflict.

Breaking the culture of silence through collage work

Within the collaborative approach with teachers in individual schools and cross-community work, EYV developed and encouraged the use of collage as a primary creative stimulus to pupils' (and indeed teachers') stories and narratives (both explicit and latent) about the political conflict as well as the collages being viewed as primary data sources in themselves.

Collage is a creative technique whereby different materials, artifacts and objects are pasted on a surface to create an artistic composition on a particular theme or topic (Butler-Kisber, 2007). Unlike drawings, collage does not generally stimulate individual concerns about artistic ability. Teachers found this to be a particularly important consideration when undertaking image-based or creative research with adolescents who may be resistant to drawing tasks. Selecting materials, images and phrases from magazines and newspapers to symbolize views on issues seems to be a more immediately engaging and practical process for many at this age – especially when it comes to portraying matters of a more sensitive nature. Individuals may undertake the task or it can be a paired or small group activity in the context of planned cross-community contact (Leitch, 2008).

Collage, in the case of EYV, was found to act as a "safe container" when used by teachers (having undertaken this process themselves previously) with individual groups/classes pupils in schools and with cross-community groups of pupils. The process of collage-making encouraged symbolic expression by young people, who produced collages that were rich, varied, powerful representations of deeply-held but frequently unarticulated hopes, confusions and fears. Young people then were provided with opportunities to reflect upon, co-interpret and share their images, stories and any meanings identified.

Despite commonly held views that children and young people born since the ceasefire have little or no awareness of the political conflict in Northern Ireland and have been relatively unaffected by it, the opposite was more frequently found to be the case as the following collage and associated narrative suggest. This narrative was attached to a collage titled *Lurgan, a Divided Town*:

> Basically, it's [the conflict] just created a division, you know. Our town is split, like, right down the middle. If you are wearing a uniform in a different

community, you could get beat up. Growing up here, if there weren't the Troubles, there'd be more mixed schools. You're also restricted in what you can say and where 'cos you don't want to offend people ... like at cross-community events, people are, like, from wearing, like, Celtic or Rangers tops and stuff like that 'cos it'll obviously offend someone ... If something does happen [in your community] you are just that scared, you don't want to tell anybody in case that stuff does happen again in the future ... and if you say anything, they'll come back and hit you or something. (Lee,[9] Year 11)

The following narrative excerpt emerged through reflection on a collage entitled *Split Religions* by Year 11 girls (Protestant and Catholic) working collaboratively in a cross-community context:

Well, we wanted to show that there is hurt on both sides but it's still split. Down the middle. It's supposed to be peace here but the dove of peace is worn out 'cos it just goes on with the politicians on each side shouting, and people are still getting killed . . . it seems to us that there will never be peace.

Using collage allowed the young people to narrate not just generalized or partisan positions regarding the conflict (though these were in evidence) but also personal narratives of the conflict that were emotional and moving. These art images also seemed to create sufficient security and energy for genuine conversations, across the divide of the two main religious groups, when engaging in cross-community work (i.e. Catholics and Protestants working together through the curriculum), focusing on reconciliation and peace-building.

Teachers' Voices

Awareness and impact of the political conflict

It was always a matter of "let's not discuss this" because this was something I felt was better, you know, never touched at all ... it's a minefield. (Female teacher, Secondary High School)

It was interesting to observe that during the baseline research participating teachers were significantly more reticent than pupils about opening up to discuss their views and experiences of how schools and young people were affected by any aspect of the past and/or present situation in Northern

Ireland. There was evidence of initial denial about any impact of the political conflict. A number of teachers were dismissive of contemporary pupils' understanding of the Troubles and the influence of these on people's lives – "they haven't got a clue" was a phrase heard repeatedly across a number of teacher focus groups, thus separating children's awareness radically from those of adults. Others relied on children and young people's resilience as a justification for not needing to address any potentially sensitive or controversial issues. However, the use of creative incident (time-line) analysis by teachers themselves opened up specific recollections – mortar bomb attacks, bomb scares, school evacuations, shootings into schools, pupil injuries, death of pupil(s), parental murder as well as, in one case, a teacher being held at gunpoint in her classroom. A considerable number of these events had occurred since 1998, as well as generic issues of concern that had arisen and which they considered to be related – pupil behaviour, e.g. hyper-vigilance; political graffiti; sectarian bullying; social deprivation; racism; disrupted learning. None of the teachers could recall any specific training (curricular or pastoral) in relation to any aspect of the Troubles and no mention could be made of any outside support (from specialist agencies) for pupils who had suffered loss, bereavement or injury. Yet, as O'Connor et al. (2006: 10) identified in their early evaluation of Citizenship Education here:

> Issues that tended to be considered as controversial were generally confined to challenging local contexts, such as religious discrimination, sectarianism and the use of violence for political ends.

As the opening teacher statement to this section suggests, teaching or touching upon any of the issues in relation to the political conflict was viewed metaphorically as a "minefield" or "hornets' nest", too controversial and thus best left untouched. Through EYV, specific development needs began slowly to be catalogued at school and individual teacher levels with participants gradually identifying how they might want to change or improve their practice in their own subject areas or pastoral roles in respect of issues relating to the conflict. This led to a range of teachers having the opportunity to be supported by the EYV team through choosing one of the three forms of support and intervention that ensued:

1 individual schools' programmes with young people;

2 cross-community schools' work with young people;

3 INSET teacher development through practitioner inquiry.

Some elements of intervention (3), the INSET, will be illustrated below, in order to demonstrate the way in which the personal development of teachers was centralized in this approach to practitioner inquiry.

INSET support programme: Teacher personal development through Practitioner Action Inquiry

The INSET support programme developed was entitled "Handling Sensitive Issues in the Context of the Northern Ireland Troubles" and comprised ten one-day sessions, held every 3–4 weeks.

Programme content was organized into units, covering such aspects as Exploring the past; Remembrance and forgiveness; Understanding emotions; Impact of trauma; Identity formation; Prejudice reduction; Creative pedagogies; Racism and Sectarianism; and Conflict resolution – critical and controversial issues, most of which had been identified through the baseline focus groups with teachers and young people and few of which were being addressed in-depth in any teacher education courses at that time. The content drew on national and international interdisciplinary fields of scholarly research on these issues to inform and scaffold the intellectual basis of practitioner-based inquiry in the programme. Thus, based on their individual and collective learning, each teacher spent time working out what classroom interventions they could progressively plan for in their own classrooms, based on their own learning and personal development. The key principle was that real change would only ensue if the teachers were willing to engage in their own self-exploration on such matters at a personal and emotional level before engaging children in classrooms.

Each INSET session was structured to ensure opportunities for the participating teacher-practitioners to present and reflect upon their successes and challenges, make changes, adapt or add new ideas to implement in a "spiral process of change". Critical to the success of the INSET programme was the creation of a safe and confidential space for the participants, not just to aid the sharing of practice but in the desire to open up genuine opportunities for self-learning and other-learning on the challenging themes raised by the programme. The EYV facilitators were sensitive to the vulnerability which might easily be felt by those who had never spoken publicly about their feelings and experiences of the conflict, never mind within a cross-community group of teachers. They were also mindful that individuals may feel exposed and uneasy when addressing the sensitive issue of the Troubles because educators when dealing with issues such as the conflict in Northern

Ireland must be prepared to encounter heightened emotions. Group contract, active learning and creative methodologies/pedagogies all played an important role in the success of this work.

For this task, each participant brought to the course session two personally important symbols significant to their cultural identity. These symbols were presented and their meanings shared within the group. On the surface this appears as a simple "trust task", in the context of a cross-community of teachers in Northern Ireland, but the personal discourse that accompanied was found to be a deeply challenging, often moving, and involving sometimes deep personal learning. As one of the participants later recorded:

> I was shocked by my own fear at the sight of some of the religious symbols that I did not understand and also by their juxtaposition on the table. I had no idea how we would handle the session but the openness and willingness to hear each others' stories was immensely powerful, not to mention emotionally draining, but I will never forget this session. It has had a huge impact on me.

Such personal engagement and subsequent reflection led on to the heart of the research debate on the relative effectiveness of "Single Identity" work versus the "Contact Hypothesis"[10] for prejudice reduction; the discussion that ensued brought life to an otherwise academic debate and invigorated subsequent reflections on classroom practice. The hugely varied range of tasks throughout the INSET programme ensured that personally engaging experiences like this were built upon, thereby encouraging the participating teachers to take on new challenges with more personal and professional confidence. Overall, formative and summative evaluations of this INSET programme, reinforced by examples from practice development by the two groups[11] of participating teachers, attest to this. This is reported elsewhere in the final report. Indicative feedback was extremely positive, in terms of the challenges undertaken and the consequences for personal and professional learning. Two examples of feedback, from many, are outlined below as testimony to the steps taken by the teacher-practitioners:

> I would always have been reluctant to speak openly about the troubles and/ or religion but over the course, I have more confidence to express myself and to pursue meaningful work in the classroom with young people as a result.

> The Enabling Young Voices project was both enjoyable and enlightening. I was unsure what could be achieved in this school having initially felt that the programme had missed its target pupils. We felt that the programme was

possibly a generation too late. I was delighted to have been proven wrong. I had the experience of gaining confidence from the course and in classrooms watching children from very different backgrounds, socially and education-ally, grow together as a group and interact so well on difficult themes. There have been very positive outcomes judging from the pupils' evaluations and I hope they can continue to build on what they have learnt.

Summary of the Impact of EYV research-in-practice

EYV was an ambitious and complex project in its vision and roll-out. This brief account of research-in-practice can only partially reflect the breadth and depth of the EYV study over time and how it combined research and practice in a dynamic form, with young people's voices at its centre and teachers' voices in support. Some of the key contributions of the project to date could be summarized thus:

- The multi-layered research methodology was influenced and ex-tended through the use of traditional qualitative methods, evaluation frameworks, practitioner inquiry, arts-based, creative and fit-for-pur-pose pedagogical methods.
- Voices of pupils and teachers were central to the work – teachers' and pupils' personal and practical knowledge informed both the research design and practice (interventions) and were crucial to the successful outcomes of the study.
- Pupils clearly indicated that they were aware of and were affected (both directly and indirectly) by the post-conflict situation. There was evidence of ongoing sectarian violence for them and the conse-quences of various losses sustained by their parents' generation that some were having to deal with, but often without acknowledgment.
- Pupils found the use of creative methodologies (such as art and drama) an enjoyable challenging means to explore, extend and narrate their views whether as individuals or in cross-community settings.
- Teachers, as adults, are reluctant to address any sensitive or controver-sial issues concerning the Northern Ireland political conflict in their classrooms despite the expectations within the new curriculum and Citizenship Education in particular. Those involved in EYV had re-ceived little or no support or training on how to handle sensitive issues within the classroom but confidence levels increased in practice when provided with "safe" and creative opportunities for raising awareness.

- When teachers in cross-community learning contexts were provided with ongoing INSET opportunities to explore and address their own views, understanding, beliefs and lived experiences through creative and practical pedagogical application, they became more confident in safely addressing sensitive issues in classrooms.

Schools are agents of transformation and change, if the cultures of schools and classrooms are opened up and supported to deal sensitively with controversial and sensitive issues. The need for system support as well as teacher personal and professional development is essential here.

Various findings of the study continue to contribute to debates about the emotional impact of conflict and violence on young people; identity theory; intergenerational impact; and prejudice-reduction and the role the arts have to play as safe vehicles for expression in both pedagogy and research.

Nevertheless, although there is a body of evidence emerging from the EYV project for a number of effective interventions and processes for responding to perceived needs of schools, teachers and young people, in relation to the impact of the protracted political conflict in Northern Ireland, it remains to be seen how those responsible for the roll-out of the new curriculum will choose to respond to the report's recommendations and sustain teachers, especially in relation to the delivery of the aims of citizenship education in this context.

To conclude, this paper has specifically addressed the various ways in which research was used in the design and development of this project to inform practice and, as a corollary, the ways in the development and evaluation of practice contributed to the knowledge base on matters such as facilitating pupil voice on sensitive matters and how to promote more pupil-centred and teacher-centred educational responses to conflict resolution and peace-building in a society emerging from conflict.

*

This chapter ends by meditating on the dilemma expressed by McEvoy (2007: 145–146) and which people in Northern Ireland, continue to ponder:

> In the fragile political context of Northern Ireland there is an inevitable tension between the desire to address the hurts of the past and a desire to ignore them. While some individuals are concerned that dealing with the past might only serve to open old wounds or negatively affect any chance of political progress, others are equally afraid that no attempt to address the past will mean the violence and injustices ... will be allowed to fester.

EYV found creative ways to ensure and demonstrate that, given the right educational conditions, the young are fearless in their understanding that to move forward in post-conflict Northern Ireland, nothing need fester.

Notes

1 263 troubles-related deaths occurred outside Northern Ireland.
2 Northern Ireland has a population of 1.6 million.
3 The Good Friday Agreement (also known as the Belfast Agreement) was a major political development in the Northern Ireland peace process. It was a power-sharing constitutional agreement signed in Belfast on 10 April 1998 (Good Friday) by the British and Irish governments and endorsed by most of Northern Ireland's political parties. It was dedicated to the 'achievement of reconciliation, tolerance, and mutual trust and to the protection and vindication of Human Rights for all' (Article 2).
4 Defined by Diagnostic and Statistical Manual for Mental Disorders IV (DSM IV). DSM IV is a handbook for mental health professionals that lists different categories of mental disorder and the criteria for diagnosing them, according to the American Psychiatric Association. It is used worldwide by clinicians and researchers as well as insurance companies, pharmaceutical companies and policy makers. Post-traumatic stress disorder (PTSD) is a term for certain severe psychological consequences of exposure to, or confrontation with stressful events that the person experiences as highly traumatic. Clinically, such events involve actual or threatened death, serious physical injury, or a threat to physical and/or psychological integrity, to a degree that usual psycholodical defences are incapable of coping with the impact.
5 It is recognized that the action research genre comprises a spectrum of approaches and, given the complexity of the project, an eclectic approach was adopted that combined a "spiral of cycles" (after Elliott, 1991) with teacher inquiry and "students as co-researchers" (after Fielding & Bragg, 2003).
6 There were also aspects of EYV in the informal education sector within youth work settings which are not reported in this account as, well as work with a variety of external agencies in the development of a resource directory for young people.
7 A distinctive feature of the education system in Northern Ireland is that it remains segregated in terms of both religion and ability (Gallagher, 2004). The education system therefore is a reflection of societal segregation with estimates of 90–95% of children attending either a Catholic or Protestant school at both primary and post-primary level (Gallagher, 1995; Cairns and Hewstone, 2002) and only 5% of pupils attending an integrated school (Smith, 2001, McGlynn et al., 2004).
8 Details of all subsamples are available in the Final Report on the Enabling Young Voices project submitted to the Department of Education for consideration, 2007.
9 Pseudonyms used throughout.
10 The Contact Hypothesis (based on Allport, 1954; Connolly, 2000) entails bringing

different identity groups into contact with one another under optimal conditions to reduce prejudice and has been the main theoretical base in Northern Ireland.
11 The course was run on two separate occasions for differing cohorts of teacher-practitioners, one of which included members from other agencies concerned with supporting children through trauma

References

Allport, G. W. 1954. *The Nature of Prejudice.* Cambridge, MA. Addison-Wesley.
Barone, T. 2001. 'Science, art and the predisposition of educational researchers', *Educational Researcher,* 30(7): 24–28.
Barone, T., and Eisner, E. W. 1997. 'Arts-based educational research.' In M. Jaeger (ed.). *Complementary Methods for Research in Education.* 2nd edn. Washington, DC. American Educational Research Association.
Birtchnell, J. 1999. 'Art as a form of psychotherapy'. In T. Dalley (ed.). *Art as Therapy: Aan Introduction into the Use of Art as a Therapeutic Technique.* London. Routledge.
Boyden, J., et al. 2002. Children Affected by Armed Conflict in South Asia: A Review of Trends and Issues Identified through Secondary Research. Working Paper series 7, Refugee Studies Centre. Oxford. International Development Centre, Queen Elizabeth House. http://www.rsc.ox.ac.uk/PDFs/workingpaper7.pdf – accessed 5 August 2007.
Bruner, J. S. 1990. *Acts of Meaning* Cambridge, MA. Harvard University Press.
Butler-Kisber, L. 2007. 'Collage in qualitative inquiry.' In G. Knowles & A. Cole (eds.), *Handbook of the Arts in Qualitative Inquiry: Perspectives, Methodologies, Examples and Issues.* Thousand Oaks, CA. Sage.
Cairns, E. 1987. Caught in the Crossfire: Children and the Northern Ireland Conflict. Belfast. Appletree Press.
Cairns, E. and Hewstone, M. 2002. 'Northern Ireland: The Impact of Peacemaking in Northern Ireland on Intergroup Behaviour.' In G. Salomom and B. Neov (eds) *Peace Education: The Concept, Principles and Practices Around the World.* New Jersey. Larry Erlbaum Associates.
Connolly, P. 2000. 'What now for the contact hypothesis? Towards a new research agenda', *Race, Ethnicity and Education,* 3(2): 169–93.
Cost of the Troubles Study (CTS). 1999. http://cain.ulst.ac.uk/cts/ – accessed 25 June 2010.
Council for the Curriculum and Examinations (CCEA). 2005. *Statements of Entitlement for Local and Global Citizenship.* http://www.rewardinglearning.com/development/ks3/implementation/docs/june06/citizenship.pdf – accessed June 2006.
Council for the Curriculum and Examinations (CCEA). 2007. *Planning for the Revised Curriculum at Key Stages 3 and 4.* http://www.nicurriculum.org.uk/docs/key_stage_3/training/Planning-KS3-Guidance.pdf – accessed 27 July 2007.
Dewey, J. 1934. *Art as Experience.* New York. Milton and Balch.
Dewey, J. 1989. *John Dewey: The Later Works, 1925–1953. Vol. 10: 1934, Art*

as Experience, ed. J. Boydston. Carbondale, IL. Southern Illinois University Press.

Eisner, E. W. 1985. *The Art of Educational Evaluation: A Personal View.* London. Falmer Press.

Elliott, J. 1991. *Action Research for Educational Change.* Milton Keynes and Philadelphia. Open University Press.

Fay, M.-T., Smyth, M. and Morrissey, M. 1997. *Mapping Troubles-Related Deaths in Northern Ireland, 1969–1994.* Londonderry. INCORE. See http://cain.ulst.ac.uk/issues/violence/cts/abstract.htm.

Fielding, M., and Bragg, S. 2003. *Students as Researchers: Making a Difference.* Cambridge. Pearson Publishing.

Gallagher, A. M. 2004. *Education in Divided Societies.* Basingstoke. Palgrave Macmillan.

Gibson, M. 2006. *Order from Chaos: Responding to Traumatic Events.* 3rd ed. Bristol: Policy Press.

Hammarberg, T. 2007. *The Impact of Conflict on Children: Healing the Past and Securing the Future.* Presentation at the Children's Law Centre Annual Lecture, Belfast, 8th February, https://wcd.coe.int/ViewDoc.jsp?id=1094643&BackColorInternet+FEC65B&BCo – accessed 6 August 2007.

Huss, E., and Cwikel, J. 2005. 'Researching Creations: Applying Arts-based research to Bedouin Women's Drawings,' *International Journal of Qualitative Methods,* 4 (December).

Kilpatrick, R., and Leitch, R. 2004. 'Teachers and pupils' educational experiences and schools-based responses to the conflict in Northern Ireland', *Journal of Social Issues,* 60(3): 563–587.

Kritskaya, O. 2003. 'Notions of the Aesthetic: definition, value and implications for educational research.' Symposium paper presented to American Education Research Association conference, Chicago, IL.

Leitch, R. 2000. 'Victims or mentors? Metaphors for twenty-first century children.' In J Gardner and R Leitch (eds). *Education 2020: A Millennium Vision: Issues and Ideas for the Future of Education in Northern Ireland.* Belfast. Blackstaff Press: 47–53.

Leitch, R. 2008. 'Researching Children's Narratives Creatively through Drawings.' In P. Thompson (ed.) *Doing Visual Research with Children and Young People,* New York & London. Routledge: 37–59.

Leitch, R,, and Kilpatrick, R. 1999. *Inside the School Gates: Schools and the Troubles: A Research Report into how Schools Support Children in relation to the Political Conflict in Northern Ireland.* Belfast. Save the Children.

Liechty, J., and Clegg, C. 2001. Moving beyond Sectarianism: Religion, Conflict, and Reconciliation in Northern Ireland. Blackrock, Co. Dublin. Columba Press.

Lindberg, D. M., and others. 2007. 'Recognizing Child Abuse during Prolonged "Low Intensity" Armed Conflict: Are We Missing the Forest for the Trees?' *Israeli Journal of Emergency Medicine,* 7(2): 62–70.

Lyons, H. A. 1971. 'Psychiatric Sequelae of the Belfast Riots', *British Journal of Psychiatry,* 118: 25–273

McAuley, J. W. 2004. 'Peace and Progress? Political and Social Change Among Young Loyalists in Northern Ireland', *Journal of Social Issues* 60(3): 541–562.

McEvoy, L. 2007. 'Beneath the rhetoric: policy approximation and citizenship education in Northern Ireland', *Education, Citizenship and Social Justice,*2(2): 135–157.

McGlynn, C., et al. 2004. 'Moving out of conflict: the contribution of integrated schools in Northern Ireland to identity, attitudes, forgiveness and reconciliation', *Journal of Peace Education,* 1(2): 147–163.

McKittrick, D., et al. 1999. *Lost Lives: The Stories of the Men, Women and Children who Die as a Result of the Northern Ireland Troubles.* Edinburgh. Mainstream.

McNiff, S. 1998. *Arts-based Research.* London & Philadelphia. Jessica Kingsley.

Melaugh, M. 2007. *Violence – Draft List of Deaths related to the Conflict in 2007,* http://cain.ulst.ac.uk/issues/violence/deaths2007draft.htm – accessed 28 July 2007.

Muldoon, O. T. 2004. 'Children of the Troubles: The Impact of Political Violence in Northern Ireland', *Journal of Social Issues* 60(3): 453–468.

Muldoon, O. T, et al. 2006. *The Legacy of the Troubles: Experience of the Troubles, Mental Health and Social Attitudes.* Belfast. Queen's University School of Psychology.

Office of the First Minister and Deputy First Minister (OFMDFM). 2002. *Reshape, Rebuild, Achieve: Developing Practical Help and Services to the Victims of Northern Ireland.* Victims, Unit, Stormont, Belfast. Stormont, Victims Unit. http://www.ofmdfmni.gov.uk/victimsbrochure-2.pdf – accessed 29th July 2007.

O'Connor, U., et al. 2002. *A Review of the School Community Relations Programme 2002.* http://www.deni.gov.uk/about/consultation/documents/Review_of_ Schools_CR_Prog.pdf – accessed November 2004.

Parlett, M., and Hamilton, D. 1975. 'Evaluation as illumination: a new approach to the study of innovatory programmes.' In D. Hamilton et al. (eds). *Beyond the Numbers Game.* London. Macmillan: 6–22.

Peace II programme: http://www.legacyofthetroubles.qub.ac.uk/

RUC statistics. 1995. *Background Information on Northern Ireland Society, CAIN – Security and Defence.* http://cain.ulst.ac.uk/ni/security.htm#deathlats – accessed 27 July 2007.

Smyth, M. 2004. *Impact of the Political Conflict on Children in Northern Ireland.* Londonderry. Institute of Conflict Research.

Stewart, D. 2001. 'Unsafety Zones: thinking about the emotional impact of the Northern Ireland Troubles on children referred to a community child therapy service'. In M. Smyth and K. Thomson (eds). *Working with Children and Young People in Violently Divided Societies: Papers from South Africa and Northern Ireland.* Belfast. Institute for Conflict Research.

Trew, K. 2004. 'Children and Socio-Cultural Divisions in Northern Ireland', *Journal of Social Issues* 60(3): 507–522.

United Nations. 1996. *Impact of Armed Conflict on Children: Promotion and Protection of the Rights of Children.* New York. United Nations.

Weingarten, K. 2004. 'Witnessing the effects of political violence in families: mechanisms of intergenerational transmission and clinical interventions', *Journal of Marital and Family Therapy,* 30(1): 45–59.

CHAPTER FIVE

THE PSYCHOLOGICAL IMPACT OF EXPOSURE TO POLITICAL VIOLENCE: COPING WITH CONFLICT

EVE BINKS

The past 25 years have seen a rapid growth in interest into the psychological effects of exposure to organized violence (Miller & Rasmussen, 2010), and with the world increasingly becoming a global village, with incidences of political conflict, armed insurgency and war still prevalent in many countries, the need to assess the psychological impact of exposure to these events is paramount. Weingarten (2004) attests to the impact of political violence extending far beyond the immediate victims, its impact being felt not only by those directly affected by the events but also passing from one generation to the next, causing lasting damage to both direct and indirect victims. Moreover, with the advent of continuous television news coverage, access to international news agencies online and an increased propensity and wherewithal to maintain contact with friends and relatives overseas, the intergenerational transmission of trauma is greater than ever.

Farhood (1999) suggests that war and other man-made disasters have tended to be less studied than their natural disaster counterparts, though in recent years the focus on war, conflict and man-made trauma has become more prevalent (for example, Khamis, 1998; Qouta et al., 2007; McDermott, Duffy & McGuinness, 2004; Pedersen, 2002).

Although conflict is traditionally defined as an interaction between the perpetrator and the victim, it would be remiss to deny the impact on the witnesses of those interactions (Gilligan, 1997), and as Herman (1997) has suggested, the victims are not the only ones left to cope with the fallout of the event: witnesses too must deal with not only the event itself, but the impact of that event upon those directly affected. Indeed, the experience of trauma occurs not only from threats to the self, but also "actual or threatened death or serious injury . . . of others" (Spitzer, 1994: 427–428).

If one can be exposed and subsequently affected not only by seeing an event first-hand but by hearing it, having access to media coverage of the event and by knowing of another person's traumatization (Buka et al., 2001), then it is possible that an event such as the 9/11 terror attacks could be responsible for millions of cases of primary, secondary and vicarious traumatization worldwide. Similarly, if being traumatized is a subjective experience (Gershuny & Thayer, 1999), the danger here is of assuming people are traumatized when they are not, and vice versa.

If we are to understand fully the impact of exposure to conflict and political violence, then care must be taken to ensure that all victims are attended to. The following chapter will, therefore, assess the impact of exposure to conflict and political violence, alongside the reactions to experiencing these events, the adequate and inadequate coping mechanisms and the steps that need to be taken in these troubled areas of the world to ensure that effective recovery and reconstruction can be achieved.

Reactions to and Coping with Trauma

When discussing the impact of, and reactions to, exposure to political violence and armed conflict, there are a multitude of factors to consider. Not only does the direct victim warrant close attention, but so do those who were victims indirectly, and those who experience incidences of secondary or vicarious traumatization (Stamm, 1999; McCann & Pearlman, 1990; Pearlman & Saakvitne, 1995). In previous years, the veracity of claims of secondary and vicarious traumatization were sometimes received sceptically by clinicians and practitioners (Auerhahn & Laub, 1998) but in more recent years the legitimacy of these claims has been recognized. Attention must be paid to the psychological and physiological fallout that can occur as a result of being exposed to such potentially deleterious events.

In terms of the negative psychological consequences of coping with conflict, Gabriel et al. (2007) suggest that post-traumatic stress disorder (PTSD) is one of the more common and intrusive psychological disorders which emerges. They further suggest that in the wake of a terrorist attack, for example, there is a significant increase in maladaptive psychological responses, with those who were directly affected demonstrating higher levels of psychological distress than those who were indirectly affected.

Weingarten (2004) suggests that people in these environments characterized by conflict and political violence are forced to cope not only with living through the conflict, but also events such as displacement, politically motivated oppression and dictatorship and fear of persecution. Necessarily, the whole spectrum of events associated with conflict has the potential to impact at a societal and individual level in a catastrophic way. Further, experience of previous traumatic stressors – even those associated with natural disasters – means that coping mechanisms may already be over-loaded and so the ability to cope with subsequent calamitous stressors is overwhelmed.

Similarly, other coping mechanisms may pose a risk of additional harm. Weingarten (2004) cautions against the use of silence as a coping strategy, suggesting that although silence may, at the individual level, be the result of a dissociative coping mechanism, or, at the societal level, the result of a community unable to speak of and therefore acknowledge the impact of the violence that has been visited upon them, its function is to transmit notions of shame and pain, to nurture fear, prolong violence and aid in the transmis-sion of trauma across generations (see also Kaufman, 1992; Gilligan, 1997). Further, this resultant shame and humiliation which victims and survivors are left to cope with in the aftermath of conflict is the key to understanding the transmission of trauma between generations (Volkan, 2000).

However, although the use of silence can be a dangerous and ill-advised coping mechanism its use is understandable, particularly at the individual and familial level. In this context, silence is used as a protective force, as a way of buffering children from the impact of the traumas that have been experienced by the parents. However, this act of withholding informa-tion, even when the goal is to conceal the unpleasant truth from children, forces those children into a situation where they are aware that a situation exists and so fill in the gaps for themselves, often imagining horrors far more upsetting than the truth. To that end, silence is rarely an effective or liberating coping experience for either the parent or the child. For the par-ent, the silence delays, or in some cases prevents altogether, the necessary psychological working through of the trauma which is crucial for recovery (Weingarten, 2004). For the child, it serves to incubate fear and helpless-ness and therefore promotes traumatization. Rather, as Bar-On (1996) and Shahini (2001) attest, remembering and grieving for the losses inflicted by conflict are the most difficult yet brave responses.

Otto et al. (2007) determined that there is a negative correlation between a free and open familial discussion of thoughts and feelings related to the traumatic event and the development and onset of post-traumatic stress dis-order (PTSD) symptoms in children. This would lend support to the findings of Kaufman (1992), Gilligan (1997), Bar-On (1996) and Shahini (2001), who suggest that greater post-traumatic pathology is related to lesser ac-knowledgement and discussion of the event.

Pedersen (2002) has suggested that the nature of war is changing and civilian populations are now more vulnerable to war-associated stressors. Indeed, the World Health Organisation (2005) suggests that living in societies where political violence is present has the potential to result in either a compromise in mental health, albeit one which would not tend to restrict day-to-day functioning; psychological distress which would lead not only to an interruption to daily activities but also to considerable emotional suffering; or mental disorders which would be characterized by specific psychiatric conditions which meet diagnostic criteria.

These related events all have the potential to lead to a variety of ruinous effects upon physical and psychological well-being. For example, Hourani et al. (1986) determined that the loss of a home following the Israeli invasion of Lebanon was correlated with psychological distress. Further, Bryce et al. (1988) found that an increase in symptoms of depression was positively associated with an increase in the number of environmental problems in a Beirut population.

As Miller and Rasmussen (2010) demonstrate, those individuals and communities that survive periods of organized violence have not only to cope with the impact of direct exposure to this violence, but also with any number of stressful events that are the result of this violence. They go on to show that daily stressors may, in fact, mediate the relationship between war exposure and poor mental health. They further suggest that "daily stressors have shown strong and significantly related main effects on mental health outcomes" (2010: 11). Miller and Rasmussen also say that previous research has suggested that daily stressors are better predictors of poor mental health outcomes than war exposure. Citing work by al-Krenawi et al. (2007), Catani et al. (2008), and Farhood et al. (1993), they suggest that family violence (including child abuse, spousal abuse, sibling–sibling abuse) is a better predictor of children's mental health than the presence or degree of exposure to war. They continue that daily stressors such as a lack or cessation of community services, poverty variables and fracturing of family units were all reported as "better predictors of distress than the constant threat of war-related violence" (2010: 11). However, although there may be a degree of evidence to support these claims, they require a cautious interpretation and further consideration.

Although daily stressors in areas of political violence affect the mental health of those exposed to them, those daily stressors – family breakdowns, economic fluctuations, etc. – are experienced to a greater or lesser extent by individuals around the globe. The difference in countries and communities in conflict is that these individuals are living in a situation where they experience real and consistent threats to their safety, their integrity, their lives and the lives of loved ones. This threat and the consistently violent conditions which they experience have the potential to overwhelm their ability to cope with the daily stressors (Herman, 1997). Once these coping mechanisms are overwhelmed, the daily events can become unmanageable. Indeed it is possible, even likely, that many of these daily stressors would not exist to the same degree if the war were not a feature of that country or community. It could therefore be said that separating these daily stressors from the war violence is ill-advised. As research has suggested, the prevalence of child and spousal abuse may be a direct result of exposure to war, and these abusive actions are often the result of a projection defence mechanism (Weiss & Weiss, 2000; Rowland-Klein & Dunlop, 1998).

Miller and Rasmussen (2010:11) continue that daily hassles "such as difficulties in maintaining contact with family and friends as a result of war were all better predictors of distress than the constant threat of war related violence". However, although this may be the case for their research, these issues may be more pressing for the individuals involved in a bid to divert focus from the violence. Additionally, in situations of chronic conflict, such as those researched by Miller and Rasmussen, psychological defence mechanisms for dealing with the actual violence, e.g. habituation (McWhirter, 1983; Solomon, 1995), are often present, leaving the individual to focus on war-related sequelae rather than the war itself (Binks & Ferguson, 2006).

In terms of child exposure, although children are at risk if they are directly exposed, research has determined that the risk is actually two-fold: their own exposure poses a risk, but they are increasingly in danger if (i) they are exposed and (ii) they bear witness to political violence executed against their parents (Cairns & Lewis, 1999; Punamäki et al., 2001; Reilly, 2002). Indeed, it is documented that the child of a parent suffering from detrimental psychological effects of exposure to political violence may be adversely affected by their parent's experiences (Weingarten, 2004).

Further, Lubit (2006: 3) suggests that if a child experiences symptoms of trauma, after a short time this is enough to interfere with their ability to participate in and benefit from social and educational opportunities and this interference has the potential to "propel the child off the normal developmental curve". Lubit also suggests that children are more harshly affected by post-disaster crisis states as the tendency during this time is for adults to be engaged in efforts to rebuild the community and they are therefore less available to support the children. Lubit goes further and suggests that because children have a greater tendency to rely on routine and structure, changes to this routine and annihilation of the relevant daily structures is more difficult for them than it is for adults. For example, while adults recognize that the loss of a church or school does not mean the loss of religion, education or friendships, this is a more difficult concept for children.

Khamis (2005) assessed the development of PTSD among school age Palestinian children and determined that of the 1000 children included in the study, 62% fulfilled the DSM-IV criterion for PTSD. This significant portion of the sample is, Khamis suggests, "comparable to the rate of PTSD found in children exposed to the stress of extreme political violence (Anthony, 1986; Goleman, 1986; Saigh, 1989)" (2005: 90). Khamis concludes that those high levels of PTSD may be the result of living under the stress of prolonged political oppression and vast and repeated experiences of death and devastation.

However it is not just those persons *in situ* during the conflict that are adversely impacted. Research has documented the impact of refugee experiences on children from areas of conflict and have uncovered troubling findings. Zureik (1996) determined that the prolonged psychological impact of exposure to politically motivated trauma and conflict was greater not only in those Palestinian refugees who had suffered subsequent persecution, but also in their children (Shuval, 1993).

Research (e.g. Ajdukovic & Ajdukovic, 1993) has suggested that refugee children demonstrate considerably higher levels of psychological symptomatology, with Almqvist and Brandell-Forsberg (1997) showing that refugee children are faced with a series of repeated exposures to traumatic stressors which range in severity. Indeed, these children living in refugee camps have often not only witnessed the conflict but also suffer from issues of familial separation, poor living conditions, economic hardship, difficult working conditions, overcrowding and inadequate subsistence (e.g. Pelcovitz & Kaplan, 1996; Kimura, 1999; Thabet & Vostanis, 2000; Birman et al., 2005).

According to Khamis (2005), children from urban and rural areas reported significantly lower levels of PTSD symptoms than those who were residing in refugee camps. Desjarlais et al. (1995) suggest that this is probably a result of related economic factors which have a negative impact on the mental health of refugees as a result of stress, and also because increased economic hardship results in a decrease of resources which would ordinarily serve to buffer the psychological impact of traumatic events.

Although the research evidence points to an increase in psychopathology in those living in refugee camps, it would seem that one of the reasons for this is the multiple trauma-exposures that this population endures. In 1989, the United Nations House Committee on Refugees reported that the women and children who reside in such camps are significantly more vulnerable to exploitation, abuse and neglect, with other research by Mollica (1990) showing that those factors lead to psychological issues of despair, helpless-ness and powerlessness, all of which are commensurate with the DSM-IV's diagnostic guidelines for the development of PTSD (Spitzer, 1994). Further, Khamis (2005) has determined that the risks of PTSD are greater for working children than they are for non-working children, and that because child labour is more prevalent in refugee camps, this also contributes to the high levels of PTSD which are identified in these camps.

However, aside from the impact and coping mechanisms witnessed at an individual level, it is important not to dismiss those which are in operation at the societal level. Research has suggested that social support is a key determinant in ameliorating the impact of intense war stress (Farhood, 1999). Further, social support has been associated with increased well-being and decreased personal problems (e.g. communication breakdowns, marital issues) (Farhood et al., 1993). Additionally, Patterson and McCubbin (1983) found that effective social support is beneficial in maintaining family cohesion and communication in countries that have been exposed to conflict.

When coping with political violence and associated stressors, Tol et al. (2010: 37) suggest the importance of "existing socio-cultural resources in mediating the consequences of political violence for psychosocial well-being and mental health". They suggest that there are a number of ways in which well-being can be promoted in a climate of violence and stress, and for those who are coping, or attempting to cope, with these issues it is important that these factors be adequately addressed. They continue that it is important

- that existing coping mechanisms are not destabilized by the introduction of new coping procedures;
- that support programmes which help sustain good psychological well-being should be increased;
- that damage caused to safety by political violence should be identified and healing should begin.

(See also Boyden & Berry, 2006.)

Galea et al. (2002) identified a high prevalence of PTSD amongst those individuals who were directly exposed to the attack, while Schlenger et al. (2002) determined that even those who were not geographically proximate to the event showed signs of PTSD. When coping with such an event, it would appear that several factors are salient in predicting effective coping, especially in children. For example, Saigh et al. (1999) determined that individual factors, familial factors and situational variables were all related to the development of PTSD following a traumatic event (see also Pelcovitz & Kaplan, 1996), while other researchers have suggested that parental pathology, family stress, poor mother–child relationship and low family adaptability and cohesion are all related to the onset of PTSD in children (Otto et al., 2007: 889, citing Brent et al. (1995), Martini et al. (1990), Kimura (1909) and Kazak et al. (1998)). However, although those factors seem to have some relevance in determining the onset of PTSD and poor coping mechanisms in children, there are also other factors that should not be overlooked.

Panter-Brick et al. (2009) point to the paucity of information pertaining to war-affected youth, suggesting that there has been a heavy focus on traumatic stress and similar outcomes of war stress, to the detriment of a comprehensive focus upon general psychosocial aspects of psychological well-being. This focus on the ruinous effects of war and conflict needs to be balanced with research which focuses on not only vulnerability to these negative aspects, but also resilience to these consequences.

Stein et al. (2005: 872) suggest that childhood trauma may be responsible for the development of effective coping mechanisms which can be used to cope with subsequent traumas in adulthood: "childhood trauma may inoculate against PTSD development when severe traumas are repeatedly experienced". This, however, is contrary to other research (e.g. Solomon & Mikulincer, 1992; Gershuny & Thayer, 1999; Spitzer, 1994) which indicates childhood trauma as being negatively correlated with consequent coping ability, and positively correlated with PTSD development.

Earlier research indicates that parents have a tendency to underestimate or to deny altogether any post-traumatic reactions that their children may be experiencing (e.g. Earls et al., 1988) and that in line with this, children demonstrate a tendency to be reluctant to display the full extent of the traumatic impact to their parents, choosing instead to protect their parents from having to witness this. The result of these actions, they suggest, is that children's post-traumatic reactions are at risk of going unnoticed and, consequently, untreated.

Weingarten (2004) and Simpson (1998) indicate that youths, especially those who are politicized and become involved with the conflict, have the ability to traumatize their parents who fear for their children's well-being. Indeed, as Hardy et al. (2002) found, Palestinian mental health care workers report that parents are seeking advice about how to stop their children becoming involved in the conflict, such is their degree of fear for their child's safety.

With regard to assessing the needs of the people forced to cope with the eventuality of and the aftermath of organized violence, Miller and Rasmussen (2010) suggest that research has, thus far, concentrated exclusively on either trauma-focused coping or psychosocial methods of coping.

Research which has detailed trauma-focused approaches has addressed specifically those direct experiences to which individuals are exposed – death, destruction, loss, assault; whereas the psychosocial focus has concentrated on those social conditions which experience deterioration as a result of armed conflict: displacement, poverty, community chasms. According to the research which addresses these approaches, trauma-focused advocates promote the use of specific clinical treatments (see Neuner & Elbert, 2007), whereas the psychosocial-focused advocates promote the improvement of stressful conditions such as community relations and the economy as the most effective way to reduce the impact of the trauma and bolster the mental health of those affected. Contrary to this, those who sponsor a trauma-focused approach suggest that once the deleterious mental health effects have been addressed, the individuals and communities in question would be better able to cope with the associated environmental stressors (Miller & Rasmussen, 2010).

Bachrach and Zautra (1985) have suggested that different coping mechanisms are often needed to address different traumas. They further suggest that when the traumatic stressor is controllable then a problem-focused mechanism might be the most appropriate, while if the stressor is less controllable or uncontrollable then an emotion-focused strategy may be more suitable.

However, Zeidner (2006) suggests a more complex picture. Research by Silver et al. (2002) determined that when emotion-focused coping was used to deal with the 9/11 terror attacks, there were significantly greater incidences of post-traumatic stress. Indeed, Zeidner and Ben-Zur (1993) suggest that an increase in emotion-focused coping caused a decrease in adaptive responses to the trauma.

In relation to the suggestion that problem-focused coping strategies are related to better mental health outcomes, Stein et al. (2005) suggest that this is probably because problem-focused strategies encourage the individual to work through the traumatic event and take some degree of control over both the experience and the self (see also Foa & Hearst-Ikeda, 1996). However, as Zeidner (2006) continues, even highly effective problem-focused strategies fail to remove the actual threat, and the tendency to put these problem-focused safety nets in place serves only to promote the avoidance of dealing with the threat or stressor and neither removes nor effectively works through the problem.

Zeidner (2006) further asserts that those individuals who demonstrate high levels of negative affect are increasingly vulnerable to external stressors, do not develop sufficient coping skills, and are more likely to experience physical symptoms when exposed to stressors. Additionally, Zeidner continues that those individuals with high levels of negative affect are more likely to utilise emotion-focused coping strategies which are associated with greater maladaptive responses (Silver et al., 2002; Zeidner & Ben-Zur, 1993). Conversely, those individuals with high levels of positive affect may experience positive emotions serving as a buffer against stress, and as an effective way of coping with stressors (e.g. Fredrickson et al., 2003).

Zeidner continues by supporting Rachman's (1980) suggestion that the maladaptive coping typified in individuals with high levels of negative effect is probably because of the related persistence of intrusive thoughts and continued fixation upon the event and, therefore, continued focus on the perceived traumatic subject matter of the event. Zeidner concludes by indicating that although initial evaluations of a potentially traumatising event or threat tend to be characterized by emotion-focused coping and the associated maladaptive responses, subsequent evaluations are more likely to result in a problem-focused approach which elicit more adaptive mechanisms.

Although there is evidence in support of both emotion-focused and problem-focused coping strategies, these methods are highly dependent upon the perspective of the individual involved in the traumatic event. As Horowitz and Lissak (1989) and Zeidner (2006) attest, the erosion of emotional resources experienced by those living in conditions of persistent stress means that there is a real risk of "social burnout and potential increase in social tension and pathology" (Zeidner, 2006: 779). This could indicate that in situations where an emotion-focused mechanism may be advantageous, the resources necessary to elicit such a response may be unavailable, leaving the individual to rely upon a problem-focused approach.

Issues of Recovery and Reconstruction

In terms of recovery and reconstruction following a period of conflict or political violence, a number of issues deserve attention. From helping the individual to cope with and recover from the horrors that have been visited upon them, to rallying the community to take stock and attempt successful reconstruction, there are challenges at all stages of recovery and reconstruction. Survivors, witnesses and practitioners alike need to be aware of these issues and to develop a thorough understanding of the recovery cycle and of what can be done at each stage of recovery in order to best promote a successful life after trauma.

Herman (1997) suggests that trauma recovery necessarily begins with establishing the safety of the individual and is, in the first instance, a practical concern. To feel safe, individuals must feel that they have some control over themselves and their environment. Initially, individuals need to establish control of themselves, often this means regaining and regulating activities such as eating and sleeping and once this has been achieved they can begin to establish some environmental control too. Here it may be that the individual makes decisions regarding living situations and mobility, and both these self and environmental control issues require not only the focus of the individual but effective social support. Establishing a safe living environment is a difficult business, especially in societies that are characterized by civil unrest or political violence, and this can be a challenging issue for these individuals. Herman suggests that progress in this area would include the ability to calculate realistically the degree of continuing threat and decide upon reasonable precautions.

During the second stage, where the exploration of traumatic memories takes place, Herman indicates the importance of re-experiencing the traumatic event and integrating it into conscious awareness. Here, the function of remembrance and mourning are to allow individuals to grieve for their losses – material, psychological and symbolic – in order that they can eventually move on to the final stage of personality reintegration and rehabilitation. Here, in this final stage, survivors should integrate the trauma into their conscious awareness in order that it, like all other experiences, becomes central to the development of the self. If this is achieved, the individual should begin to resolve the trauma issues and develop effective post-trauma coping skills. Once this has been achieved they can reconnect both with significant others in their lives and with wider society.

During these stages of recovery it is important for survivors to tell their story and to have people to bear witness to their testimony. Research by Agger and Jensen (1990) indicates the importance of this with survivors of political tyranny and suggests that there is healing in the telling of the event: testimonies given and stories told by these individuals aid both a personal recovery and a public acknowledgement, serving a cathartic and transcendent purpose for the individual. Mollica (1988) further suggests that the act of story-telling and giving voice to the experiences has the ability to transform the event into one which is more adequately typified by dignity and virtue. It is the act of story-telling which can transform the way in which the traumatic memories are processed and relief from many of the symptoms of PTSD.

During the final stage of recovery the survivors reclaim their world and in doing so often return to issues which were first encountered during the first three stages. The final stage includes an ability to consciously face danger. This is an important issue for those exposed to political violence as the danger they face is often ongoing and ever present (Herman, 1997). One of the most useful elements of this stage is the discovery of how to tell the trauma story to children. In doing so, and in avoiding or actively shunning secrecy and silence, the individual can help children develop protective mechanisms that will help safeguard them against future dangers (see also Weingarten, 2004; Volkan, 2000; Shahini, 2001). During this final stage, traumatized individuals can find a social purpose in their experience, helping similarly traumatized people, educating others and engaging in political endeavours that seek to prevent future similar traumas – all ways in which individuals can make their experiences useful and gain a sense of purpose and positive outcome from their experience.

With political violence comes a widespread impact of devastating events, and although this negative impact on multiple members of the community can have long-term pernicious consequences, there is also an element of strength in numbers. A feeling of commonality and connection to others is a vital part of human and social life, and while victims of an individual traumatic event – the rape victim for example – may find it difficult to establish this commonality, this is more readily available to survivors of widespread political violence and persecution. As Herman (1997: 124) notes, "the solidarity of a group provides the strongest antidote to traumatic experience". Connection with the group provides a sense of stability, and sense of belonging and a secure identity with which to move forward.

For this reason, it is likely that when seeking to restore and rehabilitate survivors of political violence, while individual therapeutic approaches may be necessary in some cases, group approaches to treatment often elicit better results (Danieli, 1988). However, as Herman (1997) cautions, although the therapeutic power of groups is great, the pain and anguish experienced by the members of the group can be destructive and, if not managed properly, the effects can be disastrous, with intragroup conflicts mimicking the traumatic event itself and exacerbating the traumatic reactions of the individual involved. It is also important to note that the sharing of a common experience does not necessarily make for commonality among group members: it is the common reaction to the event which binds people, not simply the physical experience of that event (see also Norris et al., 2002). The effectiveness of groups can be seen throughout all stages of recovery – from their importance in establishing safety to the emotional support during mourning and remembrance. The reduction in feelings of isolation and increase in self-esteem offered by these groups is vitally important.

Aside from the clinical and psychological interventions, when assessing the societal impact of political violence, Maclure and Denov (2009) highlight the importance of education in promoting societal reconciliation and reducing social tensions (see also Bush & Saltarelli, 2000; Tidwell, 2004). Maclure and Denov point to the stabilizing and normalizing effect that education can have on children, with the rebuilding of schools and the resuming of education being interpreted as a restoration of normality and a return to hopefulness and purpose. Further, they say that "post-war education can ... help to strengthen [children's] confidence and self-esteem" (2009: 612). Further, Pigozzi (1999) and Seitz (2004) suggest that this post-war education has transforming potential which has the ability to redress the balance in social inadequacies and injustices.

Whatever methods are used to promote recovery and reconstruction, it is important that survivors and professionals alike recognize that coping with incidences of political violence is often a long and uncomfortable road, which may require individual approaches or the support of the wider community.

Conclusion

Although recent decades have seen a burgeoning interest in the psychological effects of both acute and chronic exposure to organized violence, war and insurgency, the information available remains ambiguous. While there is evidence in support of direct and indirect trauma as a result of exposure to traumatic events, and of primary, secondary and vicarious traumatisation, there remains a danger of either over- or underestimating the impact of these events on both individuals and communities.

Research points to traumatized adults coping with their experiences in a way which puts their children in harm's way, to the collision of societal and individual coping mechanisms and to the potential deleterious and widespread effects that media coverage of traumatic events can have on populations. Additionally, with the employment of ineffective coping mechanisms – often used in a bid to protect others from the impact of one's own suffering – comes the acceleration of trauma transmission, both laterally in a community-wide spread, and inter-generationally.

The ability and inability to cope with the trauma of potential violence and war-related events can result in an exacerbation of ever-present daily stressors, intolerable interruptions to daily activities and significant emotional suffering. Coping with political violence requires more than an abil-

ity to make sense of and recover from acts of violence: Loss of community
services, economic downturns, poverty variables and familial breakdowns
all require attention. Putting coping mechanisms in place to deal with these
daily stressors which occur in addition to the violent events themselves
proves a considerable challenge to adults and children living in such environments. For those who are unable to remain in their indigenous communities, displacement provides additional stress, requiring those individuals
to cope with supplementary stressors in an environment which is alien to
them.

While not all individuals report being negatively affected by exposure to
political violence, and while there are accounts of those who do not suffer
maladaptive psychological responses to such stressors, there is clear evidence that stress related to the occurrence of war has a significant impact on
mental health. These issues must be heeded if a successful recovery is to be
made and post-trauma life is to be fruitful and uninhibited.

References

Agger, I., and Jensen, S. B. 1990. 'Testimony as ritual and evidence in psychotherapy for political refugees', *Journal of Traumatic Stress*, 3: 115–130.
Ajdukovic, M., and Ajdukovic, D. 1993. 'Psychological well-being of refugee children', *Child Abuse and Neglect*, 17: 843–854.
al-Krenawi, A., Lev-Wiesel, R., and Sehwail, M. 2007. 'Psychological
symptomatology among Palestinian children living with political violence',
Child and Adolescent Mental Health, 12: 27–31.
Almqvist, K., and Brandell-Forsberg, M. 1997. 'Refugee children in Sweden:
Posttraumatic stress disorder in Iranian preschool children exposed to organised
violence', *Child Abuse and Neglect*, 21(4): 351–366.
Anthony, E. J. 1986. 'Special section: Children's reactions to severe stress', *Journal
of the American Academy of Child Psychiatry*, 25: 299–392.
Auerhahn, N. C., and Laub, D. 1998. 'Intergenerational memory of the Holocaust.'
In Y. Danieli (ed.). *International Handbook of Multigenerational Legacies of
Trauma*. New York: Plenum Press: 21–41.
Bachrach, K. M., and Zautra, A. J. 1985. 'Coping with a community stressor: The
threat of a hazardous waste facility', *Journal of Health and Social Behaviour*,
26: 127–141.
Bar-On, D. 1996. 'Attempting to overcome the intergenerational transmission of
trauma: Dialogue between descendants of victims and perpetrators.' In R. J.
Apfel and B. Simon (eds) *Minefields in their Hearts: The Mental Health of
Children in War and Communal Violence*. New Haven, CT: Yale University
Press: 165–188.
Binks, E., and Ferguson, N. 2006. 'Legacies of conflict: Children in Northern
Ireland.' In A. Hosin (ed.). *Responses to Traumatized Children*. Basingstoke.

Palgrave Macmillan.

Birman, D., et al. 2005. *Mental Health Interventions for Refugee Children in Resettlement: White Paper II.* National Child Traumatic Stress Network. http://www.nctsn.org/nctsn_assets/pdfs/promising_practices/MH_Interventions_for_Refugee_Children.pdf – accessed 27 November 2009.

Boyden, J., and de Berry, J. 2006. 'Introduction.' In J. Boyden and J. de Berry (eds). *Children and youth on the front line: Ethnography, armed conflict, and displacement.* New York. Bergahn Books: xi–xxvii.

Brent, D. A., et al. 1995. 'Posttraumatic stress disorder in peers of adolescent suicide victims: Predisposing factors and phenomenology', *Journal of the American Academy of Child and Adolescent Psychiatry*, 47: 923–929.

Bryce, J., Walker, N., and Peterson, C. 1988. 'Predicting symptoms of depression among women in Beirut: The importance of daily life', *International Journal of Mental Health*, 18: 57–70.

Buka, S. L., et al. 2001. 'Youth exposure to violence: Prevalence, risks and consequences', *American Journal of Orthopsychiatry*, 71: 298–310.

Bush, K. D., and Saltarelli, D. 2000. *The Two Faces of Education in Ethnic Conflict: Towards a Peace-building Education for Children.* Florence. UNICEF Innocenti Research Centre.

Cairns, E., and Lewis, C. A. 1999. 'Collective memories, political violence and mental health in Northern Ireland', *British Journal of Psychology*, 90: 25–33.

Catani, C., Schauer, E., and Neuner, F. 2008. 'Beyond individual war trauma: Domestic violence against children in Afghanistan and Sri Lanka', *Journal of Marital and Family Therapy*, 34: 165–176.

Danieli, Y. 1988. 'Treating survivors and children of survivors of the Nazi Holocaust.' In F. M. Ochberg (ed.). *Post-traumatic Therapy and the Victim of Violence.* New York. Brumer/Mazel.

Desjarlais, R., et al. 1995. *World Mental Health: Problems and Priorities in Low-income Countries.* New York. Oxford University Press.

Earls, F., et al. 1998. 'Investigating psychopathological consequences of a disaster in children: A pilot study incorporating a structured diagnostic interview', *Journal of the American Academy of Child and Adolescent Psychiatry*, 27: 90–95.

Farhood, L. F. 1999. 'Testing a model of family stress and coping based on war and non-war stressors: Family resources and coping among Lebanese families', *Archives of Psychiatric Nursing*, 13(4): 192–203.

Farhood, L., et al. 1993. 'The impact of war on the physical and mental health of the family: the Lebanese experience', *Social Science & Medicine* 36: 1555–1567.

Foa, E. B., and Hearst-Ikeda, D. 1996. 'Emotional dissociation in response to trauma: An information-processing approach.' In L. K. Michaelson and W. J. Ray (eds). *Handbook of Dissociation: Theoretical, Empirical and Clinical Perspectives.* New York, NY. Plenum Press: 207–224.

Fredrickson, B. L., et al. 2003. 'What good are positive emotions in crises? A prospective study of resilience and emotions following the terrorist attacks on the United States on September 11th, 2001', *Journal of Personality and Social Psychology*, 84: 365–376.

Gabriel, R., et al. 2007. 'Psychopathological consequences after a terrorist attach: An epidemiological study among victims, the general population and police officers.' *European Psychiatry*, 22(6): 339–346.

Galea, S., et al. 2002. 'Psychological sequelae of the September 11 terrorist attacks in New York City', *New England Journal of Medicine*, 346: 982–987.

Gershuny, B. S., and Thayer, J. F. 1999. 'Relations among psychological trauma, dissociative phenomena and trauma-related distress: A review and integration', *Clinical Psychology Review*, 19(5): 631–657.

Gilligan, J. 1997. *Violence: Reflections on a National Epidemic*. New York. Vintage Books.

Goleman, D. 1986. 'Terror's children: Mending mental wounds', *New York Times*, 2 September: 15, 19.

Hardy, C., et al. 2003. 'Resources, knowledge and influence: The organisational effects of interorganisational collaboration', *Journal of Management Studies*, 40(2): 321–347.

Herman, J. L. 1997. *Trauma and Recovery: From domestic abuse to Political Terror*. London: Pandora.

Horowitz, D., and Lissak, M. 1989. *Trouble in Eutopia: The overburdened polity of Israel*. Albany, NY. State University of New York Press.

Hourani, L. L., et al. 1986. 'A population-based survey of loss and psychological distress during war', *Social Science and Medicine*, 23(3): 269–275.

Kaufman, G. 1992. *Shame: The Power of Caring*. Rochester, VT: Schenkman Books.

Kazak, A. D., et al. 1998. 'Predicting posttraumatic stress symptoms in mothers and fathers of survivors of childhood cancers', *Journal of the American Academy of Child and Adolescent Psychiatry*, 37: 823–831.

Khamis, V. 1998. 'Psychological distress and well-being among traumatized Palestinian women during the Intifada', *Social Science and Medicine*, 46(8): 1033–1041.

Khamis, V. 2005. Posttraumatic stress disorder among school age Palestinian children', *Child Abuse and Neglect*, 29: 81–95.

Kimura, M. S. 1999. 'Mother-child relationships and adjustment of children exposed to marital aggression and violence', *Dissertation Abstract International: Section B: The Sciences and Engineering*, 59: 6070.

Lubit, R. 2006. 'Responding to traumatised children: An overview of diagnosis and treatment options I.' In A. Hosin (ed.). *Responses to Traumatized Children*. Basingstoke. Palgrave Macmillan.

McCann, I. L., and Pearlman, L. A. 1990. 'Vicarious traumatisation: A framework for understanding the psychological effects of working with victims', *Journal of Traumatic Stress*, 3: 131–149.

McDermott, M., Duffy, M., and McGuinness, D. 2004. 'Addressing the psychological needs of children and young people in the aftermath of the Omagh bomb', *Child Care in Practice* 10(2): 141–154.

Maclure, R., and Denov, M. 2009. 'Reconstruction versus transformation: Post-war education and the struggle for gender equality in Sierra Leone', *International Journal of Educational Development*, 29(6):612–620.

McWhirter, L. 1983. 'Growing up in Northern Ireland: From aggression to the Troubles.' In P. Goldstein and M. H. Segall (eds). *Aggression in Global Perspective*. New York: Pergamon.

Martini, D. R., et al. 1990. 'Psychiatric sequelae after traumatic injury: The Pittsburgh Regatta accident', *Journal of the American Academy of Child and*

Adolescent Psychiatry, 29(1): 70–75.

Miller, K. E., and Rasmussen, A. 2010. 'War exposure, daily stressors, and mental health in conflict and post-conflict settings: Bridging the divide between trauma-focused and psychosocial frameworks', *Social Science and Medicine,* 70: 7–16.

Mollica, R. F. 1988. 'The trauma story: the psychiatric care of refugee survivors of violence and torture.' In F. M. Ochberg (ed.). *Post-traumatic Therapy and the Victim of Violence.* New York. Brumer/Mazel.

Mollica, R. F. 1990. 'Communities of confinement: An international plan for relieving the mental health crisis in the Thai-Khmer border camps', *Southeast Asian Journal of Social Science,* 18: 132–152.

Neuner, F., and Elbert, T. 2007. 'The mental health disaster in conflict setting: Can scientific research help?' *BMC Public Health,* 7: 275.

Norris, F. H., et al.2002. '60,000 Disaster victims speak: Part 1. An Empirical review of the empirical literature 1981–2001', *Psychiatry,* 65: 207–239.

Otto, M. W., et al. 2007. 'Posttraumatic stress disorder symptoms following media exposure to tragic events: Impact of 9/11 on children at risk for anxiety disorders', *Journal of Anxiety Disorders,* 21: 888–902.

Panter-Brick, A., et al. 2009. 'Violence, suffering, and mental health in Afghanistan: A school-based survey', *The Lancet,* 374: 807–816.

Patterson, J. M., and McCubbin, H. I. 1983. 'The impact of family life events and changes on the health of a chronically ill child', *Family Relations,* 32(21): 255–264.

Pearlman, L. A., and Saakvitne, K. W. 1995. *Trauma and the Therapist: Countertransference and Vicarious Traumatisation in Psychotherapy with Incest Survivors.* New York. Norton.

Pedersen, D. 2002. 'Political violence, ethnic conflict and contemporary wars: broad implications for health and social well-being', *Social Science and Medicine* 55: 175–190.

Pelcovitz, D., and Kaplan, S. 1996. 'Posttraumatic stress disorder in children and adolescents', *Child and Adolescent Psychiatric Clinics of North America,* 5: 449–469.

Pigozzi, M. J. 1999. *Education in Emergencies and for Reconstruction: A Developmental Approach.* UNICEF Working Paper Series. New York. UNICEF Education Section.

Punamäki, R.-L., Qouta, S., and El-Sarraj, E. 2001. 'Resiliency factors predicting psychological adjustment after political violence among Palestinian children', *International Journal of Behavioural Development,* 25(3): 256–275.

Qouta, S., et al. 2007. 'Predictors of pathological distress and positive resources among Palestinian adolescents: Trauma, child, and mothering characteristics', *Child Abuse and Neglect* 31: 699–717.

Rachman, S. .1980. 'Emotional Processing', *Behaviour Research and Therapy,* 18: 51–60.

Reilly, I. 2002. 'Trauma and family therapy: Reflections on September 11 from Northern Ireland', *Journal of Systemic Therapies,* 21: 71–80.

Rowland-Klein, D., and Dunlop, R. 1998. 'The transmission of trauma across generations: Identification with parental trauma in children of Holocaust survivors', *Australian and New Zealand Journal of Psychiatry,* 32: 358–369.

Saigh, P.A. 1989. 'The validity of the DSM-III posttraumatic stress disorder classifi-
cation as applied to children', *Journal of Abnormal Psychology*, 98: 189–192.
Saigh, P. A., et al. 1999. 'Child-adolescent posttraumatic stress disorder: Prevalence,
risk-factors and comorbidity.' In P. A. Saigh and J. D. Bremner (eds).
Posttraumatic Stress Disorder: A Comprehensive Text. Needham Heights, MA.
Allyn & Bacon: 18–43.
Schlenger, W. E., et al. 2002. 'Psychological reactions to terrorist attacks: Findings
from the National Study of Americans' Reactions to September 11', *Journal of
the American Medical Association*, 288: 581–588.
Seitz, K. 2004. *Education and Conflict: The Role of Education in the Creation,
Prevention and Resolution of Societal Crisis: Consequences for Development
Cooperation.* Eschborn. GTZ.
Shahini, M. 2001. 'Therapy, tradition and myself', *AACAP News*, 32: 181–182.
Shuval, J. T. 1993. 'Migration and stress.' In L. Goldberger and S. Berznitz (eds).
The Handbook of Stress: Theoretical and Clinical Aspects. New York. Free
Press: 641–657.
Silver, R. C., et al. 2002. 'Nationwide longitudinal study of psychological re-
sponses to September 11th' *Journal of the American Medical Association*, 288:
1235–1244.
Simpson, M. A. 1998. 'The second bullet: Transgenerational impacts of trauma
of conflict within a South African and world context.' In Y. Danieli (ed.).
International Handbook of Multigenerational Legacies of Trauma. New York.
Plenum Press: 487–512.
Solomon, Z. 1995. *Coping with War-induced Stress: The Gulf War and the Israeli
Response.* New York: Plenum Press.
Solomon, Z., and Mikulincer, M. 1992. 'Aftermaths of combat stress reactions: A
3yr study', *British Journal of Clinical Psychology*, 31(1): 21–32.
Spitzer, R. L. (ed.). 1994. *DSM-IV Casebook:A Learning Companion to the
Diagnostic and Statistical Manual of Mental Disorders, fourth edition / edited
by Robert L. Spitzer . . . [et al.].* Washington, DC. American Psychiatric Press.
Stamm, B. H. 1999. *Secondary Traumatic Stress: Self-care Issues for Clinicians,
Researchers, and Educators.* 2nd ed. Lutherville, MD. Sidan Press.
Stein, A. L., et al. 2005. 'Correlates for posttraumatic stress disorder in Gulf
War veterans: a retrospective study of main and moderating effects', *Anxiety
Disorders*, 19: 861–876.
Thabet, A. A., and Vostanis, P. 2000. 'Posttraumatic stress disorder reactions in chil-
dren of war: A longitudinal study', *Child Abuse and Neglect*, 24(2): 291–298.
Tidwell, A. 2004. 'Conflict, peace and education: A tangled web', *Conflict
Resolution Quarterly*, 21(4): 463–470.
Tol, W. A., et al. 2010. 'Political violence and mental health: A multidisciplinary
review of the literature on Nepal', *Social Science and Medicine*, 70: 35–44.
United Nations House Committee on Refugees (UNHCR) (1989) *Report on
Refugees.* New York: United Nations Publishing Services.
Volkan, V. D. 2000. 'Traumatised societies and psychological care: Expanding the
concept of preventive medicine', *Mind and Human Interaction*, 11: 177–194.
Weingarten, K. 2004. 'Witnessing the effects of political violence in families:
Mechanisms of intergenerational transmission of trauma and clinical interven-
tions', *Journal of Marital and Family Therapy*, 30(1): 45–59.

Weiss, M., and Weiss, S. 2000. 'Second generation to Holocaust survivors: Enhanced differentiation of trauma transmission', *American Journal of Psychotherapy*, 54: 372–385.

World Health Organisation. 2005. *Mental Health Assistance to the Populations Affected by the Tsunami in Asia.* Geneva. World Health Organisation.

Zeidner, M. 2006. 'Individual differences in psychological reactions to terror attack', *Personality and Individual Differences,* 40: 771–781.

Zeidner, M., and Ben-Zur, H. 1993. 'Coping with a national crisis: The Israeli experience with the threat of missile attacks', *Personality and Individual Differences,* 14: 209–224.

Zureik, E. 1996. *Palestinian Refugees in the Peace Process.* Washington, DC. Institute for Palestine Studies.

CHAPTER SIX

COMPLEXITY DYNAMICS IN POST-CONFLICT ENVIRONMENTS: WHERE THE RESEARCH AGENDA COULD BEGIN

FRANK BALCH WOOD

As an introduction to a preliminary research agenda for post-conflict situations, this essay identifies insights from neuroscience and complexity dynamics that may be useful in describing those situations and predicting their outcome. These insights may be somewhat novel and sometimes counter-intuitive, but their ultimate utility will depend on the research agenda, and the ensuing evidence base, that they could generate. Public health advance depends on continuing improvements in its evidence base; peace-building efforts by local, national, and international entities may likewise depend on a reliable and growing evidence base.

Post-conflict environments often exhibit new and unexpected characteristics. These can be peaceful and productive, or hostile and destructive; they are usually a complex combination of both. Sometimes these outcomes are the direct result of the actions or policies of the combatant groups or of international third party agencies attempting to intervene to create peaceful conditions. Often, however, new outcomes come as a surprise that contradicts deliberate efforts by various parties to "arrange" a peaceful outcome. Complexity dynamics, in brain and in social behaviour, may help explain circumstances that give rise to such surprises; more generally, they may identify important features of post-conflict environments that improve the understanding and management of such environments.

Examples in current history can serve to illustrate the general point. In South Africa, the creation of the Truth and Reconciliation Commission (TRC) provided a procedure by which amnesty was granted by the government to perpetrators of political violence who testified honestly about their crimes. Amnesty turned out to be the lesser outcome; outpourings of emotion at the TRC hearings included overt expressions and acts of forgiveness that were as unexpected as they were moving. TRC chair Archbishop Desmond Tutu's book *No Future Without Forgiveness* (Tutu, 2000) not only chronicled these but insisted that forgiveness, not simply amnesty, were essential in the social response to violence. In the context of the bitter struggle against apartheid, the book is – to say the least – a surprise, notwithstanding objections to the notion of forgiveness from within and from outside South Africa.

Iraq, with its swirling mix of constructive and destructive factors, has exhibited surprises more in the negative direction. The violent outbreaks in the aftermath of the invasion by mostly US and British military forces in 2003 were not only individually shocking but also surprising in their number and sheer variety. They ranged widely: torture of detainees by US and UK soldiers; spectacular bombings of individual political and religious institutions; destruction and pillage of museums and ancient sites that are foundational for Islam, Judaism and Christianity alike; killing of hundreds of academics and professionals from all political parties and religious persuasions; and forceful intimidation and expulsion of civilians, resulting in a massive refugee crisis in neighbouring Syria and Jordan.

The question arising from post-conflict situations such as those above is a fundamentally serious one: have we no better understanding of the dynamics of such situations than simply to hope that this or that policy will succeed in creating and maintaining peace and avoiding surprises? Where should we look for answers?

In contemporary science, some features of internal brain dynamics seem to resemble those of complex dynamics in society. Complexity by definition involves many interacting parts, with corresponding difficulty in accurately predicting some types of future outcomes; and these are features equally true of brain and society. In a sense, brains and societies are two levels of description of the same complex phenomenon of human life in the world. Let us consider six complexity-dynamic features, observable both in brain activity and in society at large, that may be useful in understanding post-conflict situations.

Relevant Features of Similarity between Brain and Society in Complexity Terms

Massive networks of intercommunication between parts of the brain

Cortical neurons – i.e., individual cells in that large outer layer of the brain where most of the brain's computing is done – generally have perhaps a thousand times more connections to each other than to the outside world.

Most of the brain's "work", therefore, is about what its different parts are saying to each other; not what the world is saying to the brain or the brain to the world (Braitenberg and Schüz, 1991).

Societies at national and local levels are similar to brains in their preponderance of internal dialogue and discussion. Citizens talk and listen much more often to each other than to those who are from outside, i.e. "foreign". That is true even when the society is on land occupied by foreign invaders; over history such invaders have learned that they ignore the massive internal dialogue at their peril. Brutal attempts to suppress internal societal dialogues may produce unexpected, and sometimes undesired, consequences.

The "small world" nature of interactions between neurons

In the vast network of brain neurons, each neuron has up to 10,000 synaptic connections to other neurons (Breitenberg and Schüz, 1991). The "small world" designation means that these connections are not random across the entire network, but instead have a preponderance of local connections that constitute sub-networks of their own. More distal connections, while a minority of the total, are also functionally highly important and allow any one cortical neuron to connect to any other through as few as three or four synapses, i.e. connections between individual neurons (Watts and Strogatz, 1998, and Bassett and Bullmore, 2006, provide useful reviews).

The small world model has also repeatedly been argued as applicable in human society. The classic first popular formulation by Milgram (1967) illustrated a surprisingly short sequence of acquaintances that might suffice to transfer a communication between almost any two individuals, unknown to each other. Simply put, A is asked to send a message to F. So A contacts acquaintance B, who contacts acquaintance C (not an acquaintance of A), and the sequence then continues until F gets the message. As an example, "ordinary" citizens in Nebraska were asked to send a package to an unknown but named investment broker in Boston. Though many factors – including ethnic or linguistic divisions – can certainly affect the path length, the average number of connections required to communicate between two such distant individuals appeared to be unexpectedly small: just over five.

More critically, the particular balance of local and distal connections is critical, as Kleinberg (2000) has pointed out from a purely mathematical perspective. Good decisions require strong activity in the smaller networks (cell assemblies in brain and neighbourhoods in society); these actually drive the larger decisions. Society is defined as a network of intercommunications between its members; if those fail, there is no society and therefore no society-wide cultural or governmental influence that can promote peace or inhibit violence. One or two particular types of network impairment or damage may be particularly worth considering in this light, as in the following comparison of children and adolescents to adults.

Restriction of network size in children and adolescents, compared to adults

While impaired network communications are known to be caused by a variety of congenital factors, acquired brain lesions and learning itself, it is the limitation of the immature brain that is particularly interesting for understanding post-conflict situations. It has long been known that fibres to, from and within some areas of the brain – particularly in the frontal lobes – do not develop full functioning until well into adolescence, indeed sometimes the early twenties. Thus, it is only then that prefrontal brain areas become fully adept at high speed communication with other brain areas. See Yergelun-Todd (2007) for a review of the changes and their overall significance for emotional and cognitive behaviour. See also Supekar, Musen & Menon (2009), showing a general trend whereby longer distance axonal fibres become more prevalent in young adults than in children.

Among the areas of brain showing increased connectivity in adults compared to children, the combined orbital-ventromedial frontal (OVF) cortex takes prominence. This cortex is on the base and lower inside surface of each of the two frontal lobes. The OVF cortex is widely understood as the brain's principal support apparatus for decision-making, notably including decisions not to behave in a certain way, i.e. inhibitory or self-repressive decisions (see especially Rolls & Grabenhorst, 2008). There is general consensus that – at any given moment – the decisions the brain is considering are represented across the expanse of OVF cortex. There, the various options for decisional choice are evaluated and compared as to their cost-benefit properties, and a single final "go" choice is adopted.

The capacity of the OVF cortex to represent the full range of choices is related to the fact it is the only area of the brain that receives full input from all five brain sensory areas as well as from areas where emotional drives or intentions, some types of abstract cognition and all types of updated memories are produced. The OVF cortex is therefore well equipped to represent the reward value and predicted emotional satisfaction to be expected from each of the variety of the decisions available to the individual. Because the

OVF cortex is still immature in adolescence, youthful age itself becomes a risk factor for impulsive or insufficiently thoughtful behaviour.

Independent of age, the OVF cortex damage has long been understood as a risk factor for violent or anti-social behaviour. See the reviews by Bechara and Van der Linden (2005) and by Davidson, Putnam and Larson (2000); also the full book by Raine (1993), showing a consistent trend that associates violent criminal behaviour with OVF damage.

The societal analogy is straightforward. When the communication infrastructure is damaged or destroyed, the multiplicity of influences necessary for an accurate cost-benefit decision is unavailable. Post-conflict environments characteristically impair all electronic or print publications, telephone contact, and even safe travel to speak with neighbours, family and friends. In the present analysis, these disruptions are the analogous to OVF brain damage in individuals and impose a significantly overlooked risk for violence.

As information sharing becomes even less efficient, the remaining network devolves to even smaller subsets – these being increasingly defined by strong familial, ethnic, religious or ideological ties. Soon, the only sub-networks left are those with pre-existing strong ties, which then dominate the local dialogue. The sense that a larger society even exists is lost or becomes at least increasingly tentative. Gone also are the opportunities for a consensus – on anything – within the occupied society. A vague purposelessness ensues, and it becomes increasingly difficult to re-energize the fragments of the network and give any impetus to the creation of repaired or new networks. Such deteriorated networks can then slide into recurrent maladaptive destructiveness.

Attractors

Consider marbles rolling around inside a bowl. The entire bowl is the *basin of attraction*. If the bowls are recessed into a flat table-top surface, with no "edge" between the bowl and the flat surface, then a marble rolling free on the table top is not constrained to enter the bowl, but if it does so it is trapped in that basin and will not escape unless it or the bowl is strongly agitated.

In the brain, as in society, these attractor basins appear to be better understandable as networks that over time repeatedly "settle" on a given behaviour, which defines the attractor. Small networks within the brain may precipitate or even dominate that settling, but ultimately the whole brain – or a large part of it – adopts the settled behaviour. Habit (what William

James called the "great flywheel of society" that keeps people working) or recurrence of a particular behavioural pattern (what Sigmund Freud called "repetition compulsion") are other well known terms describing such an attractor basin.

In terms of the analysis of the social significance of the attractor basins operating in individual brains, Walter Freeman (1995, 1998, 2006) has presented what is probably the most penetrating analysis in modern neuro-science – certainly the one most directly related to issues of war and peace. It occurs in the publication of his invited lectures from the Spinoza chair at the University of Amsterdam (Freeman, 1995). In this relatively brief but expansive book, Freeman discusses life-long attractor basins including their propensity toward love and hate, noting that these are such powerful attrac-tors, i.e. relatively large basins with steep sides, that only intense activity can stand a chance of dislodging behaviour from such basins.

For Freeman, the vigorous music and dance activities of some socie-ties, such as those of the few remaining hunter-gatherers groups in southern Africa, are particularly potent in providing the intense level of multisensory and whole body stimulation required to motivate behaviour toward an en-during pattern of prosocial affiliation. If music and dance rituals are not the daily repetitive activity of modern industrial and post-industrial societies, various vigorous whole body expressions, sometimes accompanying music or singing, are still observable in many contexts, e.g. sports arenas, certain kinds of religious assemblies, and some political expressions such as march-ing or protesting in the streets. In keeping with Freeman's analysis, these all involve strong levels of commitment to a group, an idea or a cause.

Changes toward hate from love or at least from social cohesion, are equally well known. Riots – again, for example, in sports settings or in strong political protests – are certainly vigorous and intense whole-body expressions that seem to tip behaviour into at least a temporary anti-social basin. The outraged screams and shaking of fists by survivors of aerial or artillery bombardments, police brutality or torture of family members – all inflicted by a bordering or opposing armed force – are certainly enough to shift the behaviour of some individuals into a powerful attractor basin repre-senting enduring hatred toward the enemy inflicting those outrages. Often, however, the shift to hatred occurs after genuine reflection by the individual who ultimately shifts, as Ferguson, Burgess and Hollywood (2008) have so instructively pointed out from their interviews of militant individuals in Northern Ireland. When, and to whom, these shifts will occur is unpredict-able, but if there are more than a very few individuals thus shifted, then the social version of the same attractor basin predicts that they will find each other. Thereupon, they will constitute a stable group that is dedicated to, and reinforces, hatred toward and aggression against those viewed as the enemy, whether that enemy is perceived as local or as foreign. This coalescing into attractor basins of hatred brings us to our last two points of analysis.

Non-linear acceleration of the intensity of behaviour, especially arising from positive instead of negative feedback situations

The classic example of negative feedback is a thermostat that regulates a gas-fired heating system in a house by responding in a direction opposite to the direction of change in the ambient air temperature. As air temperature declines, the thermostat increases gas flow to the heater and air temperature soon rises. Conversely, as the air temperature rises, the thermostat reduces the gas flow to the furnace, which soon lowers the air temperature. Negative feedback thus achieves stability within a range. Positive feedback, however, is dangerous at best and often catastrophic – as when a thermostat responds to increased air temperature by increasing the gas flow to the furnace. Moreover, air temperature does not simply rise steadily in a straight line; instead, the more the loop continues, the faster is the rise in air temperature. The critical consequence is that the inevitable explosion of flames comes sooner than expected, because expectations are typically linear, not exponential.

The socially relevant positive feedback loop is the uncontrollable rage reaction, in which a brain moves quickly from processing small and seemingly insignificant stimuli toward processing a rapidly intensifying internal dialogue, the verbal version of which is something like: "the more I think about what you (the policeman) did (brutalize my brother) the angrier I get, and the angrier I get the more I focus on what you did". The speed by which the conflict intensifies can nevertheless be variable: see again Ferguson, Burgess & Hollywood (2008) for the reflectivity that often precedes the decision; also Fisher and Keashly (1991) and Spillman and Spillman (1991) on the power of images of the enemy to accelerate an ongoing self-perpetuating drive to violence. Whatever the time course, the ensuing explosion can be vicious indeed and might generalize to anyone resembling the enemy or any humans. The suddenness of the explosion is due to the non-linear, exponential rise in intensity. The overgeneralization to all humans, as in a seemingly random killing spree, is due to the emotive quality of the outburst, because emotions are essentially omnidirectional and not well targeted; they broadcast an individual's internal emotional state in a "let all beware" mode. See Yakovlev (1948) for this classical insight into the nature of emotion. The killing of academics and professionals in Iraq, without regard to their racial, ethnic or political identities, illustrates the kind of indiscriminate overgeneralization that can arise from non-linear complexity dynamics in a post-conflict environment. That overgeneralization (whether limited to any member of the hates ethnic group or inclusive of all humans) is not contradicted by the fact that it is sometimes cool, and methodical.

In certain cases, one additional characteristic can emerge, as follows:

Chaos

Chaos is a technical mathematical term describing a complex system showing one or more additional characteristics related to the difficulty with which future outcomes can be predicted. Outcomes in many complex systems can be predicted with suitable precision: as when infection by a certain virus reliably leads to a characteristic cluster of symptoms, notwithstanding the full complexity of the biological processes going on inside the host. See, for example, Bolker and Grenfell (1993) for an excellent analysis of the simplicity-complexity polarity in measles. Circumstances do sometimes yield pathways of prediction that are delicately dependent on fine details of their starting points, where initially small differences can ultimately result in large differences in outcome. This *sensitive dependence on initial conditions* can make two seemingly very similar pathways diverge toward outcomes that are not only different but altogether surprising. The differences at the start may be immeasurably small – but nonetheless entirely real. The pathways – however intricate – are deterministic, not random; but they are unpredictable on account of imprecision of measurement of the initial conditions. The simple consequence of the practical unpredictability is that the outcomes seem "chaotic". The social version is aptly conveyed in folklore as "the law of unintended consequences" or as the familiar "for want of a nail the shoe was lost, for want of a shoe the horse was lost . . . (etc., until) . . . the kingdom was lost."

It may well be that in any situation characterized by the first five of the above six features, chaotic dynamics are almost inevitable although not necessarily widespread or common. Particularly when surprising or unpredicted events occur – as they began to occur in Iraq within days of the 2003 invasion – then chaotic mechanisms may be suspected.

Let us then consider some possible hypotheses that might flow from the complexity-analytic perspective.

Preliminary Hypotheses: Toward a Research Agenda

Maintenance of communication networks, in all areas, is a primary goal of any government seeking peace

Given that societies, like brains, are ordinarily massively interconnected, a post-conflict society has by definition sustained major stresses if not outright fractures in its network properties. A government, local or foreign, does well to avoid additional stresses that will impair the local communication networks. In the context of small world networks, any time local interconnectivities (e.g. neighbourhoods) are disrupted, communications cannot efficiently reach through an entire population, and social cohesion begins to deconstruct.

For example, when the Coalition Provisional Authority in Iraq banned former Ba'th party members from government service, any potential gain was offset by the fact that this manoeuvre displaced the existing well established networks, forcing both the Ba'thists now unemployed, as well as the new government employees just employed, into situations where the networks in which they would subsequently operate were fractured and lacking in small-world properties. Criticism of banning Ba'thists from the government is not new; but the unique contribution of a complexity analysis is to identify the costs as fracture of the local connectivity within a small-world network.

Similarly, the ubiquitous tendency of governmental authorities, or occupying armies, to wall off and segregate ethnically identifiable neighbourhoods "for their own protection" is by complexity analysis certain to be counterproductive inasmuch as it prevents the very intercommunication networks that are required if a society is to survive. In this view, walls and fences, whether in Berlin, Gaza or Sri Lanka, are doomed to eventual destruction; otherwise, they destroy the societies they are intended to protect (see Ferguson and Cairns, 1996).

Inter-group and inter-institutional connectivity must not only be facilitated but enriched by contributions from cultural institutions

If the network of connectivities in post-conflict societies is either immature or damaged, then impulsive behaviours are inadequately restrained by reflective thought that includes values and emotional intentions. Every society has sources for such values and intentions, including pressures for peace and against violence. These include many formal and cultural institutions that promote historic values in the context of present realities. If these are disconnected, discouraged or unprotected, they obviously can have no influence. Encouraging the expression of those pressures is the societal equivalent of providing that wider range of cognitive and emotional influences to which an individual's OVF cortex becomes receptive as it matures. In the absence of those more mature cultural expressions, the society remains childish.

An open, tolerant, and challenging educational system, with high engagement and participation from students, is virtually a sine qua non of reconstruction and peace-building, not to mention sustained peace

Adolescent mentality as a characteristic of post-conflict society is also equally important at the level of individuals. If some adolescent individuals are prone to respond impulsively to provocations from government or occupying authority, then truly vigorous efforts may be required in order to enhance the expression, to them, of the full range of factors that determine desirable outcomes for them.

While difficult to achieve in any society, the prospects for effective education are nonetheless much better if recurrent maladaptive or destructive behaviour, an attractor basin, has not yet taken hold. On the other hand, persons or groups whose maladaptive behaviours are not only impulsive but also recurrent, are trapped in an attractor basin that is worse than simple impulsivity, hence the next point.

Recurrent violence must prompt immediate and intensive counter-measures

As an attractor basin for social behaviour, impulsively driven violence not only recurs but is by definition unlikely to change. Instead, its destructive impact can increase as the individual or group is unable to satisfy the demands of the attractor except through increasingly spectacular destructive acts. The stakes go up with each repetition of a violent act.

Consistent with Freeman's (1995) discussion of vigorous "whole body" engagement; an approach from complexity dynamics would be to drive up the intensity of activity, both within networks and within individuals. For example, instead of covering up the acts of violence, they can instead be vividly described, displayed and fully represented in all media of communication. Rituals of remembrance of victims can attract a wide audience, as can a variety of cultural communications – religious and political as well as literary and artistic. Gatherings of individuals to protest the violence are influential. Diverse cultural leaders across religion, politics, art, and literature – separately voicing and demonstrating their intolerance of the violence – can be effective, at least in arousing heightened senses of internal conflict within groups of individuals. It may take years, even decades, to mobilize an enduring cultural campaign against repetitive violence so that the forces against the violence are strong enough to have an impact.

Rage reactions may start a chain of repetitive violence, and two particular characteristics additionally inform their management. First, since rage is initially omnidirectional it cannot be stifled by preventing any single behaviour or group of behaviours – any more than a gas and fire explosion in a house can be stifled by closing the doors. In the long run (and sometimes in the short run) violent rage simply cannot be suppressed, however vigorous the policing response. Secondly, since rage reactions tend to accelerate unexpectedly quickly toward behavioural explosions, then any attempt to intervene to stop the acceleration must necessarily come as early as possible. Ideally, then, at the first signs of violent outbursts, the vigorous and intense cultural countermeasures described above should commence.

The perspective of complexity dynamics thus offers an unconventional proposition, contrasting with the common and understandable instinct to suppress the news of violence.

It is usually feared that such news will simply provoke further rage. The counter principle is that vigorous countermeasures also depend not only on accurate but intense communication of the reality of the violence. Balancing these two concerns – fear of provoking rage and the need to arouse peacemaking motivations – is obviously difficult. Providing credible evidence on where the line should be drawn is even more difficult. But history can be sifted with this question as the sieve; and it is possible that laboratory researches or even mathematical simulations would be possible. As a balance against ill-considered presentations of the horrors of any situation, Gilbert (2007) presents an interesting discussion of a subtler version of the problem – the use of "slum" nomenclature in urban renewal – that can alert us to the risks of thoughtless descriptions of undesirable situations. More broadly, the technique of publicizing acts of violence should be fully descriptive of the acts, but not prejudicial or emotionally slanted in its description of the persons involved.

The final strategy is to identify a vision that is compelling enough to say "yes" to

It is important to remember that failure of inhibitory control of violence, both in the brain and in societal networks, is probably related to a corresponding failure to perceive sufficient reward value in the pro-social options. The brain is perhaps not wired in such a way that it can easily "just say no" – at least not to specific and destructive behavioural plans that are under consideration. Instead, it may say "no" to destructive choices mainly by means of the cross inhibition that arises from the constructive choices to which it has said, or could say, "yes". See the classical account by Pribram and McGuiness (1975), and more recent accounts by Freeman (1995 and 1998). But to engage a population on a journey driven by a strong and enduring "yes" to hopes for a more humane and enriching life together is the single most difficult task of any society, post-conflict or not. (See Tutu (1999) for one attempt at that vision.)

Three Possible Starting Points for Research

The above considerations suggest some obvious programmes of research that a complexity theory could stimulate. Readers will doubtless conceive others. First, a systematic series of brain imaging studies in 18 to 22 year olds could examine the details of the individual differences in structural and functional connectivity involving the orbital-ventromedial frontal (OVF) cortex. Previous work has shown that is possible on a voxel by voxel basis to map the full set of the many thousands of connectivities calculable in a set of MRI brain images. These have confirmed the appropriateness of small-world network models, and to date such high resolution connectivity mappings have also generally replicated the large functional maps of brain regions that have been developed over the last 25 years. Important individual differences are seen in these connectivity maps, however, and it is especially important to investigate whether those differences correlate with behavioural characteristics such as impulsivity within typical late adolescent/young adults. See Wood and Flowers (1999) for one earlier version of such studies.

A second area of research would involve the attempt to clarify and specify many of the key terms of a complexity or chaos model as they would apply in the types of post-conflict situations that are described above. Of critical importance would be the types of data that could be used, and how such data would be collected. For example, archival documents (South Africa's or Sierra Leone's Truth and Reconciliation records) or literary works (German writers before and after WWII) might yield to techniques so simple, yet so potentially powerful, as frequency analyses of key words, statistically improbable phrases and similar constructs. These might trace changes in attitudes across post-war years, which could then be followed by full-fledged traditional literary and historical analyses.

An entirely different approach might be to develop complexity-based models of the known outbreaks of new and emerging disease in certain post-conflict environments. These are particularly well documented in Iraq. As a general definitional matter, small-world network properties in a population do facilitate the more rapid spread of disease, and since there are good data on psychiatric as well as physical disease it could be informative to compare them. Two features might particularly inform such an analysis of psychiatric epidemiology: (1) local or regional trauma, analogous to an initial infection in the population; and (2) the notion that much human mal-adaptive or destructive behaviour is normal or commonplace (see Bartlett, 2005, for a particularly illuminating and wide-ranging discussion from that perspective). These two somewhat contrasting notions might therefore re-quire a very different descriptive methodology, but maps of the spread of the psychiatric consequences of violence – whether novel or commonplace in a given population – may well inform us about their mechanisms; so, too, might corresponding maps of the spread of pro-social countermeasures.

Finally, in many ways the most important of all the potential applica-tions to new research on post-conflict environments would come from educational research, both in the laboratory and in the field. One approach could test small modular curricula, varying in the scope and intensity of their emotional and cognitive content, for the degree to which learners with varying characteristics on the impulsivity dimension could receive and master given curricula. Field trials of longer semester and whole year ap-proaches might study the impact of much more comprehensive educational techniques that include specific teacher-training features, optimally efficient reallocation of scarce resources such as textbooks, and various techniques, especially including music and drama, that foster engagements with stu-dents that are both more emotionally expressive and more cognitively rich. It should not be forgotten that a major task of society is also the education of adults: all the above considerations call for intentional and sustained ef-forts to train adults in leadership roles continually to facilitate dialogue and communication within their groups.

Complexity approaches might particularly focus on looking for the tipping points – when the multiplicity of influences finally coalesces to produce a major new self-understanding in individuals regarding their prospects for assisting in building and maintaining peace. While such points are difficult to quantify, they are often not difficult to recognize and their natural history alone, including the types of situations in which they occur and the forces seeming to be in play, need full documentation to begin to answer the question: under what conditions do students find themselves engaged in sustained quest for peace? Creative outcomes can also be the result all the complexity mechanisms reviewed above, including chaos. Even case history data can uncover the sort of factors that generate that kind of creative insight. Education bids fair to be an expanding frontier of peace studies.

References

Bartlett, S. J. 2005. *The Pathology of Man: A Study of Human Evil*. Springfield, IL. Charles C. Thomas.

Bassett, D., and Bullmore, E. 2006. 'Small-world brain networks', *Neuroscientist* 6: 512–523.

Bechara, A., and Van Der Linden, M. 2005. 'Decision-making and impulse control after frontal lobe injuries.' *Current Opinion in Neurology*, 18(6): 734–739.

Bolker, B., and Grenfell, B. 1993. 'Chaos and Biological Complexity in Measles Dynamics', *Proceedings of the Royal Society of London. B*, 251: 75–81.

Braitenberg, V. and Schüz, A. 1991. *Anatomy of the Cerebral Cortex. Statistics and Geometry*. Berlin. Springer Verlag.

Davidson, R. J., Putnam, K. M., and Larson, C. L. 2000. 'Dysfunction in the neural circuitry of emotion regulation: A possible prelude to violence', *Science*, 289: 591–594.

Ferguson, N., Burgess, M. and Hollywood, I. 2008. 'Crossing the Rubicon: Deciding to Become a Paramilitary in Northern Ireland', *International Journal of Conflict and Violence*, 2(1): 130–137.

Ferguson, N., and Cairns, E. 1996. 'Political violence and moral maturity in Northern Ireland', *Political Psychology*, 17(4): 713–725.

Fisher, R. J., and Keashly, L. (1991). 'A contingency approach to third party intervention', in R. J. Fisher (ed.), *The Social Psychology of Intergroup and International Conflict Resolution*, pp. 211–238. New York. Springer-Verlag.

Freeman, W. 1995. *Societies of Brains: A Study in the Neuroscience of Love and Hate*. Hillsdale, NJ. Erlbaum.

Freeman, W. 1998. 'Emotion is essential to all intentional behaviors.' In M. Lewis & I. Granic (eds), *Emotion, Development, and Self Organization: Dynamic Systems Approaches to Emotional Development*: 209–235.

Freeman, W. 2006. 'A cinematographic hypothesis of cortical dynamics in perception', *International Journal of Psychophysiology* 60(2): 149–161.

Gilbert, A. 2007. 'The return of the *slum*: does language matter?' *International Journal of Urban and Regional Research*, 31(4): 697–713.

Kleinberg, J. 2000. 'Navigation in a small world', *Nature* 406: 845. doi:10.1038/35022643

Milgram, S. 1967. 'The small-world problem', *Psychology Today* 1: 61–67.

Pribram, K., and McGuinness, D. 1975. *'Arousal, activation, and effort* in the control of attention', *Psychological Review* 82(2): 116–149.

Raine, A. 1993. *The Psychopathology of Crime: Criminal Behavior as a Clinical Disorder.* San Diego. Academic Press.

Rolls, E.T., and Grabenhorst, F. 2008. 'The orbitofrontal cortex and beyond: from affect to decision making.' *Progress in Neurobiology*, 86(3): 216–44.

Spillmann, K. R., and Spillmann, K. 1991. 'On enemy images and conflict escalation', *International Social Science Journal*, 43(1): 57–76.

Supekar, K., Musen, M. and Menon, V. 2009. 'Development of large-scale functional brain networks in children', *Public Library of Science Biology.* doi: 10.1371/journal pbio. 1000157.

Tutu, D. 1999. *No Future Without Forgiveness.* London. Rider.

Watts, D. and Strogatz, S. 1998. 'Collective dynamics of "small-world" networks', *Nature*, 393: 440–442. doi: 10.1038/30918.

Wood, F., and Flowers, D. 1999. 'Functional neuroanatomy of dyslexic subtypes: A survey of 43 candidate regions with a factor analytic validation across 100 cases.' In: D. D. Duane (ed.), *Reading and Attention Disorders: Neurobiological Correlates*: 131–161.

Yakovlev, P. 1948. 'Motility, behavior and the brain; stereodynamic organization and neural coordinates of behavior', *Journal of Nervous and Mental Disease*, 107(4): 313–335.

Yurgelun-Todd, D. 2007. 'Emotional and cognitive changes during adolescence.' *Current Opinion in Neurobiology*, 17(2): 5–13.

CHAPTER SEVEN

BRIDGE-BUILDING IN MOSTAR: FROM
FRAGMENTED STUMBLING BLOCKS TO
OVERARCHING NARRATIVE SOLUTIONS

PADDY GREER

Site specific art has often been perceived as a reaction to the self-referential nature of modernist art. It resists both the museum culture – "white cubing" – and the commercial drive of the art market. In more ways than one it became grounded and bolted to specific locations, denying attempts to dislocate and/or relocate to alternative venues. However, this myth of the unmoveable became unhinged with the dismantling and subsequent removal of Richard Serra's *Tilted Arc* from the Federal Plaza in New York, to which he vehemently objected. The uncoupling of the *Tilted Arc* from its location generated a debate around the nature of the "site". Site specificity eventually expanded into a larger discourse with socio-economic ramifications and political efficacy. In so doing "different cultural debates, a theoretical concept, a social issue, a political problem, an institutional framework, a community or seasonal event, a historical condition and even particular formations of desire are deemed to function as sites now" (Kwon, 1997)·

Rosalyn Deutsche discusses the various issues surrounding the removal of Serra's *Tilted Arc* and recounts the events leading up to its destruction (Deutsche, 1996). What is interesting are the questions she raises concerning the nature and significance of "public", "public spaces" and "public use" as well as the issues surrounding public authorities' homogenizing outlook on public spaces, the public and specific sites. She suggests that such universal terms suppress conflict and leave the way open to exploitation of public sites by public authorities. Furthermore, homogenizing the "general public" as a conceptual and legal entity is surely political manipulation. Indeed, she says, this goes right to the core of the definition of democracy.

But perhaps more disturbing is the haste to redevelop and gentrify dilapidated and neglected areas of the city. Rundown areas seem to awaken nostalgia for the secure and predictable way things were and people want to restore the sites to their original pristine, essentialist state.[1] Both the homogenizing of the peoples of Mostar (leaving aside the assumption that there are two clearly distinct "homogenous" groups, Bosniak and Croat), and the gentrification of the war-torn centre of old Mostar are germane to this discussion. The debate about public art and hence public space and public performance is a debate about democracy, about openness, participation, inclusion and accountability.

Whether one creates or removes an art object (a performance in itself), a new space will always be created. The new space of course perturbs the urban psychogeography, whether it is understood aesthetically, politically, historically or culturally. What this paper tries to do is to examine, not only the removal of a Tilted Arc, but both the removal and the performative reconstruction of a most famous Bosnian arc, the Mostar Bridge, and its effect on the people of the city of Mostar. The site of the bridge and the space it creates is the location for multiple interpretation and hermeneutical intrigue. But first allow me digress and cast some light on aspects of bridging in Bosnia.

Bridges in Bosnia

In 'Blowing up the "Bridge"', the introduction to the collected essays on the Balkans entitled *Balkan as Metaphor: Between Globalization and Fragmentation*, Dušan Bjelić acknowledges the figurative language of the metaphor in understanding Balkanism. The very concept of "metaphor" itself implies etymologically a translation or transition. And the question arises from where or what to where and what. Bjelić succinctly replies:

> For the Ottomans, as well as for Western colonial cultures, the Balkans formed a "bridge" between the East and the West, a metaphor naturalized by Ivo Andrić in his Nobel Prize-winning novel, *The Bridge over the Drina*.[2] That metaphor of the "bridge" induces endless hermeneutical circles which transform a "bridge" into a "wall", dividing rather than connecting. (Bjelić & Savić, 2002: 15, 16)

Mark Thompson (1992) devotes a whole chapter to "The Bridges of Bosnia". As we shall see, the bridge in Bosnia connotes much more than an access passage or a wall. However, Andrić, in the person of the *hodja,* considering the impassable nature of the mountainous region between the Balkan[3] Mountains and the Dinaric Alps, explains how bridges came into being.

When Allah the Merciful and Compassionate first created the world, the earth was smooth and even as a finely graven plate.[4] That displeased the devil who envied man this gift of God. And while the earth was just as it had come from God's hands, damped and soft as unbaked clay, he stole up and scratched the face of God's earth with his nails as much and as deeply as he could. Therefore, the story says, deep rivers and ravines were formed which divide one district from another, and kept men apart[5] . . . When the angels saw how unfortunate men could not pass those abysses and ravines to finish the work they had to do, but tormented themselves and looked in vain and shouted from one side to the other, they spread their wings above those places and men were able to cross. So men learned from the angels of God how to build bridges, and therefore, after fountains, the greatest blessing is to build a bridge and the greatest sin to interfere with it,[6] for every bridge, from a tree trunk crossing a mountain stream to this great erection of Mehmed Pasha, has its guardian angel who cares for it and maintains it as long as God has ordained that it should stand. (Andrić, 1994: 208)

What is of particular interest in the story by the hodja is the *tabula rasa* reference concerning the original pristine nature of the world – "the Real" as Lacan would describe it – before the devil's inscriptions – the Lacanian Symbolic order. This blank space without any symbolic markings is devoid of meaning. The ensuing psychological longing for the merger with the "other", with the world of symbiotic union, or desire for the *objet petit "a"* (Lacan, 1977) is also echoed in the ancient Roman notion of the *Pontifex Maximus*, the Great Bridge Builder, a title now appropriated by the Roman Pontiff. The Pontifex Maximus was a personal bridge between this world and the other – "the me" and "the not me" – to ensure the Pax Deorum or the peace of the gods.

However the sense of permanence of the bridge remains –"but the bridge still stood, the same as it had always been ... or so it seemed", but does "not share the fate of the transient things of this world" (Andrić, 1994: 214). This is not the case with the bridge at Mostar.

Maria Todorova emphasizes the "in-betweenness" of the Balkans, and affirms that Balkan is neither here nor there but in between. She claims that "Unlike Orientalism,[7] which is a discourse about an imputed opposition, Balkanism is a discourse of imputed ambiguity", a site "constructed not as 'other' but as an incomplete 'self'" (Todorova, 1997: 17). This notion of liminality[8] is further attested to by the then British Prime Minister, Mr Tony Blair, when he referred to the Balkans as "on our doorstep in Europe"[9] (literally the *limen*). Greer et al. (2005) refer repeatedly to the multiple levels of transition or liminality experienced by the former Communist countries such as Bosnia & Herzegovina and Serbia & Montenegro, as well as Bulgaria and Romania. For instance, Bosnia is not only moving from a regime of centralized government to participatory democracy, from a war-torn country to peaceful co-existence, a transition to a market economy as well as a route between East and West, but also is currently seeking membership of the EU with its economic assurances. This in-betweenness is a place of growth and national individuation and is fraught with societal anxiety and risk; it is the site generated by the trauma of war. The disjunctive feature of liminality experienced by people on the move reminds us of the postmodern aphorism to "make the border your territory", or a "communitas" as Victor Turner (1974) would suggest. Life in Mostar is not that simple.

Other bridges in the former republic of Yugoslavia besides the one in Višegrad have been immortalized. For instance the famous "Battle for the Wounded" in Jablanica in 1941–1945 is deeply reverenced by a generation of Southern Slavs. The Yugoslav national liberation forces, the Partisans, though completely outnumbered and caring for 4000 sick and wounded, devised a strategy to evade both the German strafing offensive and the barrage of gunfire from both the Chetniks and the Ustaši. Faced with having to cross a railway bridge and being decimated, they decided to blow up the bridge and build a smaller one with the remnants and then cross the river Neretva, and so outwit the enemy. Shortly after the war Tito insisted that the broken bridge remain as it was as a testimony to the bravery of the anti-fascist partisans.[10] The aestheticizing of this bridge extends also to the building of a memorial museum above the bridge and a remembrance café in the German bunker. However, once more, this contrasts significantly with the story of the bridge at Mostar.

The Story of Mostar

The city of Mostar gets its name from the very old Ottoman single arched stone bridge built in 1566 after nine years of labour[11] – the *Stari Most* or Old Bridge. Sometimes the word *Stari* has been used to personify the "Old Man" or guardian angel of the bridge. This was, and to some extent, still is the city's greatest symbol. During the Bosnian war of 1993–1995 fighting between Croats and Bosniaks intensified particularly around Mostar.[12] On 9 November 1993 the Croat commander, Slobadan Praljak, is alleged to have given orders to destroy the famous world heritage bridge in Mostar, supposedly saying that he would see to it that an "even older and more beautiful bridge" would be built. Militarily, from a logistics point of view, the bridge was not significant.[13] The destruction was intended to destroy the heart of the people of Mostar. And that is what it did. "A group of Bosnian Croat soldiers videoed the climax of this orgy", a psychotic act that represented the "utter senselessness and misery of the entire conflict" (Glenny, 2000: 646) As the citizenry had based their identity for many centuries on the permanence of this symbol, like those in Višegrad, its destruction and the constant bombardment of the city in no short measure traumatized the people of Mostar.

The visual imagery of the truncated stumps of the bridge and the brokenness of the city's heart can easily be romanticized as was the case for the other bridge over the same river Neretva at Jablanica. However, Braco Peza, a local artist, issued to the newspaper *Pobjeda* a statement regarding the bridge: "Now the Old Bridge reminds us of an invalid of war, whose arms were amputated almost at its shoulders" (the Halebija and the Tara fortified towers). The spectacle of its destruction and the traumatic and disabling effect it has had on the citizens, both physically and psychologically, remains largely unaddressed.

On 10 March 1994, the Director-General of Unesco launched an appeal for its reconstruction. On 23 July 2004, the bridge was finally rebuilt, inaugurated and officially opened by Britain's Prince of Wales. Unesco's justification for the rebuilding of the bridge is set forth thus:

> With the "renaissance" of the Old Bridge and its surroundings, the *symbolic* power and meaning of the City of Mostar – as an exceptional and universal *symbol* of coexistence of communities from diverse cultural, ethnic and religious backgrounds – has been reinforced and strengthened, underlining the unlimited efforts of human solidarity for peace and powerful cooperation in the face of overwhelming catastrophes.

The reconstruction was financially supported by the international community, particularly Italy, Turkey, the Netherlands and France, and managed by the World Bank with the backing and support of the Council of Europe and the European Union. The celebrations surrounding the event echoed the thunderous spectacle of its destruction. Many heads of state and international celebrities were invited to the event. Although the Imaginary order of the city (citizens identifying with the original bridge), and its Symbolic order (the bridge as symbol of coexistence) are evident, the Lacanian Real (the possibility for genocidal eruption) remains.

Guy Debord (1994: 1–2) says that

the spectacle presents itself simultaneously as all of society, as part of society, and as *instrument of unification* . . . [it] concentrates all gazing and all consciousness ... and the unification it achieves is nothing but an official language of generalized separation ... The spectacle's form and content are identically the total justification of the existing system's conditions and goals. The spectacle is also the *permanent presence*[14] of this justification.

This is precisely what Deutsche refers to as homogenizing and the denial of democracy. The art object (in this case the new bridge) is a residue of the spectacular performance and is effortlessly appropriated, colonized and commodified.

However, this prosthetic new bridge remains and will remain merely a replica of the old one. The Mostar Bridge is gone. There remains a lack, and consequently, a desire to be fulfilled, but which can never be realized. There will always be a communal rift between the experience of that bridge and its discourse. There will always be a lack which remains elusive. Consider the following reflection by a local Mostar citizen at the opening of the new bypass:

> You make one mistake concerning this bridge. It is not Turkish bridge. This is Bosnian bridge but build by the Turkish constructor. Like you know they succeed to rebuild bridge but it is not same at all. I whose [= was] there few days before grand opening. It look like completely new bridge with old shape. It is not the same and newer [= never] will be. The people from Mostar don't have same feelings to the bridge like before. This bridge has special meanings to the people of Mostar and hi [= it] connected to sides of river and people on both sides. Hi whose [= it was] unifier of community in Mostar. Now it is not the same. That means with this action of blowing up the bridge they succeed to divide people of Mostar and they will newer be united community any more like this new bridge will never be the old one.

Bridge as Simulacrum

The mimetic reconstruction of the bridge implies a form of prosthesis, without any feeling – a lack of sensation – but assumed to be real. This perverse attempt by the international community to embrace "authentic" performance by reusing the original desecrated stones of the destroyed bridge, supplementing them with more masonry cut from similar quarries as the original ones, as well as the construction process, conspire to lead one to believe in the re-presentation of the original Stari Most. But this can only be a simulacrum. Baudrillard (1994: 6) reminds us that "whereas representation attempts to absorb simulation by interpreting it as a false representation, simulation envelops the whole edifice of representation itself as a simulacrum".

While the new bridge itself has been rebuilt, it remains a simulacrum marking the absence of the peace it professes to symbolize. It has a discursive life of its own. For instance the peace award "Mostar 2004"[15] and "Mostar 2005" etc is a miniature replica of the new bridge under construction. It has a derived value with an energy of its own but oddly enough it resembles a prosthetic limb. It is not the bridge, not the rebuilt bridge, but is a replica of a replica, a double derivative sign of peace, a simulacrum. Ultimately, the "New Old Bridge" marks the absence of the original one; it marks the Lacanian "lack". It will forever awaken the desire for the times before the destruction of the bridge. There is now a complete and irrevocable separation from the past. We enter a new realm of discourse, where the bridge has been mythologized, derivatized, and ultimately forgotten. The new bridge, a mere simulacrum, has created a chasm with the past. The new construct is now available for recolonization; once again Mostar has been disempowered.

Bridge as Metonym

It has already been mentioned that the bridge can be been seen as a metaphor for connecting peoples or for separating them. We have also seen how Todorova and others have bridged many concepts with this idea. However, in the case of Mostar and the destruction of the old single-arched bridge, its loss and reconstruction ensure a sense of loss. This loss or lack can never be supplied. The bridge is gone for ever. However, the desire to replace it, to reach out and reclaim it, or simply to wish it back, is the key to understanding the metonymic nature of the new bridge – the mimesis. The new bridge symbolizes the need to pursue one's desire to be at one with the mother city before the cataclysmic and traumatic separation. This union can never happen. The split is permanent and replacing the bridge is simply a metonymic replacement, an attempt to be at peace in a way the city was before the war. No amount of mimetic reconstruction or urban gentrification can alleviate the trauma. Nonetheless the international community has decided to build the replica despite the psychological consequences of this venture to the citizens of Mostar. In so doing, the international community stands accused of being perverse and insensitive to the plight of the citizens of Mostar and their unvoiced trauma.

Bridge as Liminal Space

The term "liminal" was first used by the French anthropologist A. van Gennep (1960), in his study on the rites of passage in relation to transitions between one social order and another. It denotes both a temporal and spatial sense of crossing, the elements of site-specific performance. It is where community members leave the everyday, the familiar or profane and enter a sacred space which Victor Turner refers to as liminoid. Turner sees the liminoid space as an opportunity for creativity, of ambiguity where one can defamiliarize the familiar and blur the boundaries between ethnic discontinuities. Where two communities meet in a common space like this the opportunity for creating something beyond the dreams of either is possible. Such was the case in Mostar upon this bridge, where both Croat and Bosniak met and created a sense of commonality, as the characters in Andrić's novel allegedly did upon the bridge over the Drina at Višegrad.

Turner employs Paul Goodman's (1947) term "communitas", used in reference to town planning, from the citizens' point of view rather than merely the "cold stone" construction. This essentially means a relational quality of full, unmediated communication, between people who find themselves thrown into the same situation. The communitas finds presence in the liminoid space between a "going" and a "coming", a sacred space. The I-Thou exchanges by the people of Mostar often found expression upon the bridge, which became a place of community growth, exchange, creativity, a place apart. Needless to say, this sense of communitas was irrevocably destroyed in 1993.

A Lacanian Interpretation

Jacques Lacan is considered a Freudian psychoanalyst, clinically related to the psychodynamic school of therapy, and relies heavily on a well-grounded theory of the unconscious. However Lacan dismantles the entire Freudian edifice which he considered anchored in a historico-cultural interpretation of society's value system. In his now famous "Rome Discourse" he announced that the unconscious is structured like a language (Lacan, 1977: 30–113). This assertion was predicated on the work of Saussure and Lévi-

Strauss. For instance, he felt that in all discourse we tend to string signifiers sequentially or syntagmatically. He described this structure as metonymy and equated it to Freud's "displacement". Similarly he related Freud's "condensation" with the metaphoric choices we make by selecting alternative but more encompassing signifiers. This structure of the unconscious involving both metaphor and metonymy has roots in the work of the linguist Roman Jakobson and his studies of aphasias (Jakobson, 1968).

The theory of Lacanian psychoanalysis is predicated on a triple ordering system: the *Real,* the *Imaginary* and the *Symbolic* orders. All three are interrelated and influence and compete with each other. The Real (as distinct from "reality", a coherent and self-consistent set of socially constructed beliefs or basic meanings) is difficult to describe, simply because it is beyond language and defies articulation. However it is that which erupts traumatically in our lives and disrupts our notion of a coherent reality. It is the unexplained, unforeseen, unpredictable intrusion into our everyday reality, such as war, environmental disaster, economic meltdown or sudden illness. The Real obeys no rules or laws. The fear it generates is the result of its cataclysmic unpredictability that cannot be controlled, as was the case in the senseless destruction of Mostar during the war. The Real is the undifferentiated amorphous mass – "smooth and even as a finely graven plate" – that resists articulation and the creation of meaning.

For Lacan, the Imaginary is the specular image we have of ourselves, a sense of self generated by our relationship with the (m)other, "learned from the angels". The citizens of Mostar derived their sense of collective self from the manner in which they related to their city, particularly that "public space" in the vicinity of the old bridge. This self, albeit false, is continually seeking approval from, and constantly adapting to the desire of the (m)other. When the (m)other is disfigured or even destroyed, the loss of identity is traumatic, generating a lack that can only be replaced metonymically. A substituted New Old Bridge cannot satisfy the city's desire nor can it reconstruct the lost sense of identity. A new identity may emerge for later generations which can only be sustained by communal repression of the city's trauma.

Perhaps the easiest part of the triad to explain is the Symbolic order. This of course is the realm of language and other systems of signification and relies on the development of meaning through a system of signifiers. Young children enter the Symbolic order when they acquire language and leave the Real for ever. All meaning, values and laws are constructed and mediated through language, "scratched the face of God's earth with his nails". It is the Symbolic that tries to put shape on the Real, although there always remains some residual Real that cannot be articulated. Laws, regulations and decrees of right and wrong are encoded by the language of the other – the authority. The international community as the Other has decreed that "with the 'renaissance' of the Old Bridge and its surroundings, the symbolic power and meaning of the City of Mostar – as an exceptional and universal symbol of coexistence of communities – are restored" (Unesco, 2005). The citizens of Mostar are left to make sense of the imposition.

Like his predecessor, Lacan was continuously faced with the dilemma of knowing which patients would benefit from his psychoanalytical treatment. In brief, he needed to know which patients were psychotic, and who therefore would benefit little if at all from his treatment, which patients were neurotic and who were more amenable to intervention and which were perverse (these latter would never consider needing help). He was also constrained by the considered fact that the only way to diagnose these differences was through the medium of language. Consequently, Lacan's theorizing and his aetiology of psychological disturbance is intimately associated with the patient's entry into the world of language, which he terms the Symbolic order, and its consequences. In other words the entry of the child into society and its cultural demands necessitates an adjustment on his/her part and is irreversibly predicated on the acquisition of language and the abandonment of the sense of the Real.

Lacan states that the development of language like this starts with the child's acquisition of the "Name-of-the-Father" or the Paternal Metaphor, which causes a necessary primal repression of the feeling that s/he is the sole object of the mother's desire. Instead the child learns to move from a state of *being* the object of the mother's desire to *having* the object of the mother's desire. This is referred to by Lacan as the metonymy of desire. In the Symbolic order we are forever cut off from the Real and must negotiate our desire through the medium of language, which is usually addressed to another. This split (*Spaltung*) from the Real compels us to seek a unifying meaning amid the sea of floating signifiers, i.e. with the use of what Lacan calls the Master Signifier. The Master Signifier is that anchoring signifier which assists us to interpret or to mediate meaning to ourselves – the so-called "quilting function". That constant doubt or missing reassurance is what Lacan referred to as the "Lack". There is always an unfathomable rift between the speaker and addressee (the "other"), between one side of the bridge and the other, between the Old Bridge and the new one. Failure or traumatic difficulty in this primal repression gives rise to an aetiology of psychic economies such as psychosis, neurosis or perversion.

From a therapeutic point of view, Lacan needed to distinguish between these various symptoms on the basis of linguistic criteria. For the psychotic, language – the signifying chain – is completely uncoupled from the underlying signifieds; there is no apparent necessity to involve a master signifier, "nothing is unsure within what is being transmitted; sentences are one-dimensional, a word does not carry any other meaning than that which is presented by the word itself (Nobus, 2000). The same can be said about other signifiers such as the "Old Bridge". The psychotic has no need to seek the truth; it is already clear to him/her. An aetiology of psychosis is explained by the failure to repress the primal desire, the failure of the paternal metaphor and a virtual absence of desire.

Neurotic patients, on the other hand, succeed in this repression, which induces an extreme anxiety or confusion. They therefore seek amelioration or alleviation of the symptoms through seeking the truth from others whom they deem knowledgeable. "The passion of ignorance which sustains the neurotic repression is thus paired with a desire to know the truth behind the symptoms – the return of the repressed" (Nobus, 2000: 34). This allows symbolic transference to occur for the neurotic. In contrast, the psychotic, because he has not repressed, does not seek help; he has no need to seek the knowledgeable other.

It is symptomatic of the pervert that he denies reality and is driven towards fetishism. The other(s) in close relationships are reduced to mere objects or fetishes. He is often characterized by a defiant disposition and by transgression of the law. What distinguishes him from the neurotic is his peculiar involvement of the other in his recouping of his lost enjoyment. The perverse person refuses to suppress the primal desire and sees himself as the object of everyone's desire.

The dialogue which ensues, between the traumatized community neurosis and the controlling perverse community, enables a co-dependent relationship, which remains unhealthy for the people of Mostar. The psychotic person has no value on the symbolic nature of the bridge; for him the catastrophic removal of the bridge has no meaning. For the Mostar community the master signifier, the creator of identity, enables them to generate a sense of communal meaning. Their loss accompanying the destruction of the bridge compels them to seek the "truth" from the other. However when the other is perverse the manipulation is complete. The perverse behaviour of the international community, in this respect, is displayed by their disregard for the longing by the citizenry for an explanation – to symbolize the real. The pervert always generates his (almost invariably male) own discourse with his own accompanying master signifier; he makes his own rules. Thus the dialogue remains one-sided and so the trauma endures. The lack of psychological integration brought about by evading therapeutic dialogue and by the imposition of a surrogate identity is tantamount to the denial of democracy, as Deutsche suggests.

Individuals are destined to re-enact what they cannot remember, and so too are groups. Maintaining silence about traumatic and disturbing collective events such as the destruction of Mostar, including its famous bridge, may have the counter-effect of making memory even more potent and dangerous. The lack of debate about public art and hence public space and public performance in this case is a foreclosure of the debate about democracy, openness, participation, inclusion and accountability.

Conclusion

The "Bridge", whether a *Tilted Arc* or not, is more than a bridge which spans a ravine. It is metaphor, metonym, liminal space, site of communitas, simulacrum, a site for democratic free play; or it can become a gentrified commodity and a place for colonization. This particular bridge in Mostar is a potential site for local participatory democracy; but instead the political perversion of the international community has disenfranchised the citizens of that city in that regard. The aesthetics of site-specific public art performances in public spaces need careful examination. Inducing democratic citizenship by such performances may lead to the very opposite if the underlying psychological currents are ignored for the sake of the unifying spectacle.

The aesthetics of repression is not unknown in Bosnia. Emir Kusturica in his movie *Underground* (1995, the date of cessation of Bosnian violence) describes a group of citizens in Belgrade who decide to go underground during the Second World War and prepare for the resistance under Tito. This movie encapsulates the repression of the trauma inflicted on the citizens like those in Mostar and elsewhere and its re-emergence in another form simply because it has not been addressed appropriately. Bosnia's trauma will always return until it is suitably addressed. Unfortunately little is being done in this way. Was Tito right to leave the bridge at Jablonica as it was, as a constant reminder of the nation's trauma, or was the international community right in building a replica bridge and deny the nation's trauma? The co-dependency of the perverse international political community and the distraught and traumatized citizenry needs careful examination.

Notes

1   The Lacanian "Real".
2   Sokollu Mehmed Pasha Bridge, Višegrad, Bosnia and Herzegovina.
3   "Balkan" derives from the Turkish word for "mountains".
4   For the Lacanian "Real" order, see p. 127.
5   For the Lacanian "Symbolic" order, see p. 127.
6   For the Lacanian "Imaginary" order, see p. 127.
7   Said, 1979.
8   For Victor Turner, see p. 126.
9   http://www.pbs.org/wgbh/pages/frontline/shows/kosovo/interviews/blair.html
    – accessed 25 May 2010. This reference entails a singular ingression from the
    East; are there are no doorsteps in the West?
10 A replica bridge was rebuilt by the film crew of the *Battle on the Neretva* in 1968
    only to be blown up once more.
11 Kodža Mimar Sinan (1489–1588), a renowned Ottoman architect, who during
    his 50-year career built a great many bridges, of which the best known is the
    bridge of Mehmed-Pasha Sokolović over the Drina at Višegrad already referred
    to. Sinan's apprentice was Mimar Hajrudin, builder of the Old Bridge at
    Mostar.
12 UN observers registered up to 1000 Croat shells a day fired at the eastern,
    Muslim side of the city.
13 Praljak is said to have been relieved of his command on the previous day, 8
    December. However, because the BiH army had been using the bridge as a
    supply route Praljak said he would rather blow up three such bridges than let
    one of his soldiers lose one finger.
14 Compare Homi Bhabha's "metonymy of presence" and Lacan's "metonymy of
    desire" (= lack).
15 The Peace Award "Mostar 2004" was designed and constructed by the Austrian
    and Bosnian artists Pühringer and Kutragic. It is a miniature of the bridge under
    reconstruction. The trophy is made of brass and precious metals and placed on
    a fragment of the original Old Bridge stone. It seems that the bridge and its
    signification have been appropriated by the international community.

References

Andrić, I. 1994. *The Bridge over the Drina*, trans. from the Serbo-Croat by L.
    F. Edwards. London. Harvill Press. Originally published 1945 as *Na Drini
    Cuprija*.
Baudrillard, J. 1994. *Simulacra and Simulation*, trans. S. F. Glaser. Ann Arbor.
    University of Michigan Press. Originally published Paris 1981.
Bjelić, D., and Savić, O. 2002. *Balkan as Metaphor: Between Globalization and
    Fragmentation*. London. MIT Press.
Debord, G. 1994. *The Society of the Spectacle*, trans. Donald Nicholson-Smith. New
    York. Zone Books. Originally published Paris 1967 as *La Société du Spectacle*.
Deutsche, R. 1996. *Evictions: Art and Spatial Politics*. London. MIT Press.

Gennep, A. van. 1960. *Rites of Passage*. London. Routledge & Kegan Paul. Originally published Paris 1909 as *Les Rites de Passage*.

Glenny, M. 2000. *The Balkans, Nationalism, War and the Great Powers*. London. Granta.

Goodman, P., and Goodman, P. 1947. *Communitas: Means of Livelihood and Ways of Life*. Chicago, IL. University of Chicago Press.

Greer, P., Murphy, A., and Øgård, M. 2005. *Guide to Participatory Democracy in Bosnia and Herzegovina and in Serbia and Montenegro*. Brussels. Council of Europe Publishing.

Jakobson, R. 1968. *Child Language, Aphasia, and Phonological Universals*, trans. A. Keiler. The Hague. Mouton. Originally published 1944 as *Kindersprache, Aphasie und allgemeine Lautgesetze*.

Kwon, M. 1997. "One Place after Another – Notes on Site Specificity" *October*, 80, Spring: 85–110.

Lacan, J. 1977. *Ecrits: A Selection*, trans. A. Sheridan. London. Tavistock Publications. Translation of nine essays from *Ecrits*, published Paris 1966.

Nobus, D. 2000. *Jacques Lacan and the Freudian Practice of Psychoanalysis*. London. Routledge.

Said, E.W. 1979. *Orientalism*. New York. Vintage Books.

Thompson, M. 1992. *A Paper House: The Ending of Yugoslavia*. New York. Pantheon Books.

Todorova, M. 1997. *Imagining the Balkans*. New York. Oxford University Press.

Turner, V. 1974. *Dramas, Fields, and Metaphors: Symbolic Action in Human Society*. New York. Cornell University Press.

Unesco. 2005. Inscription 946: http://whc.unesco.org/en/list/946/ – accessed 2 June 2010.

CHAPTER EIGHT

PEACEBUILDING IN LIBERIA AND SIERRA LEONE: A COMPARATIVE PERSPECTIVE

JOHN M. KABIA

Far from the linear model of transition from civil war to post-war peace-building and reconstruction suggested in the conflict resolution literature of the early 1990s, the transitional period between the signing of peace agreements and consolidation of fragile peace has been fraught with difficulties and uncertainties. From Angola to Sierra Leone, Liberia to Cambodia, peace settlements have unravelled a few years after coming into effect. There have however been notable success stories in places like Mozambique, Namibia, and El Salvador. But what counts as success in a peace process? What is the role, if any, of regional and international actors in the process? There is a burgeoning body of literature over the past decade focussing on the determinants of a successful peace process and transitional period; see, among others, Darby & MacGinty (2003), Stedman et al. (2002) and Hampson (1996). But such studies have been hampered by the wide variety of contexts and intervening factors involved.

This chapter (drawing on Kabia, 2009) compares the peacebuilding interventions in Liberia and Sierra Leone and evaluates the efforts of domestic, regional, and international actors in building sustainable peace. The chapter begins with a review of the literature on peacebuilding with a view to defining success in a peace process. The next section provides a background on the conflicts in both countries to understand the context within which peacebuilding is taking place. This is followed by an analysis of the peacemaking process in both countries, bringing out the successes and failures. Next, we assess peacebuilding in Liberia and Sierra Leone focusing on the following areas: governance and economic reform, Disarmament Demobilisation and Reintegration (DDR) and Security Sector Reform (SSR). We conclude by looking at the prospects and challenges for durable peace in Liberia and Sierra Leone.

Defining Success in Peace Processes: Theoretical Insights

The definition of success in a peace process has been hotly debated in the theoretical literature and there appears to be no consensus on the subject. Downs and Stedman (2002) use two variables to determine success in peace implementation: (1) the termination of large scale violence while the implementers are present; (2) termination of war on a self-enforcing basis so that the implementers can go home without fear of a resurgence of fighting. This definition classifies a mission as a failure if war resumes in two years after the departure of implementers. These variables however tend to be more focussed on short-term measures to halt violence and are mostly focussed on the role of international actors, disregarding the key role played by local civil society groups. In his *An Agenda for Peace,* former UN Secretary-General Boutros Boutros-Ghali links peace implementation to peacebuilding which he defines as "actions to identify and support structures which will tend to strengthen and solidify peace in order to avoid a relapse into conflict" (1992: 11). This broad definition determines success in a peace process in terms of long-term measures to address the political, economic and social underlining causes of war.

Miall et al. (2005) distinguish the two definitions above in two phases: transitional and consolidation. This is also in line with Galtung's (1981) classification of "negative" and "positive" peace. The transitional phase involves efforts aimed at preventing a relapse into violence (negative peace), whereas the consolidation phase deals with the removal of structural and cultural violence (positive peace). The transitional phase (negative peace) represents the most urgent tasks facing peacebuilders. As it aims at preventing a relapse into violence, it includes measures such as compromises and trade-offs to factional leaders. In this context, the transitional phase is about who gets what in the post-war period.

As Ramsbotham (2000) rightly observes, this short-term aim of preventing violence is often at odds with, and may adversely affect, the long-term goal of building sustainable peace. However, despite this dark side, this phase still remains vital to peacebuilding since post-war reconstruction is only possible in a violence free environment. On the other hand, the consolidation phase is the most important stage and involves tasks such as strengthening the institutional base, security sector reform, promoting economic development, building social capital and addressing the psychosocial needs of the society. Only when the necessary political, social and economic structures are in place and there is some notion that the root causes of the original tensions have been addressed can a fuller and holistic concept of peacebuilding be proclaimed. Drawing from the above analysis, this chapter defines success in a peace process as preventing a relapse into violence and laying of foundations for the achievement of long-term peacebuilding objectives. It therefore adopts a medium-term perspective of success representing a compromise between Stedman's short-term goal and Boutros-Ghali's long-term objectives.

Background to the Conflicts in Liberia and Sierra Leone

Liberia and Sierra Leone share a common border along the West African coast and its people have similar cultures. Both countries were founded as settlements for freed slaves. Liberia was founded by an American charity, the American Colonisation Society, to resettle freed slaves from the Americas, whilst freed slaves from Britain were relocated to Sierra Leone. Although Liberia was never formally colonized, the country looks up to the US as its 'big brother'. Sierra Leone on the other hand was a British colony until independence in 1961.

Both countries were plunged into brutal wars in the early 1990s that lasted for between 11 to 14 years. Although the two conflicts have context specific causal factors, however, the main factor underlying both is the years of misrule that resulted in massive corruption and suppression of the opposition. The consequence for the people of both countries was a state of declining social services, dilapidated infrastructure, weak and collapsing economy and widespread poverty. The increasing 'informalization' of the state also led to a weakening of state institutions and subsequently state failure and collapse. The political and economic discontent generated by this collapse sowed the seeds of the conflicts in both countries and indeed in most conflicts in Africa.

In Liberia, though the triggers of the conflict lay in the decade-long misrule and excesses of its military leader, Samuel Doe, its roots can be traced back to the 1820s when freed slaves from America were settled in the country. The "apartheid" policy of the settler Americo-Liberians sowed the seed of the years of brutal conflict that were to come. Comprising less than 5% of the country's 1.8 million people (Mackinlay & Alao, 1995), the Americo-Liberians dominated all aspects of the country's political, social and economic life and effectively marginalized the indigenous population. Since gaining independence from the American Colonisation Society in 1847, only the settler-dominated True Whig Party ruled the country till Samuel Doe's military coup in 1980. The euphoria that greeted the Doe coup did not last long as he merely replaced Americo-Liberian dominance with Khran rule. Even though they were poorly educated and represented only about 4% of the total population, Doe placed his Khran people and their Mandingo allies into all the strategic positions of the land and marginalized the other ethnic groups. Thus what started as a united front soon fragmented. By 1983, Doe had eliminated most of his supporters including his academic allies, the Movement for Justice in Africa (MOJA) and all 16 non-commissioned officers with whom he had staged the coup (Mackinlay & Alao, 1995). Corruption became endemic and the economy virtually collapsed. Doe rigged the 1985 elections and transformed himself into a civilian president. Opposition to his rule was crushed with ruthless brutality.

A coup staged by his former friend Thomas Quiwonkpa in November 1985 was met with unprecedented reprisals and intimidation of his Gio and Mano ethnic groups of Nimba County. Three thousand people, including women and children, were reportedly massacred (Mackinlay & Alao, 1995). This heavy-handed treatment created a strong anti-Doe movement. As a brother-in-law of Quiwonkpa, Charles Taylor, a former official in Doe's government, exploited the resentment of Gios and Manos and recruited the bulk of his forces from this area and used the region as the launching pad for his rebellion in December 1989.

The spill-over effects of the Liberian War were first felt in Sierra Leone where an obscure former army corporal, Foday Sankoh, and his Revolutionary United Front (RUF) invaded the country on 23 March 1991 with the tacit support of Charles Taylor and Libya's Colonel Qadafi. State collapse and conflict became inevitable due to massive corruption, the mismanagement of public funds, political and economic marginalization of the rural areas, intimidation and suppression of the opposition, politicization of the military and the widespread abuse of human rights. William Reno coined the term "shadow state" to explain the relationship which existed between corruption and politics in Sierra Leone (Reno, 1998).

This state of affairs can be traced as far back as 1968 when President Siaka Stevens took over power. He effectively turned politics in Sierra Leone into an affair for and on behalf of supporters of the ruling All Peoples' Congress (APC) party. The state was virtually privatized within a patrimonial network of unscrupulous Lebanese businessmen and close associates of the ruling circle. Public services and corporations withered in the midst of neglect and massive corruption. The ensuing economic hardship caused thousands of unemployed and disgruntled youths to drift to the diamond-producing region of Kono where they became socialized in a climate of violence, drugs and crime (Pratt, 1999). With endemic poverty and growing unemployment, most of the country's youths became easy prey for disgruntled politicians keen on furthering their political ambitions. The RUF were therefore able to recruit the bulk of their fighters amongst these disillusioned youths; in fact onetime RUF Field Commander Sam "Maskita" Bockarie was one of such youths. In the absence of opportunities and avenues for organized forms of democratic opposition and dissent, violence becomes the only means to seek redress.

The Nature of Peace Processes in Liberia and Sierra Leone

Peace processes in both countries are characterized by repeated failures, disregard for human rights and intransigence by warring parties. In Liberia, between 1990 and 2004, a total of 15 peace agreements were signed by warring parties, whilst five major agreements were signed between 1996 and 2000 in Sierra Leone. Following years of failed peace agreements and frustrated efforts, the Comprehensive Peace Agreement (CPA) signed in Accra in August 2003 is the most notable of the 15 peace treaties of the Liberian conflict. The CPA provided for the establishment of the National Transitional Government of Liberia (NTGL) and a transitional legislature. Made up of representatives of the various rebel groups and civil society representatives, the transitional government was tasked with the responsibility of implementing the peace accord and conducting elections.

However, the NTGL was made ineffective by lack of capacity and massive levels of corruption. Most of the members of the NTGL were warlords who lacked political experience and were more interested in jobs and the wealth and prestige that followed. For instance, arguments over ministerial appointments rendered the NTGL ineffective for most of the period since it was established. The cabinet was only sworn in on 23 March 2004, five months after inauguration of the interim Chairman. The high level of corruption led to the establishment of the intrusive Governance and Economic Management Assistance Programme (GEMAP) by the UN, World Bank, IMF, Economic Community of West African States (ECOWAS) and the European Union. The programme involves the placement of foreign financial experts in key revenue generating departments.

The agreement also calls for the establishment of a number of commissions to oversee compliance of factions to the accord. These include: (1) the Joint Monitoring Commission to supervise the implementation of the ceasefire; (2) the Implementation Monitoring Committee to ensure effective implementation of the accord; (3) the National Commission for Disarmament, Demobilisation Reconstruction, Resettlement and Reintegration (NCDDRRR) to organize and implement the DDR programme; and (4) a Truth and Reconciliation Commission.

The delegates also proposed that the Transitional Government offer a general amnesty to perpetrators of war crimes during Liberia's long civil war. Like previous peace agreements in the sub-region, this amnesty provision guarantees impunity for war crimes and encourages a repeat of the past. Considering the level of violence perpetuated by all factions in Liberia, a Truth and Reconciliation Commission alone was not enough to heal the wounds of victims whilst perpetrators are seen in government offices and parastatals.

Momentum for the peace process in Sierra Leone was kept alive by the combined efforts of both domestic and international actors. At home, the peace process was facilitated by civil society groups such as the Inter-religious Council, the Civil Society Movement, Campaign for Good Governance and the government's National Commission for Democracy and Human Rights. At the international level, the process has been boosted by the involvement of the UN and the British-led International Contact Group on Sierra Leone. However, it is the role of the regional body, ECOWAS, that stood out prominently. This is in line with its policy of using diplomatic carrots and military sticks to elicit compliance from the warring factions.

The Sierra Leone peace process itself is a story of failed and often frustrated attempts that resulted in several flawed agreements. The most notable of Sierra Leone's peace agreements is Lomé. Signed in the Togolese capital on 7 July 1999, the accord called for the broadening of the government's power base to include rebels in a power-sharing deal and a blanket amnesty for all perpetrators of the decade-long civil war. The RUF leader was rewarded with the chairmanship of the Board of the Commission for the Management of Strategic Resources with vice-presidential status. This controversial appointment served to legitimize Sankoh and ceded to his control the diamonds that had financed his campaign. The RUF was transformed into a political party with four ministerial and four deputy ministerial positions. The UN, ECOWAS and Sierra Leone's Western backers became the subjects of widespread criticism for facilitating an unfair peace deal. The agreement was criticized for rewarding the rebels' political violence with a power-sharing deal (Francis, 2000).

The blanket amnesty sparked domestic and international outrage for the impunity accorded to war crime perpetrators. By failing to address the issue of justice, the Lomé Accord set the stage for the obstacles that the peace process was to later face. Under a well-orchestrated plan, RUF combatants attacked UN peacekeepers stationed at the Makeni Disarmament Centre, following the voluntary disarmament of ten of its members. The Makeni incident sparked a wave of RUF attacks on UN peacekeepers deployed all over the country and resulted in the kidnapping of more than 500 peace-keepers and the killing of four soldiers. UNAMSIL was only saved from total collapse and humiliation with the timely intervention of British para-troopers and Special Forces, who helped to forestall the RUF advance on the city and stabilized the situation.

International Intervention and Support to Peacebuilding in Liberia and Sierra Leone

As most post-war countries lack the resources and capacity to implement the terms of peace agreements, the active support of the international com-munity is very critical of the success of peacebuilding programmes. In addition to the various interventions by regional organizations, the UN, NGOs and other bilateral and multilateral agencies, there is an emerging consensus that points to the pivotal role played by so-called "lead nations" and International Contact Groups in peacebuilding.

The sub-regional body, ECOWAS, played a major part in stabiliz-ing both countries. It deployed its peacekeeping troops, the ECOWAS Monitoring Group (ECOMOG), to both countries in the 1990s and also played a key role in facilitating the peace processes of either country. But the lack of financial, human and military resources to undertake an effec-tive peacekeeping and humanitarian operation undermined the efforts of ECOWAS to resolve the conflicts.

The UN also deployed peacekeeping missions in both countries with similar Standard Operating Procedures characteristic of post-Cold War peacekeeping missions. The United Nations Mission in Sierra Leone (UNAMSIL) was deployed in October 1999 following the signing of the Lomé Peace Agreement. However, following the near-collapse of UNAMSIL in May 2000 and the constant comparison with international response to the Kosovo and East Timor crises, the peace process received a fresh lease of life from the international community. The humiliation suf-fered by the UN forces necessitated a critical rethink of the whole concept and practice of peacekeeping in the form of various reviews and reports. Consequently, the force was bolstered from 11,000 to 17,500 troops and given a more robust Chapter VII mandate. With additional troop numbers and a robust mandate, the mission was able to deploy country-wide thereby helping the Freetown-hostage government to extend its authority.

UNAMSIL withdrew in December 2005 and was replaced by the United Nations Integrated Office in Sierra Leone (UNIOSIL), a political mission tasked with consolidating the gains of UNAMSIL, helping the government to strengthen its human rights record, meeting the Millennium Development Goals, and holding free and fair elections in 2007. UNAMSIL's exit strategy was successfully linked to meeting the mission's mandate. The mission implemented a phased drawdown plan to enable the Sierra Leone government to take responsibility for security. The government was also assisted in extending its authority including decentralization, rule of law and judicial reform. To ensure continued engagement with the country, Sierra Leone was chosen alongside Burundi to become the first beneficiaries of the UN Peacebuilding Fund. Although the role of the international community in reconstructing Sierra Leone is highly commendable, care should be taken to minimize the dependency syndrome gripping the country. Sierra Leone today is effectively a donor driven state with international NGOs and aid agencies providing key amenities.

In Liberia, acting on the recommendation of the Secretary-General, the Security Council on 19 September 2003 adopted resolution 1509 that established the United Nations Mission in Liberia (UNMIL) with mandated troop strength of 15,000 including 1115 civilian police. Like UNAMSIL in Sierra Leone, UNMIL was given a robust Chapter VII mandate with responsibilities ranging from monitoring the cease-fire, overseeing the DDR programme to restructuring of the Security Sector and extension of government authority. The involvement of troops from developed countries like Sweden and Ireland also bolstered the capability of the force, as is the involvement of a permanent member of the Security Council, China. UNMIL is in the process of implementing its Consolidation, Drawdown and Withdrawal Plan. However although the mission has met some of the indicators in its four benchmarks of security, rule of law and governance, economic revitalization and basic services and infrastructure, there still remain major challenges. These include reform of the justice and security sectors and human rights (UN, March 2008).

The power and resources that strong and wealthy nations bring into the peace process are crucial to the success of peacebuilding. Because of their global influence, these countries can help to galvanize international support and commitment to the peace process. Lead nation status is often rooted in a country's historical, political and economic ties with the country in conflict and achieved by the willingness of the country in question to devote significant resources to leading international efforts. Thus, the US and UK were expected to provide the leadership needed to move forward the peace processes in Liberia and Sierra Leone respectively. There are significant differences in the levels of commitment and involvement by both countries.

As noted above, US-Liberia relationship goes as far back as the 1820s when the country was founded as home for freed slaves by the American Colonisation Society. However, despite the close ties during the Cold War, the US did not play an active role in the resolution of the first phase of the Liberian conflict. Britain's special interest in Sierra Leone stems from the fact that it was that country's colonial power and leader of the International Contact Group. In sharp contrast to the US in Liberia, the British government played a more active role in the Sierra Leone peace process. However, this role only started in the late 1990s. Before this period, British involvement in the conflict was minimal. This limited British involvement can be linked to the Blair government's opposition to the Abacha regime in Nigeria, the dominant player in the regional peacekeeping force. Direct British assistance for ECOMOG was interpreted as boosting the international standing of Abacha.

Following the withdrawal of ECOMOG in May 2000, the British started playing a more active role. In addition to the military stabilization role mentioned above, the UK policy in Sierra Leone set out to maintain the momentum of the peace process and build and equip a reformed and accountable military. Such a policy is set against the backdrop of New Labour's "ethical foreign policy" (Williams, 2001). As leader of the International Contact Group on Sierra Leone, the British government has managed to keep international attention focussed on rebuilding the country. The presence of so-called "over-the-horizon" forces presented a credible deterrent to would-be "spoilers" whilst making the security situation conducive to security sector reform. As previous attempts to reform the military ended in failure, British efforts in this respect were of major importance. Later sections of this chapter will look at UK's contribution to the security sector reform programme.

Governance and Economic Reform in Liberia and Sierra Leone

Governance reform is a key factor in sustaining peace in transitional societies. As most of these conflicts are rooted in unjust and incompetent governance structures and processes, the need for governance reform cannot be overemphasized. This need is often embedded in the provisions of various peace accords. However, attention has been mostly limited to the holding of elections. But governance reform goes beyond the periodic holding of elections to encompass issues such as a genuinely representative government, building of key political institutions, strengthening of civil society and accountability and economic propriety. Follow-up action and monitoring of the post-agreement governance system must focus on these issues. Both Sierra Leone and Liberia are failed states that require radical transformation of governance structures and institutions. At various stages, they were effectively UN protectorates. However, the process of state reform is progressing at a steady pace, although major challenges remain.

As provided for in the Comprehensive Peace Agreement, elections were held in Liberia in late 2005 and Ellen Johnson-Sirleaf, a Harvard graduate and former World Bank official, was elected president. However, a good number of the legislative seats went to the same old guard known for destabilizing the country. Key names include Jewel Howard-Taylor, ex-wife of Charles Taylor; Prince Johnson, a former rebel leader who was responsible for the brutal murder of President Doe; Adolphus Dolo, a former Taylor Commander also known as 'General Peanut Butter'; Edwin Snowe, a former Taylor associate and son-in-law who became the speaker of the House of Representatives. This outcome is characteristic of post war elections which tend to empower predatory elites and reinforce the same wartime power structures. Notwithstanding President Johnson-Sirleaf's good image, the composition of the legislature is a negative indicator for the governance reform process. The lack of a government majority in the legislature also means that the government is often forced to make deals and form coalitions with other parties.

Under President Johnson-Sirleaf, Liberia's economy appears to be doing well with a 9 per cent growth rate in 2007 and public revenue amounting to $163 million (UN, March 2008). This is partly due to the lifting of the UN ban on the export of Liberia's diamonds and timber. The country has also benefited from a number of debt cancellations by major financial institutions and bilateral partners. For instance, the World Bank and the African Development Bank have agreed to clear $671 million of the country's $4.8 billion debt arrears and the IMF has forgiven $920 million of debt (UN, March 2008). Consequently, the government has been able to undertake a limited programme of rebuilding infrastructure and delivering basic services. For instance, piped water and mains electricity have been restored to parts of Monrovia.

However, unemployment continues to be a major challenge for the government's economic recovery programme. Corruption also continues to be a problem despite efforts by the Johnson-Sirleaf government to curb it. In June 2007, Liberia's independent Auditor-General alleged that the current administration is three times more corrupt than its predecessor (UN, August, 2007). Although this allegation was not substantiated, the president herself admitted that corruption continues to undermine her government's efforts to respond to the needs of the Liberian people (Butty, 2008).

Consolidation of state authority and the decentralization process have been hit by lack of funds and capacity. Local council and chieftaincy elections had to be delayed in 2007 because the government could not afford the estimated $19 million to organize them (UN, August, 2007). The President had to appoint municipal officials instead. Justice sector reform poses another big challenge to the governance reform process. The judiciary is severely constrained by lack of capacity, adequate infrastructure and poor conditions of service. The government's inability to manage the growing land disputes also poses another threat to the fragile peace. With the return of tens of thousands of refugees, there has been an escalation in the number of violent attacks and community disputes over land. Some returning refugees have found their land and homes taken over. In June 2008, one such incident resulted in the killing of at least 12 people in a farm some 35 miles south-east of Monrovia (BBC, June 2008).

Since the official end of the war in 2002, Sierra Leone has made significant progress in rebuilding governance structures and consolidating the fragile peace. These include the creation of a National Revenue Authority (NRA) which has developed enhanced revenue collection mechanisms; an ongoing decentralization process; justice sector reform programme; security forces subject to democratic control, and free and fair elections in 2002, 2004 and 2007. The economy also appears to be doing well with a reported 7% growth rate in 2006 and 2007 (ICG, July 2007). With the implementation of the Kimberley Process Certification Scheme, the government's income from diamond exports soared from $10 million in 2000 to $160 in 2004 (Sola-Martin and Kabia, 2007).

However, despite the considerable international donor support and impressive macro-economic figures, the country's social and economic indicators continue to make grim reading. Youth employment is estimated at around 80% with over 70% of the population living under the poverty line (ICG, July 2007). The 2009 UNDP Human Development Index ranks the country 180 out of 182 countries. Despite the setting up of an Anti-Corruption Commission (ACC), corruption remains high. Whilst the ACC has been able to raise awareness about corruption, it has been hamstrung by political interference and lack of capacity by the judiciary to prosecute those accused of corrupt practices. Public perception of corruption amongst government officials was a key factor responsible for the defeat of the former ruling party in the August 2007 elections. The new president, Ernest Bai Koroma, has made the fight against corruption his top priority and has declared zero tolerance. However, it remains to be seen how effective his government will be in tackling this menace.

Disarmament Demobilization and Reintegration (DDR) of Ex-Combatants

Since the end of the Cold War, DDR programmes have been at the centre of international peacebuilding efforts in war-torn societies. These programmes have formed part of comprehensive peace settlements signed by parties to the conflicts, usually under the auspices of international and/or regional organizations. Considering the widespread militarization of the society and the proliferation of arms in both countries, DDR is key to the success of peacebuilding.

Following previous half-hearted attempts at disarmament in Sierra Leone, the DDR programme restarted in May 2001; by January 2002, a total of 72,490 ex-combatants had been disarmed and 42,300 weapons and 1.2 million rounds of ammunition recovered (Kai Kai, 2004). On January 2002, the UN and government of Sierra Leone declared the war over, symbolically burning surrendered weapons. The success of this programme was highlighted by the unusually violence-free elections conducted in May 2002. However, despite the success of the disarmament and demobilization phase of the DDR programme, reintegration remains a major doubt. Although most ex-combatants have been given skills training, the continuing economic hardship means there are few jobs available to absorb the thousands of skilled youths. As past experiences in Liberia and Sierra Leone have shown, half-hearted reintegration programmes can lead to a resurgence of conflict.

After stabilizing the fluid security situation in Monrovia and its environs, UNMIL embarked on disarming an estimated 38,000 ex-combatants. However, the initial attempt to start disarmament in December 2003 failed due to lack of planning, logistics and co-ordination between the UN and humanitarian agencies. In a bid to impress donors before the February 2004 donors' conference, the UNMIL leadership decided to start disarmament on 7 December 2003. This premature start to the DDR programme did not take into account the low level of troops on the ground and the unavailability of logistics and finance to support the programme. In fact the ICG reported that key stakeholders did not meet until few days before the start of the programme. The original plan called for the setting up of cantonment sites targeting 1000 combatants from each faction. But after advice from the military component of UNMIL that its troop strength was insufficient to cover all the three factions, it was decided to start with the former government forces. UNMIL could not cope with the big turnout – about 12,000. When fighters discovered that there was no cash for weapons, they rioted and erected roadblocks on the streets of Monrovia. At the end of the disturbances, nine people were killed and one UNMIL soldier sustained injuries. UNMIL suspended the programme on 17 December 2003.

The programme restarted in April 2004 and by the end of 2004 had succeeded in disarming over 100,000 ex-combatants. However, despite this high number, there were serious problems. The number of weapons surrendered fell far short of expectations and there are worrying signs that they were transported across the border to neighbouring countries (UN, May 2004). The most likely place is Cote d'Ivoire where ex-combatants are paid about US$975 for surrendering their weapons as compared to the US$300 given to Liberians. There are also reports of ex-combatants giving their surplus weapons to civilians for them to collect the $300 on offer.

Another problem facing the DDR programme is lack of sufficient funds for reintegration. This is partly due to the discrepancy between the initial estimates of 38,000 and the actual figure of over 100,000. This led to a funding shortfall of $58 million. Furthermore, although disarmament and demobilization are budgeted for within UNMIL, reintegration is funded through voluntary contributions. However, as in other post-conflict countries, donor countries are very slow in honouring the pledges they made at the Liberian Donor Conference in February 2004. As a result, UNMIL and Liberia's Disarmament and Reintegration Commission are struggling to reintegrate the thousands of ex-combatants who have gone through the disarmament programme. At some point, up to 4000 ex-combatants were expelled from various schools and colleges across Liberia due to UNMIL's failure to pay fees. There is a growing sense of frustration and disappointment amongst ex-combatants and this has caused sporadic unrest in Liberia.

Security Sector Reform

Since the mid 1990s, the international donor community, aid agencies, policy makers and academics have increasingly underlined the importance of security sector reform to the overall success of peace processes. The security sector 'includes all those organisations which have authority to use, or order the use of, force, or the threat of force, to protect the state and its citizens, as well as those civil structures that are responsible for their management and oversight' (Chalmers, 2000: 6). It includes a wide array of security actors ranging from military and paramilitary forces, intelligence services and police to judicial and penal services and civilian oversight mechanisms such as ministries of defence and executive and legislative organs. Weak and ineffective security structures form part of the underlying causes of most conflicts in the developing world and also have negative development implications. In this respect, some analysts now argue that what is actually needed is not 'reform' but overall transformation of the security sector (Le Roux, Dornelles & Williams, 2004). In this context, security sector reform or transformation therefore represents international and national efforts to rebuild the security sector within the wider framework of good governance and democratization.

There continues to be a funding gap with the UN Security Council expecting so-called 'lead nations' to take the lead in implementing such programmes. In Liberia and Sierra Leone, the UN led on police reform whilst army reform was led by the US and UK respectively. In a joint effort with the Commonwealth, UNAMSIL recruited and trained 3500 police officers. By 2005 when UNAMSIL withdrew from the country, the strength of the Sierra Leone Police Force stood at 9500 with 4000 of that number having gone through basic police training, human rights, computer literacy and middle and senior management training (Sola-Martin and Kabia, 2007). By the end of 2005, the police had 74 police stations and 112 posts across the country. The relationship between the police and the public has improved considerably with the introduction of the concept of Local Needs Policing which seeks to involve the community in policing matters. This is a big departure from the pre-war image of the police as corrupt human rights abusers. However, despite the support for the police, the force continues to suffer from logistical constraints and the poor conditions of service threaten to undermine the professional integrity of the force.

In Liberia, the UN police had to start from scratch in rebuilding the Liberian National Police (LNP). Unlike Sierra Leone which had a functioning albeit weak and ineffective police force, the LNP was virtually destroyed after years of conflict. The challenges for UNMIL were therefore enormous. In addition to recruiting, retraining and equipping the force, UNMIL had to work alongside the skeletal LNP in maintaining law and order. The task of rebuilding the LNP was hampered by lack of funds. The US had to provide $500,000 to UNMIL to help with recruiting and training 3500 officers. By August 2007, a total of 3522 officers had been trained at the National Police Academy (Malan, 2008). However, the LNP remains ineffective due to a shortage of essential logistics ranging from vehicles and communications equipment to handcuffs and raincoats. There is also a critical shortage of leadership and management skills within the LNP and morale is low and discipline very poor. Consequently, crime continues to be a major problem in Liberia with increasing incidents of robbery and sexual and gender based violence. The inability of the police to tackle the rising crime rate led the Liberian Justice Ministry to urge civilians to organize local vigilante groups to stem the armed robbery.

Working with the International Military Assistance Training Team (IMATT), Britain has trained and equipped a new Sierra Leonean army and also assisted in the UNAMSIL-Commonwealth-led police reform programme (Malan, 2003). The army reform programme in Sierra Leone involves the integration of serving British officers within the Sierra Leone Armed Forces as trainers and advisers. The UK also took a leading role in establishing the Office of National Security and producing a national security strategy and defence policy.

In Liberia, the US contracted private security companies DynCorp International and PAE to recruit, train and equip a 2000-strong army. In a sub-region where private security companies and mercenaries are notorious for their role in fuelling conflicts, the US decision to use private firms is insensitive. Whilst private companies may be good at providing infantry training, they lack the ethos and values of a professional army. The SSR programme itself has been hit by delays caused by funding problems. Although the figure for reforming the army is put at $210 million, according to Malan, 'the SSR programme in Liberia was never fully funded, that funding to date has fallen far short of this figure, and that money even when forthcoming, has been disbursed in dribs and drabs' (2008: 41). Considering that the failure of SSR was one of the causes of Liberia's relapse into war in 2002, the need to prioritize its implementation cannot be overemphasized. UNMIL has therefore put SSR as one of its benchmarks for the drawdown and withdrawal of the mission and continued delays will not only disrupt that plan but will also undermine the huge efforts to build sustainable peace in Liberia.

Conclusion

Liberia and Sierra Leone have made remarkable progress in consolidating the fragile peace and put in place structures to ensure its sustainability. Both countries have benefited from substantial international support with the deployment of large UN peacekeeping missions and donor support of peacebuilding programmes. Consequently, significant achievements have been made in rebuilding governance institutions, reviving the economies, disarming and demobilizing ex-combatants and reforming the security and judicial sectors.

Despite the achievements discussed above, there still remain considerable threats to peace in Liberia and Sierra Leone. In Liberia, problems with reforming the security sector pose a formidable challenge. The need to prioritize SSR cannot be overemphasized. The failure of SSR after the first phase of the Liberian conflict in 1997 was partly responsible for the country's relapse into conflict. In both countries, problems with reintegration of ex-combatants are posing major threats to peace. Half-hearted reintegration efforts and the prevailing high youth employment are causing discontent amongst former combatants and young people in both countries and threaten to unravel the major gains achieved so far. Corruption in both countries also undermines economic recovery efforts and robs the population of the expected peace dividend. Although the macro-economic figures are impressive, however, the pervasive poverty and poor social and economic indicators pose the biggest challenge to peacebuilding.

The situation in neighbouring Guinea and Cote d'Ivoire also pose a significant threat to the peace in Liberia and Sierra Leone. Considering the interconnectedness of actors in these countries, conflict in any one is bound to have far reaching security implications for the others. As past experiences have shown, a resurgence of conflict in either Cote d'Ivoire or Guinea risks unravelling the fragile peace in both countries and any long term peacebuilding programme should be cognisant of this.

References

BBC. 2008. 'Liberians Killed in Farm Massacre' available online at http://news.bbc.co.uk/1/hi/world/africa/7448970.stm, accessed June 2008.

Boutros-Ghali, B. 1992. *An Agenda for Peace*, New York: United Nations.

Butty, J. 2008. 'Liberia's President Sirleaf Asks Cabinet to put Corruption Fight in Writing', *The African News Journal,* available online at http://www.anjnews.com/node/696, accessed in June 2008.

Chalmers, M. 2000. *Security Sector Reform in Developing Countries: An EU Perspective.* London. Saferworld.

Darby, J. and R. Mac Ginty (eds). 2003. *Contemporary Peacemaking: Conflict, Violence and Peace Processes.* Basingstoke. Palgrave Macmillan.

Downs, G., and Stedman, S. J. 2002. 'Evaluation Issues in Peace Implementation'. In Stedman, S. J., et al. (eds), *Ending Civil Wars: The Implementation of Peace Agreements.* London. Lynne Rienner.

Francis, D. J. 2000. 'Torturous Path to Peace: The Lome Peace Agreement and Post-war Peacebuilding in Sierra Leone', *Security Dialogue,* 3(3): 357–373.

Galtung, J. 1981. 'Cultural Violence', *Journal of Peace Research,* 27(3): 291–305.

Hampson, F. O. 1996. *Nurturing Peace: Why Peace Settlements Succeed or Fail,* Washington, DC. US Institute of Peace.

ICG. July 2007. *Sierra Leone: The Election Opportunity.*, Africa Report No. 129. Dakar/Brussels. ICG.

Kai Kai, F. 2004. 'Executive Secretariat Report'. Freetown. NCDDR. Available on-line http://www.dacosl.org/encyclopedia/5, accessed September, 2004.

Kabia, J. M. 2009. *Humanitarian Intervention and Conflict Resolution in West Africa: From ECOMOG to ECOMIL.* Aldershot. Ashgate.

Le Roux, L., Dornelles, J. R. and Williams, R. 2004. 'Establishing a Common Understanding for Security Sector Transformation'. In Fitz-Gerald, A. and Lala, A. (eds), *Networking the Networks: Supporting Regional Peace and Security Agendas in Africa.* Shrivenham. Global Facilitation Network for Security Sector Reform.

Mackinlay, J., and Alao, A. 1995. *Liberia 1994: ECOMOG and UNOMIL Response to a Complex Emergency,* United Nations University Occasional Paper Series 2. Available online at http://www.unu.edu/unupress/ops2.html, accessed June 2008.

Malan, M. 2003. 'Security and Military Reform'. In Malan, M., et al., *Sierra Leone: Building the Road to Recovery,* Monograph No. 80. Pretoria. ISS.

Malan, M. 2008. *Security Sector Reform in Liberia: Mixed Results from Humble Beginnings.* Carlisle. Strategic Studies Institute.

Miall, H., et al. 2005. *Contemporary Conflict Resolution: The Prevention, Management and Transformation of Deadly Conflicts.* 2nd ed. Cambridge. Polity Press.

Pratt, D. 1999. *Sierra Leone: The Forgotten Crisis.* Ottawa. Canadian Centre for Foreign Policy Development.

Ramsbotham, O. 2000. 'Reflections on UN Post-Settlement Peacebuilding'. In Woodhouse, T., and Ramsbotham, O. (eds). *Peacekeeping and Conflict Resolution.* London. Frank Cass.

Reno, W. 1998. *Warlord Politics and African States.* London. Lynne Rienner.

Sola-Martin, A., and Kabia, J. M. 2007. *UNAMSIL Peacekeeping and Peace Support Operations in Sierra Leone.* Bradford. University of Bradford Press.

Stedman, S. J., et al. (eds). 2002. *Ending Civil Wars: The Implementation of Peace Agreements.* London. Lynne Rienner.

UN. May, 2004. *Third Progress Report of the Secretary-General on the United Nations Mission in Liberia,* S/2004/430.

UN. August, 2007. *Fifteenth Progress Report of the Secretary General on the United Nations Mission in Liberia.* S/2007/479.

UN. March, 2008. *Sixteenth Progress Report of the Secretary General on the United Nations Mission in Liberia.* S/2008/183.

Williams, P. 2001. 'Fighting for Freetown: British Military Intervention in Sierra Leone', *Contemporary Security Policy*, 22(3): 145.

CHAPTER NINE

DISARMAMENT, DEMOBILIZATION, REINSERTION AND REINTEGRATION: THE NORTHERN IRELAND EXPERIENCE

NEIL FERGUSON

Disarmament, demobilization, reinsertion and reintegration (DDRR) processes have become a common and critical aspect of post-conflict reconstruction initiatives (Knight, 2008). Formal disarmament, demobilization and reintegration (DDR) programmes have been operational since 1989 and have been a key part of multidimensional UN peacekeeping operations in El Salvador, Cambodia, Mozambique, Angola, Liberia, Sierra Leone, Guatemala, Tajikistan and many other states. The scale to these operations is highlighted by Forman and Patrick (2000), who suggest that DDR initiatives during the 1990s received pledges of over $100 billion from over 30 different nations. This chapter will explore some of the key features of these DDR programs and build on research with former combatants from Northern Ireland to explore and evaluate DDR in Northern Ireland in comparison to other programs in Central America and Africa.

DDR is a key piece of the peacebuilding and post-conflict recovery jigsaw (Berdal, 1996) having the potential to increase the peace by reassuring opposing sides that progress towards a permanent cessation of violence is ongoing. The United Nations Integrated DDR Standards offers clear operational definitions of DDR in addition to guidance and training:

> The objective of the DDR process is to contribute to security and stability in post-conflict environments so that recovery and development can begin. The DDR of ex-combatants is a complex process, with political, military, security, humanitarian and socio-economic dimensions. It aims to deal with the post-conflict security problem that arises when ex-combatants are left without livelihoods or support networks, other than their former comrades, during the vital transition period from conflict to peace and development. Through a process of removing weapons from the hands of combatants, taking the combatants out of military structures and helping them to integrate socially and economically into society, DDR seeks to support ex-combatants

so that they can become active participants in the peace process. (UN DDR Resource Centre, 2010: 1–2)

The same document defines disarmament as the collection, control and disposal of small arms, ammunition, other larger weapons and explosives. Demobilization is a controlled discharge of active combatants from armed groups. This often involves the temporary cantonment or quartering of combatants for processing before offering support packages to assist with their reinsertion into civilian life. After disarmament and demobilization come reinsertion and reintegration. Reinsertion usually involves the provision of assistance during the transitional period between demobilization and reintegration, usually extending to help to meet the basic needs (food, clothing, shelter, medical services, training etc.) of the combatants and their families for up to a year after demobilization. Reintegration is viewed as a much longer term process over an open time frame, during which the ex combatants gain civilian status and gainful sustainable employment.

The reintegration of combatants into productive civilian life is viewed as key to both post-conflict security and recovery. Kingma (2000) outlines four fundamental reasons for engaging in DDR:

- humanitarianism – many combatants are victims of the conflict in addition to being perpetrators of violence;
- compensatory justice – soldiers have done their duty and expect compensation because of
- their potential contribution – ex-combatants can be a major force in rebuilding war-torn societies; and
- they are potential 'spoilers' who can jeopardize the peace process or engage in criminal activities which threaten economic and democratic stability.

There is a general consensus that DDR improves the prospect of democracy and improved economic performance in post-conflict societies (Humphreys & Weinstein, 2007). As mentioned, the DDR processes can be a highly visible piece of this peacebuilding jigsaw (Knight & Ozerdem, 2004). Indeed, Berdal (1996) views the relationship between DDR and peacebuilding as symbiotic, or in other words, one can not be fully achieved without the other.

However, not all DDR programmes are identical and some have been much more successful than others. One measure of success commonly used is simply to count the numbers of combatants successfully demobilized. For example, the largest demobilization was of 509,200 Ethiopian combatants (Kingma, 2000), but there is a need to look beyond the numbers to explore the success of the reintegration of combatants into civilian society and this becomes much more difficult, particularly when researchers try to understand the micro or individual level determinants of successful demobilization and reintegration (see Humphreys & Weinstein, 2007 for an illustration of this complexity). The main problem is trying to see the wood for the trees in that DDR programmes are one aspect of various local, regional, national and international peace-building and post-conflict recovery processes taking place simultaneously that are managed and delivered by a plethora of agencies and individuals. So while the consensus is that these processes are fundamental to building peace, increasing security and assisting in economic post-conflict recovery (Doyle & Sambanis, 2000), their complex nature makes it difficult to distinguish which strategy or intervention makes which specific beneficial contribution (Humphreys & Weinstein, 2007).

One avenue which may offer some assistance in understanding which aspects are vital and which are superfluous is to analyse various approaches to DDR by exploring case studies from different conflicts in different regions. Kabia (this volume) and McGarry (this volume) in conjunction with this chapter offer three different approaches to the issue of DDR that illustrate the experiences from Africa and Europe, from failed states and within mature democracies. The case of DDR in Northern Ireland is unique in terms of traditional DDR and does not fit cleanly with the multidimensional UN peacekeeping operations which have taken place in Africa or Central America.

The "Troubles" in Northern Ireland (as the political violence in the North of the island of Ireland is colloquially and euphemistically known) began just over 40 years ago when a banned march of approximately 400 people on 5 October 1968 to demand electoral, employment and housing reform were confronted by the Royal Ulster Constabulary (RUC) who blocked their route at Duke Street in Londonderry and baton-charged the demonstrators. This event proved to be the point when Northern Ireland crossed its Rubicon, and began a destructive spiral to near civil war in the following years (Purdie, 1990).

The resulting period of political violence led to the deaths of over 3600 people and the injury of an additional 40–50,000, but given the small population of 1.68 million and the small geographical area of 5,456 square miles this conflict had a substantial impact on the population (Fay, Morrissey & Smyth, 1998). The low-intensity conflict involved three sides:

- the British Army, the RUC and the local militia (Ulster Defence Regiment (UDR), later merged into the Royal Irish Regiment (RIR));

- the Irish Republican Army (IRA) and other smaller Republican armed groups; and
- pro-British Loyalist paramilitary groups such as the Ulster Volunteer Force (UVF) and Ulster Defence Association (UDA).

However, most of the casualties of this three-way conflict were uninvolved civilians (Mac Ginty, Muldoon & Ferguson, 2007).

The Troubles are widely perceived as a primordial ethnic or religious conflict between Protestants and Catholics; however, these religious labels are used as badges of convenience in what is effectively a political struggle between those who wish to see Northern Ireland remain within the United Kingdom and those who desire a reunification of the island of Ireland (Darby, 1983). The majority of Unionists who wish to remain within the UK are also Protestants, while the majority of Nationalists who desire to reunify Ireland are Catholic, so the religious labels reflect these political aspirations, but are by no means exclusive, with as many as 28% of Catholics holding pro-union attitudes (see Darby, 1997; Leach & Williams, 1999).

The political violence in Northern Ireland continued for decades without either side gaining any clear advantage or achieving military domination of the others. Then during the early 1990s secret dialogue between the British and Irish Governments and the IRA began to lay the foundations for a peace process, the IRA and Loyalist ceasefires in 1994 built on these foundations, Bill Clinton's visit to and interest in Northern Ireland, coupled with the election of Tony Blair's Labour Party in 1997 energized the stalling peace process and in 1998 after protracted negotiations chaired by Senator George Mitchell the Belfast (or Good Friday) Agreement (Agreement, 1998) was reached and accepted by a large majority in an all-Ireland referendum.

While the agreement had international elements, with the involvement of the United States administration and President Bill Clinton and some input from the EU in terms of finance for post-agreement peace-building, there was no role for the UN or World Bank, so international involvement was limited in comparison with most multidimensional peace-building programmes, although much of the Agreement was modelled on the peace process which took place earlier in South Africa (Mac Ginty & Darby, 2002).

The Belfast Agreement made provision for the release of prisoners who were part of paramilitary groups on ceasefire within two years of the ratification of the Agreement. There was to be the 'normalization' of security arrangements, which included the removal of military bases and installations and a reduction in troop numbers to garrisoned peacetime levels, in addition to the reform of the militarized police force and the removal of emergency powers legislation. The Agreement also acknowledged that the decommissioning of all paramilitary weapons was an "indispensable" (1998: 20) part of peace-building; the Independent International Commission on Decommissioning (IICD), staffed by international observers, indicated that all illegal armed groups should aim to achieve decommissioning of their weapons within two years.

Decommissioning and Demobilization in Northern Ireland

While the Agreement included provision for decommissioning, security normalization and the release of politically motivated prisoners, it did not include a detailed strategy or plan for these processes to reach completion. The first step in this process saw the early release of prisoners within two years of their group's officially recognized ceasefire; this process led to the eventual release of 452 prisoners; of these 197 were Loyalist, 242 Republican and 13 non-aligned (Northern Ireland Prison Service, 2010). It must be remembered that this final release of prisoners is only a small proportion of the 15,000 Republican and 12,000 Loyalists who were imprisoned throughout the Troubles (Conflict Transformation Papers, 2003). To help alleviate fears in the general public about the mass release of former combatants, the prisoners were released under licence, which meant they could be returned to prison if they (a) supported an organization not on ceasefire, (b) became involved in the commission, preparation or instigation of acts of terrorism or (c) became a danger to the public (Shirlow & McEvoy, 2008). Since the early release of prisoners only 23 have had their licence suspended and been returned to prison, and of these 23, only 10 had been returned for involvement in terrorist offences (Northern Ireland Prison Service, 2010). This recidivism rate of 5% is surprisingly low, considering that the normal recidivism rate for Northern Irish prisoners is 48% (Shirlow & McEvoy, 2008).

However, the timely release of political prisoners was not matched by the decommissioning of paramilitary weapons. This mismatch between the complete release of combatants and lack of verifiable paramilitary disarmament posed a series of political problems for both the British and Irish Governments and the local political parties which led to the delay in establishing the Northern Ireland Executive and a working cross-party devolved Assembly; then when the governing institutions were established the lack of process on IRA decommissioning bought about the suspension of the Assembly on three occasions, in 2000 and 2001, while alleged

IRA spying activity at Stormont led to the collapse of the Assembly from 2002 till 2007. The complete decommissioning of paramilitary groups on ceasefire was not reached until 2010, with the mainstream Provisional IRA "fully" disarming[1] in 2005, the UVF in 2009 and UDA in 2010.

These acts of decommissioning were paralleled by military normalization which saw the British Army dismantle military installations in reaction to IRA decommissioning, while reducing troop numbers to garrisoned peacetime levels in addition to disbanding the local RIR home battalions, reforming the police force and either removing the intelligence gathering services from Northern Ireland or taking them out of the control of the local police constabulary.

Reinsertion and Reintegration

The reintegration of ex-prisoners was formally written into the Belfast Agreement (Agreement, 1998: 25) which stated that

> The Governments continue to recognise the importance of measures to facilitate the reintegration of prisoners into the community by providing support both prior to and after release, including assistance directed towards availing of employment opportunities, re-training and/or re-skilling, and further education.

However, the reintegration of prisoners has been highly divisive in Northern Ireland. For former prisoners who are returning to their communities and joining the thousands of other former prisoners in their communities the idea that they need to be reintegrated to communities which they went to prison to defend is absurd, while for their many victims the idea that they would be rewarded for their violence was abhorrent (Shirlow & McEvoy, 2008). In reality the depth of governmental assistance in the reintegration of former combatants has been very shallow: there was no strategic or comprehensive programme of reintegration. Instead, the funding of prisoner reintegration came from the European Union and the Community Foundation for Northern Ireland (CFNI, previously titled Northern Ireland Voluntary Trust), a local NGO. Between 1995 and 2003 the CFNI distributed £9.2 million in EU funding to ex-prisoner groups, which was about 0.9% of the total Peace I and II monies (Rolston, 2007; Shirlow & McEvoy, 2008).

The individual reintegration projects were managed by groups which broadly represented the paramilitary groupings the former combatants belonged to. Coiste na n-Iarchimí was the umbrella group (*coiste* is the Irish word for umbrella) for former Provisional IRA prisoners, EPIC served former UVF and Red Hand Commando (RHC) prisoners, UDA and Ulster Freedom Fighters (UFF) used Prisoners Aid, An Eochair works with Official IRA prisoners, Expac works mainly with Republican prisoners based in the Republic of Ireland and Teach na Failte services Irish National Liberation Army (INLA) former prisoners. The reintegration projects were diverse and included counselling and training for former prisoners, self help initiatives, advocacy work, restorative justice projects, youth and community work, community capacity building, conflict transformation initiatives, dispute resolution at community interfaces, not-for-profit employment etc (see McEvoy & Mika, 2002; Shirlow & McEvoy, 2008).

In contrast with these developments the groups which service these paramilitary prisoners feel that the civic and political elite are antagonistic to the former prisoner community, ex-prisoners are discriminated against in the labour market and face legislative barriers which curb their full rights as UK citizens (Conflict Transformation Papers, 2003). Ex-prisoners face barriers in terms of ineligibility for employment in many sectors of employment, restrictions on international travel, problems securing bank loans and access to Public Service Vehicle (PSV) licences; they are ineligible to adopt or foster children and have restricted pension entitlements.

In addition to facing discriminative legislation the former political prisoners face both similar and unique problems with resettlement as those experienced among other long term prison populations (Jamieson & Grounds, 2002; Shirlow & McEvoy, 2008; Spence 2002). These experiences include estrangement from their families and friends, emotional stress for both the ex-prisoner and their family with the readjustment of the absent father returning to the family, readjustment to the world they now find themselves in which is culturally, technologically and physically different from the one they left behind, the sadness and guilt of leaving their friends and comrades behind on release, feeling isolated and alien in the community they had fought to protect, difficulties managing the practical day-to-day realities of living outside prison (e.g. household budgets, bank accounts, mortgages), finding and keeping meaningful work, personal safety issues with working outside their local community area, difficulty establishing new relationships, lack of skills (or skills and qualifications no longer valid in the labour market) and psychological problems such as anxiety, PTSD, depression, alcohol misuse – these psychological problems are in turn reinforced by the macho culture of being a combatant which hinders many from seeking treatment, for fear of appearing weak (see Ferguson et al., 2010).

These problems contribute to high unemployment rates amongst ex-prisoners, and a reliance on employment in the informal low paid cash-in-hand economy. For example, Shirlow and McEvoy (2008) surveyed both Republican and Loyalist ex-prisoners and found the rate of unemployment to be 40% for Republican and 29.3% for Loyalist ex-prisoners sampled from an area of Belfast with an average rate of unemployment running at 14%. These figures clearly indicate the overrepresentation of ex-political prisoners among the unemployed and the disadvantage their convictions and incarceration have on successful reintegration.

Role in the Maintenance and Transformation of Conflict

As mentioned previously only 10 prisoners on the early release scheme have been re-imprisoned for involvement in terrorist offences; however, that does not mean that the armed groups which these prisoners belonged to have followed a purely peaceful path from the ceasefires in the mid 1990s or the signing of the Belfast Agreement in 1998 until the paramilitary organizations finally disarmed. For example, mainstream Republicans linked to the Provisional IRA have been linked to nine murders since they resumed their ceasefire in 1997, Loyalist groups have killed 79 people since they went on ceasefire in 1994, mainly due to inter-faction feuding, and other Republican groups have been responsible for the murder of 58 people since the Belfast Agreement (this includes the 36 people killed in the Omagh bomb in 1998 (see Sutton, 2010)). These figures demonstrate that the conflict in Northern Ireland did not end when the ink dried on the Belfast Agreement, but they do indicate a significant reduction in the level of political violence in the last decade (83 people killed in the last 10 years were due to the conflict, while 530 were killed in the 10 years previous to 1999). So while some of the supposedly former combatants have been and are still engaged in political violence with the threat from dissident Republican groups currently at its highest level since the Omagh bombing in 1998 (BBC, 2010) the conflict is not as intense or widespread as it has been and the general population are much more positive about the future of Northern Ireland. For example, 65% of people surveyed in 2008 believed that relations between Catholics and Protestants were better now than they were five years ago and 59% believe that relations between the two communities will improve further in the future (Northern Ireland Life and Times, 2010).

However, behind these negative headline-grabbing figures many ex-prisoners are involved in positive conflict transformation initiatives which are actively improving the prospects of peace and improving community cohesion and capacity in Northern Ireland (for an evaluation of projects see Mika, 2006). These projects are diverse, from involvement in truth recovery and story-telling, co-ordinating restorative justice programmes, setting up mobile phone contacts to diffuse interface tension, developing sports and community activities, promoting racial tolerance, etc. These projects have helped transform grass roots attitudes towards violence, build bridges between and within the communities and with governmental structures and assisted in community development (Rolston, 2007; Shirlow & McEvoy, 2008). While having former combatants actively working in conflict transformation seems counterintuitive, their "macho" and violent past offers them a certain credibility when they are encouraging others to turn their back on violence, that can be lacking in someone who has never experienced or engaged in violence firsthand. It could also be argued that the former combatants are more active in peacebuilding than the middle class moderate politicians who advocate peace at the elite level – a position well articulated by a former UVF prisoner we[2] interviewed in 2003:

> Had we waited for politicians to create a peace process, we'd have waited for a very long time, in fact we did. The truth of the matter is the paramilitarists created the peace process – almost the reverse of the way politics is supposed to work. We bring our soldiers home, politicians bring the soldiers home. While here the soldiers got out of the trenches, some people don't recognize them as soldiers but they still got out of the trenches and the politicians said "why are you getting out of the trenches, get back in the trench", we said "fuck off".

However, even when the ex-prisoners are actively engaged in conflict transformation they still are the subject of stigmatization and distrust from other mainstream groups who are active in peacebuilding and community development, which makes their task more difficult.

Discussion and Conclusion

The DDR experience in Northern Ireland is clearly different from the other experiences illustrated in this volume and from the general experiences from Central America and Africa reported elsewhere. The first main difference is that the majority of the combatants were already integrated into the local communities and only a minority of the 27,000 political ex-prisoners were released and reinserted into the civilian population after the paramilitary ceasefires and Agreement negotiations.

The disarmament process, which was initially due to take two years, took almost 12 years to reach completion for the groups on ceasefire, and was only finally completed when the armed groups began to the face the prospect of the IICD mandate expiring on 9th February 2010. The expiration of the IICD mandate would have led to the possibility that any weapons found after this date would be subject to forensic tests and the evidence gathered could be used to seek a conviction in court, and the organizations were issued with a letter that enabled them to move weapons legally up to the deadline. The disarmament and demobilization process has not resulted in the complete cessation of paramilitary activity in Northern Ireland and Northern Ireland's peace process still faces a serious threat from dissident Republican groups. Additionally, the fixation on decommission resulted in a lack of trust between Unionists and Republicans which jeopardized and delayed the normal and prolonged functioning of the devolved Northern Irish Assembly till 2007.

In relation to reinsertion and reintegration, the promises written into the Belfast Agreement to facilitate reinsertion and assist with reintegration were never fulfilled. Instead this work was left to the creation and/or development of self-help initiatives set up by the prisoners which found support from the CFNI and finance from the EU in the shape of the Peace I, II and III funding programmes without any comprehensive or strategic approach by the British or Irish Governments to oversee ex-prisoner reintegration. The research (Jamieson & Grounds, 2002; Shirlow & McEvoy, 2008; Spence 2002) discussed earlier clearly indicates that prisoners are suffering problems which are compounded by lingering criminalization and legislative barriers which curb their full rights as UK citizens and restrict their ability to gain meaningful employment.

As the contribution of ex-combatants to peacebuilding is a key reason for engaging in DDR (Kingma, 2000) how has Northern Ireland fared in respect to this? While the headlines are captured by the resurgent Republican dissidents, behind the scenes there are many former combatants engaged in conflict transformation and community development. This activity is fundamental to improving relations between the two communities, offering alternatives to violence, and has made significant progress on conflict transformation (Shirlow & McEvoy, 2008). However, Northern Ireland remains a deeply divided society (Jarman, 2005; Mac Ginty et al., 2007) and much still needs to be done to build peace and reconciliation. The former combatants will be essential in this process because of the credibility their rejection of violence holds in both the Loyalist and Republic working class communities which still face the realities of sectarian division and inter-community hostility on a day-to-day basis.

DDR is thought to play a role in improving the economic performance of post-conflict societies (Doyle & Sambanis, 2000). While it is difficult to distinguish which particular DDR effort makes a specific economic improvement (Humphreys & Weinstein, 2007), it is clear how the economic performance of Northern Ireland has benefited from the Peace Process. There has been increased economic growth and growing employment, while long-term unemployment decreased for the decade after the Belfast Agreement. However, while the economic picture in Northern Ireland is improving, the region still lags behind the UK average (*Northern Ireland Economic Bulletin,* 2006).

While Northern Ireland provides a unique look at DDR, there are lessons that can be learned and potentially put to work in future DDR processes. The first lesson is that the proposed timeframe is likely to fracture and the process is potentially going to take decades rather than months or years to achieve. The long-term nature of this project is clearly illustrated by the nature of the EU Peace funding programmes, as these programmes have been repeatedly extended with the current programme of Peace III funding due to run until 2013, some 15 years after the Belfast Agreement.

Secondly, an retrospective examination of the Belfast Agreement demonstrates that the text of the DDR agreement may not be acted on, or in the case of much of the Belfast Agreement the text with be fudged so that the sentences will hold different meanings for different readers This ambiguity and the bad faith it generates will potentially hold up peacebuilding and derail post-conflict reconstruction. This is most clearly illustrated in the Belfast Agreement in relation to assistance for prisoner reintegration discussed earlier and in the phrasing of the requirement for paramilitary groups to disarm within two years after accepting the Belfast Agreement and to adopt purely democratic, non-violent means. The text of the Belfast Agreement (p. 8) demands that members of the Assembly "should use democratic, non-violent means" which was seen by some as "must" and by others as "ought". While the section on decommissioning (p. 20) saw decommissioning as an "indispensable part of the process" but only asked the signatories to "use any influence they have, to achieve the decommissioning of all paramilitary arms within two years" something which is much easier to claim than actually producing stocks of arms for verifiable decommissioning. These ambiguities led to a game of political cat and mouse between Unionists, Sinn Fein and the British Government which led to the collapse of the Northern Irish Assembly on a number of occasions and delayed the proper functioning of the devolved assembly for almost a decade.

Thirdly, the ex-combatants are often viewed with suspicion as spoilers or at least potential spoilers of any DDR or peace-building process, and this was most certainly true in Northern Ireland. However, while I would not seek to claim that all former combatants are engaged in conflict transformation activities, there are many diligently working within their communities, on the interfaces between the communities or directly with the other community to increase the likelihood that Northern Ireland will not return to its violent past. These activities have made a significant impact on conflict transformation in Northern Ireland (see Shirlow & McEvoy, 2008) and their importance should not be discounted or ignored.

The peace process in Northern Ireland borrowed from the peace process in South Africa and the Basque separatists in turn looked to Northern Ireland and borrowed much. These processes can not be studied in isolation, and many future peace and DDR processes will take much from all these examples and many more, in order to find a potential solution to the problems that resonate with that particular conflict. This case study and the other case studies in this volume will shed some light on these processes and hopefully assist in both the analysis of current and the development of future DDR processes.

Notes

1   Some estimate that only 60% of IRA weapons were decommissioned (*Belfast Telegraph,* 2010).
2   Mark Burgess and Ian Hollywood were also involved in this series of interviews.

References

Agreement, The: Agreement reached in multiparty negotiations. (1998). Belfast: HMSO.
BBC. 2010. 'Dissident threat level increases', http://news.bbc.co.uk/1/hi/northern_ ireland/8638255.stm, accessed 26 June 2010.
Belfast Telegraph. (2010). More IRA guns uncovered in PSNI raids. Retrieved from http://www.belfasttelegraph.co.uk/news/local-national/more-ira-weapons-uncovered-in-psni-raids-14772056.html
Berdal, M. 1996. *Disarmament and Demobilization after Civil Wars.* Adelphi Paper 303. London. IISS.
Conflict Transformation Papers. 2003. *Ex Prisoners and Conflict Transformation.* Belfast. Regency.

Darby, J. 1997. *Scorpions in a Bottle: Conflicting Cultures in Northern Ireland.* London. Minority Rights Publications.

Darby, J. 1983. *Northern Ireland: The background to the Conflict.* Belfast. Appletree Press.

Doyle, M. W., and Sambanis, N. 2000.' International Peacekeeping: A Theoretical and Quantitative Analysis', *American Political Science Review*, 94(4): 779–801.

Fay, M. T., Morissey, M., and Smyth, M. 1998. *Northern Ireland's Troubles: The Human Costs.* London. Pluto.

Ferguson, N., et al. 2010. 'Who are the Victims? Victimhood Experiences in Post Agreement Northern Ireland', *Political Psychology.*

Forman, S., and Patrick, S. 2000. 'Introduction.' In S. Forman and S. Patrick (eds), *Good Intentions: Pledges of Aid of Postconflict Recovery.* Boulder, CO. Lynne Rienner: 1–34.

Humphreys, M., and Weinstein, J. M. 2007. 'Demobilization and Reintegration', *Journal of Conflict Resolution*, 51(4): 531–567.

Jamieson R., and Grounds, A. 2002. *No Sense of an Ending: The Effects of Long-term Imprisonment amongst Republican Prisoners and their Families.* Monaghan. Seesyu.

Jarman, N. (2005). *No Longer a Problem? Sectarian Violence in Northern Ireland.* Belfast: Institute for Conflict Research.

Kingma, K. 2000. *Demobilization in Sub-Saharan Africa: The Development and Security Impacts.* Basingstoke. Macmillan.

Knight, M. 2008. 'Expanding the DDR Model: Politics and Organisations', *Journal of Security Sector Management*, 6(1): 1–18.

Knight, M., and Ozerdem, A. 2004. 'Guns, Camps and Cash: Disarmament, Demobilization and Reinsertion of Former Combatants in Transitions from War to Peace', *Journal of Peace Research*, 41(4): 499–516.

Leach, C. W., and Williams, W. 1999. 'Group identity and conflicting expectations of the future in Northern Ireland', *Political Psychology*, 20(4): 875–897.

McEvoy, K., and Mika, H. 2002. 'Restorative justice and the critique of informalism in Northern Ireland', *British Journal of Criminology*, 43(3): 534–563.

Mac Ginty, R., and Darby, J. 2002. *Guns and Government: The Management of the Northern Ireland Peace Process.* Basingstoke. Palgrave.

Mac Ginty, R., Muldoon, O., and Ferguson, N. 2007. 'No war, no peace: Northern Ireland after the Agreement', *Political Psychology*, 28(1): 1–12.

Mika, H. 2006. *Community Based Restorative Justice in Northern Ireland: An Evaluation.* Belfast. Queens University of Belfast Institute of Criminology and Criminal Justice.

Northern Ireland Economic Bulletin. 2006. Belfast. DETI.

Northern Ireland Life and Times. (2010). Northern Ireland Life and Times Survey 2008. Retrieved from http://www.ark.ac.uk/nilt/2008/

Northern Ireland Prison Service. 2010. *Early Releases: Accelerated Release Scheme. http://www.niprisonservice.gov.uk/index.cfm/area/information/page/earlyrelease* – accessed 27 June 2010.

Purdie, B. 1990. *Politics in the Streets.* Belfast. Blackstaff Press.

Rolston, B. 2007. 'Demobilization and reintegration of ex-combatants: The Irish case in international perspective', *Social and Legal Studies*, 16(2): 259–280.

Shirlow, P., and McEvoy, K. 2008. *Beyond the Wire: Former Prisoners and Conflict Transformation in Northern Ireland.* London. Pluto.

Spence, L. 2002. *Unheard Voices: The Experience and Needs of the Children of Loyalist Political Ex-Prisoners.* Belfast. Epic.

Sutton, M. 2010. *An Index of Deaths from the Conflict in Ireland.* http://www.cain.ulst.ac.uk/sutton/chron/index.html – accessed 26 June 2010.

UN DDR Resource Centre. 2010. *Integrated Disarmament, Demobilization and Reintegration Standards,* www.unddr.org/iddrs/01/download/IDDRS_110.pdf – accessed 18 June 2010.

CHAPTER TEN

ACCEPT IT AND FORGET IT: DEMOBILIZATION,
REINTEGRATION AND THE MILITARY HOMECOMER

ROSS MCGARRY

The homecomer is not the same man who left. He is neither the same for
himself nor for those who await his return. (Schuetz, 1945: 375)

Introduction

This chapter discusses the British soldier in the context of the United Nations
Integrated Disarmament, Demobilization and Reintegration Strategy. By
first highlighting the unchanged experiences of a British military homecomer of war, this chapter highlights a requirement for the demobilization and
reintegration of British veterans within a post-military society following an
often abrupt process of disarmament from the British armed forces. Using
input and extracts from interviews with several British veterans (A, B, C,
D) who served in Iraq, some experiences and consequences of conflict are
proposed followed by a synopsis of the services available to British military
personnel. This is then contrasted with some of the difficulties British veterans face upon leaving the armed forces, showing that what is available is
inadequate to cater for the experiences of the homecomer.

New war, Old Problem

Service personnel have been returning from war and conflict for centuries.
Campaigns have ranged from the resistance of the home front against invading Nazi Germany to the global protection from the amorphous danger of
Al Qaeda, set against differing political, social and economic backdrops.
Throughout the centuries at the tip of such national and international defence has been the soldier. Having been encouraged to bond, train and fight
collectively, each soldier must return to civilian life as autonomous as he
once left it.

During the inter-war period following the Great War, British soldiers returned home to a variety of both success and failure. Some returned to middle class employment with family business; others faced unemployment and destitution (McCartney, 2005). Many families faced the return of a man physically or mentally ravaged by war; while others had to adjust to the emotional and economic hardships from the loss of a husband, father and breadwinner (Barker, 1992; McCartney, 2005). Following the end of World War Two those demobilized from service faced similar hardships upon returning to their civilian lives. Families and soldiers faced with trepidation their reunion after leading separate lives during the war effort, and public interest in British veterans began to wane due to the prolonged process of their homecoming (Allport, 2009). Again, many soldiers bore the physical and psychological scars of war; some employers worried about recruiting soldiers who would perhaps be too institutionalized to think independently, and many veterans found their military experience incompatible with civilian work (Allport, 2009). During this period Schuetz (1945), focussing on US soldiers returning home from World War Two, wrote of the "home-comers", those who departed from their locality for extended periods and returned to find once familiar surroundings changed in their absence. The demobilized homecomer returns to a civilian world without the guidance of authority; he is stripped of the status afforded him by uniform and rank, and has to adapt to an environment that fails to recognize military nuances and is often without the need for the skills and abilities which armed service has furnished him with (Schuetz, 1945). This context of the military veteran as homecomer is one which still perhaps resonates in the setting of modern conflicts.

The terrorist attacks in New York on 11th September 2001 (9/11) signified the first large scale threat to US homeland security since World War Two; its consequences were felt globally (Martin, 2003). The "War on Terrorism" was described as the "first war of the twenty-first century" (Bush, 2003, cited in Spence, 2003: 284) and some Western nations sanctioned military action in Afghanistan 26 days later (Lumley & Templeton, 2002). Now, in a world committed to a long and sanguinary battle in the War on Terrorism, British soldiers have once again begun leaving their lives and families behind to fight, and die, in Afghanistan and Iraq. Since 2001 the UK has committed British forces to these conflicts in long periods of overseas service, asking much of them mentally and physically. Upon their initial homecoming the British military remains their carer with a responsibility to support and cater for those affected by their experiences. However, once discharged from the bosom of the armed forces British veterans fall into the arms of an unfamiliar civilian world more detached from the realities of their conflicts. Although the wars may have changed, the demobilized homecomer has not.

The War on Terrorism and Post-military Society

Following conflicts in recent decades, international parties such as the United Nations have become involved in the reconstruction of countries affected by war (Rolston, 2007). A compulsory element of such intervention and peacekeeping efforts is the implementation and promotion of disarmament, demobilization and reintegration (DDR), developed in 2005 into a set of integrated DDR standards (IDDRS) (United Nations, 2006). A precursor to the implementation of IDDRS is the brokering of a ceasefire and signing of a peace agreement by warring factions (United Nations, 2006). Following this the IDDRS sets out a framework for the seizure, control and disposal of weapons (disarmament), followed by the regulated discharge of combatants from armed service (demobilization) and the long process of supporting ex-combatants back into productive civilian lives (reintegration) (United Nations, 2006). Within recent UK history, Northern Ireland has undergone a process of post-conflict DDR following the signing of the 1998 Belfast Agreement, achieved without UN involvement (Rolston, 2007). The British armed forces were involved throughout the Northern Ireland conflict and many conflicts since, including the Gulf, Bosnia, Kosovo, Afghanistan and Iraq. However, although DDR may have featured alongside UN intervention in an attempt to maintain peace and disband warring factions, little consideration has been given to the requirement of a DDR process for British soldiers serving in these recent conflicts.

Technological advances in communication and warfare are employed by nations to implement socio-military strategies to protect their citizens (Castells, 2000). Within this context the War on Terrorism can perhaps be assimilated with Castells' (2000: 484) concept of "instant wars" – military strategies using professional armies to move quickly and precisely to defeat an enemy with minimal destruction; keeping much of the devastation hidden from public view by presenting them as superficial victories (Castells, 2000). This specific approach to the conflicts in Afghanistan and Iraq has perhaps not kept the conflicts from public view nor successfully minimized the destruction of either country's infrastructure. However, Shaw (1991) suggests that modern conflict such as "instant wars", based on technological advances, has perhaps contributed to the demilitarization of certain Western democratic societies by putting a distance between war-fighting and the public. In doing so, the pre-war preparations and the rise of militarism witnessed in the build-up and durations of the World Wars, in addition to the more recent conflict in Northern Ireland, have not been necessary in contemporary society during the War on Terrorism.

Despite the violence experienced by Western nations through international terrorist activity there has been little requirement for a rise in militarism in nations such as the UK against mobilized armed forces. Instead, asymmetric warfare, such as the London bombings on 7th July 2005 (7/7), has led to a rise in self governance and vigilance within a political climate of fear (Black, 2005; Furedi, 2005). However, despite the War on Terrorism continuing in Afghanistan, the UK is perhaps best seen as a post-military society in which members of the British armed forces return following an unceremonious disarmament from combatant to civilian (Shaw, 1991). The discharge from service of members of the British armed forces involves them relinquishing all equipment and uniform as a matter of course, and any ammunition and weaponry will have been long since returned to the safe confines of a station armoury. What is left is a continuing global war against terrorism being fought in Afghanistan, from which scores of British veterans are returning to a post-military environment in need of post-conflict demobilization and reintegration.

The Consequences of Conflict: Catering for British Troops

For British service personnel who have served in Iraq and Afghanistan, the reality of witnessing traumatic incidents and having to engage and kill the enemy is no longer an abstract prospect. The morally binding agreement of the British Military Covenant states:

> Every soldier is a weapon bearer, so all must be prepared personally to make the decision to engage an enemy or to place themselves in harm's way. All British soldiers share the legal right and duty to fight and if necessary kill, according to their orders, and an unlimited liability to give their lives doing so. This is the unique nature of soldiering. (Ministry of Defence, 2005: chap. 1, para. 0101)

And within the context of this "unique nature of soldiering", before continuing to discuss demobilization and reintegration, it is first worth encountering some of the experiences British soldiers have had to face during these recent conflicts, highlighting some potential consequences of conflict and identifying the support structures available to British military personnel during their service.

During an incident in the early months following the invasion of Iraq, participant B attended the scene of an aftermath of rising insurgent violence. Arriving at a smouldering vehicle he initially had difficulty identifying the burnt remains of an Iraqi father and his young son who had been executed – disembowelled and lobotomized by gun shot wounds. Such scenes are described as "like something out of a horror film" and serve as examples of the brutality which was witnessed by 27% of British soldiers during the conflict in Iraq (Hotopf et al., 2006). Additionally, participant D recounts an occasion when he witnessed a young British soldier shot and killed; he knew the young man was dead by his "empty" eyes and by a fellow soldier's urgent screams for a "medic". Such experiences are reported to have been witnessed by 45% of British soldiers in Iraq: over 400 British military deaths have been witnessed by British soldiers in Afghanistan and Iraq since 2001 (Hotopf et al., 2006). Such experiences may produce psychological harm (ibid.). Iverson and Greenberg (2009) assert that Post-Traumatic Stress Disorder (PTSD) is a less common psychological consequence of British soldier's experiences than depression, alcohol misuse and anxiety, but Corbet and Blatchley (2007) state that although the population of British soldiers at risk from PTSD is small, those deployed in Afghanistan and Iraq are at a significantly higher risk[1] of PTSD than other soldiers; a noteworthy observation given that "the person does not have to be threatened, or be harmed themselves, to develop the disorder [PTSD]; witnessing such circumstances is enough" (Wilson, 2007: 4). If witnessing stressful or traumatic events can be enough to cause the onset of PTSD, then it is reasonable to suggest that soldiers who have served in violent conflicts may have the potential for to be psychologically harmed through what they have witnessed and experienced.

As British soldiers in conflict Participants B and D participated in combat by fulfilling "the consummation of their training" through engaging with enemy soldiers (Keegan & Holmes, 1985: 261). Participant B rationalizes his role as a soldier by electing to kill only those who "deserved to be killed" and "limiting his actions" in line with the rules of engagement. This justification of killing may also be linked to the psychological harm of Perpetration-Induced Traumatic Stress (PITS), deriving from symptoms of PTSD and induced by the "causal participation" of an individual's actions (MacNair, 2005). Here it may be suggested that a soldier who elects to kill during conflict becomes a causal participant, and some psychological harm suffered by soldiers post conflict could emanate from electing to kill the enemy. However, despite much attention acknowledging psychological harm as the main consequence suffered by British soldiers during recent conflicts, it is also important to recognize the potential physical harm that they may encounter. An example of this occurred during participant D's second tour of Iraq. Whilst attending the scene of an incident, participant D was shot in the face by a sniper, severely wounding him and leaving him with lifelong visual impairment. He is one of over 500 seriously injured service personnel to sustain a severe injury whilst serving in the British military in Afghanistan and Iraq; many of whom suffer from a range of life changing injuries from facial and bodily scarring to multiple amputations (Defence Analytical Services Agency, 2009 & 2010).

Nevertheless, it would be incorrect to suggest that the Ministry of Defence does not take the mental and physical health of its service personnel seriously. The Defence Medical Service (2007: 6) states that its aims are threefold: to ensure that, "every Serviceman and woman enjoys a level of health that is appropriate for the tasks they are required to perform by the Chain of Command", by providing "a Medical Service that maximises the potential of our people through the provision of excellent health services for the defence population at risk" in order to "maximise the numbers of Servicemen and women who are medically fit for their operational task". Whilst serving in the UK, members of the British armed forces are provided with a range of primary health care in medical centres on most UK military bases, in addition to access to a variety of secondary medical care,[2] rehabilitation[3] and mental health assistance[4] (Select Committee on Defence, 2008; House of Commons Defence Committee, 2008). This level of both physical[5] and psychological[6] health care is also extended to overseas combat operations in Iraq and Afghanistan catering for over 7000 Field Hospital Admissions and over 5000 medical evacuations (Select Committee on Defence, 2008; House of Commons Defence Committee, 2008; Defence Analytical Services Agency 2009 & 2010).

This commitment by the Defence Medical Service (2007) has been scrutinized by the government and is a pledge taken seriously by the British military; however, returning to the concept of DDR, it is worth drawing parallels between the services available to serving military personnel and the experiences of British veterans once they leave the armed forces.

British Veterans: Fallout and Barriers to Care

There is little doubt that British service personnel who are affected by their military experiences in conflict have adequate support structures available to them during service. However, focussing on post-service experiences a critical point to note is that "central to DDR is the demobilization/reintegration aspect, returning combatants ... to productive civilian life" (Rolston, 2007: 260). Despite the British state pledging "justice, fair rewards, and life-long support to all who have soldiered", it can be suggested that this promise – relative to a process of demobilization and reintegration – has not been fulfilled (Ministry of Defence, 2005, chap. 3, para. 0311). It is here that this chapter gains its key significance in looking at some of the UN guidance on demobilization and reintegration and comparing it with some experiences of British veterans of Afghanistan and Iraq upon returning to civilian life.

Psychological Costs

The United Nations (2006) IDDRS states that pre-discharge awareness should be made available to combatants to inform them of challenges that they may face in the transition from military to civilian life, including access to available services. In terms of gaining healthcare upon discharge from the British armed forces "when personnel leave military service their healthcare becomes the responsibility of the NHS" (Select Committee on Defence, 2008, paragraph 54). As of 2008 the Department of Health for England announced that priority NHS would be granted to all veterans of the British armed forces if their mental or physical injury is deemed to be caused by military service (Veterans UK, 2008). A dedicated Medical Assessment Programme (MAP) is available for British veterans who have served on military operations since 1982, including recent veterans who served during Afghanistan and Iraq, in addition to a Community Based Mental Health Service pilot for Veterans[7] being run in conjunction with the NHS, Health Departments and ex-services mental health society Combat Stress (Veterans UK, 2008).

Research by Iversen et al. (2005) does perhaps indicate that this level of care is necessary for demobilized British veterans as they found that 43.8%[8] of "vulnerable" armed service leavers had a psychiatric diagnosis, the most common disorder being on the depressive spectrum. In addition, many were found to suffer from anxiety disorders, PTSD and probable alcohol dependence, indicating correlations with research by Jones et al. (2006) who found that PTSD cases also had a diagnosis of probable alcohol dependence (Iversen et al., 2005; Jones et al., 2006). However, although such research does shed some light on the mental health issues faced by British veterans, Iversen et al. (2005) suggest there is still little detail known about it.

One key implication emerging from this research is the reluctance of British veterans to seek help either during or after their service, largely because of military culture being based on machismo, resilience and military personnel believing they should deal with their own issues without support (Iversen et al., 2005). These points are reiterated by both Greenberg, Langston & Jones (2008) and participants B and D who comment on the attitude of help seeking derived from the British military,

> after the event, if you said yes to anything . . . it's not an impression that was created by the military but if you said "yes I've got a problem" to anything, you possibly might not be getting on the . . . plane and going home . . . you just wouldn't out of self preservation approach, you just would not answer . . . "yes", not a chance.

> Accept it and forget it. There, there was time to grieve and time to think about it later on, that wasn't the time . . . there was too many other things to think about . . . you don't think about it then, you think about it later, and I think that's probably one of the post traumatic stress things.

However, in tandem with this reluctance to seek help is the growing demand for support from organizations such as the ex-service mental welfare charity Combat Stress[9] who have seen a 66% increase in new referrals since 2005 (Combat Stress, 2009a). The majority of British veterans currently being treated by Combat Stress are those who served in the Northern Ireland[10] conflict, with relatively low numbers of British veterans from Afghanistan[11] and Iraq.[12] However, it is reported that it takes a British veteran an average of 14 years to seek help with Combat Stress from the time they are discharged from the British military, demonstrating widespread reluctance within vulnerable sections of the veteran community to seek help (Combat Stress, 2009b). Suicide is one of the most serious consequences of this, say Iversen et al. (2005). They highlight data from the Defence Analytical Service Agency which indicated that young male members of the Army have higher rates of suicide than their civilian counterparts (Fear & Williamson, 2003). The continued existence of this issue is perhaps evidenced in relation to the conflicts in Afghanistan and Iraq by Combat Stress reporting a 26% rise in its case loads since 2003, to increasing cases of homelessness in ex-soldiers and 17 confirmed suicides (cited in Judd, Goodchild & Johnson, 2007). In addition, research by Kapur et al. (2009) has shown that young male British veterans who are discharged from the British armed forces are at an increased risk from suicide (although it is acknowledged that this could be due to vulnerabilities acquired prior to service).

Therefore, despite the availability of priority NHS treatment to British veterans Iversen et al. (2005) have stated that the healthcare system in the UK is not meeting the needs of those ex-members of the British military who require treatment and help for their mental illnesses. They have encouraged the British armed forces to develop a culture that combines resilience with an acceptance that help may be sought if needed by its personnel, in addition to faster access to the requisite health care for British military veterans (Iversen et al., 2005).. However, Sareen and Belik (2009) suggest that that preventative strategies in reducing veteran suicides should include pre-demobilization preparation and screening for British service leavers. Therefore it is worth considering if British veterans would benefit from elements of the IDDRS identifying reintegration needs prior to demobilization, making important links between government authorities (e.g. the NHS) and communities (e.g. Combat Stress) to assist veterans' transition from the military to the civilian world, reducing the stigma and reluctance to seek help (United Nations, 2006).

Social Costs

Despite these problems, Gee (2007) states that the majority of British ex-service personnel lead successful civilian lives following their service. This is the case for participants A and B who used their military skills and capabilities to find work in a civilian sector where they can make good use of them, and participants C and D successfully used their resettlement opportunities to retrain for different civilian occupations from those which they had during their service. However, Sareen and Belik (2009) indicate that veterans who are disenfranchised from society are less likely to make efforts to seek help and take up the opportunities available to them. With this perspective, the social and economic aspects of "comprehensive reintegration" become essential in forming part of the demobilization process in the IDDRS (United Nations, 2006, sec. 2.10, p. 6). As with demobilized homecomers of the two World Wars, veterans often lack qualifications, and the skills and abilities they do have are not always transferable to civilian

life (Rolston, 2007). Gee (2007: 1), in a discussion on early restricted economic life choices of veterans prior to service, aligns this with consequent
"social and economic disadvantages after discharge" from the British military. These points are reiterated by participant C who says that

> after being medically discharged … I felt pretty much unemployable … that
> my experiences and … lack of qualifications were a hindrance to any future
> employment, combined with the now physical requirements that I have, so I
> didn't even look for work.

Although efforts are made within the British military to offer resettlement courses to assist with the transition back into civilian life there
is an impression that this is lacking in coherence and suitability. To this
end the IDDRS highlights the importance of retraining and re-educating
combatants; without it, veterans may face circumstances leading them to
such extremes as homelessness or crime – and during times of recession
crime is said to increase (Johnsen, Jones & Rugg, 2008; Rolston, 2007;
Croall, 1998). Evidence of this is presented by research from Napo (2009)
who found that 12,000 British veterans were under the supervision of the
Probation Service and 8,500 ex-service personnel were in custody with a
criminal conviction (Napo, 2008; Ministry of Defence, 2010). In addition
Napo (2009) noted that most of the soldiers within their case studies were
suffering from PTSD or depression, which is consistent with research from
Iversen & Greenberg (2009) who found that many veterans are discharged
from the British military with serious mental health problems. Within their
recommendations they state that if there was a support outlet available to
British service personnel upon demobilization then alcohol, drug and criminal related issues could perhaps be largely avoided (Napo, 2009). Again,
this point adds credibility to suggestions of applying a DDR process in the
transition of British veterans from civilian to military life; one which is at
present devoid of any form of inspectorate within the armed forces to moni-
tor British veterans demobilized from armed service (Napo, 2009).

Discussion

Some of the issues discussed have been addressed by the Ministry of
Defence (2003b) who highlight a range of issues pertinent to veterans such
as informing ex-members of the armed forces about the services available
to them as civilians and reporting any problems that arise for veterans as a

result of their service in the British armed forces. This strategy is set to be updated every two years with improvements to the information made available to current serving members of the British military about their future as veterans and to ensure current veterans feel that they are valued and their needs are being met by the British Government (Ministry of Defence, 2003a). The result of this approach can perhaps be understood within the context of the IDDRS and various studies discussed in this chapter to not only improve health care and treatment for serving members of the British armed forces, but also unite organisations in raising awareness of veterans' needs within society and highlighting the treatment and care available to them (Ministry of Defence, 2003a). However, although such efforts indicate positive steps to caring for veterans and raising their profile within public consciousness, there is still an element of distance placed between the Ministry of Defence and ex-members of the British armed forces. The *Strategy for Veterans* states:

> The primary role of the MOD is as the former employer of veterans. Its responsibilities to those leaving the Armed Forces include the provision of resettlement advice and training, and of pension and compensation benefits ... The MOD's other main role is to provide secretariat support to the Minister for Veterans with a remit to ensure a coherent and integrated policy towards veterans across Government. (Ministry of Defence, 2003a: 4)

At no point does it indicate that its responsibilities include the mental or physical health care of veterans. The Ministry of Defence undertakes research and informs the public about the needs of the veteran but leaves their actual care, treatment and welfare to the NHS and to voluntary organizations such as Combat Stress and the Royal British Legion. It can be suggested that more care and attention should be afforded to the demobilized homecomer from Afghanistan and Iraq through DDR by helping rebuild the lives of soldiers once civilians again following conflict. The IDDRS makes further recommendations about creating public awareness of the experiences of discharged ex-combatants. It also recommends issuing a discharge document to ex-combatants to record the value of their services and to inform help associations of their veteran status (United Nations, 2006). Similar strategies have been adopted in the UK with advertising campaigns such as Help for Heroes, and the recent issue of Veterans' Badges to all service leavers. However, each scheme works in isolation, resulting in a disjointed resource that continues to fail in recognizing the needs of a century of demobilized military homecomers.

Conclusion: In Their Words

Despite the decades of conflict that the UK has been involved in, from
The Great War to the War on Terrorism, one would be forgiven for assuming that strategies such as the UN's IDDR are adopted and used widely to
great effect with British military service leavers. This would be logical and
potentially valuable in the post-conflict reconstruction of British military
veterans' lives, but the adoption of such a strategy would perhaps have the
political ramification of acknowledging the UK as a failing state. It would
also no doubt be an expensive endeavour, one unlikely to be undertaken
by a government committed to reducing the funding for the British armed
forces. Once soldiers have their webbing – rather than apron strings – cut,
they return to civilian life without the predictability and routine that the
military provides, and often without the "justice, fair rewards, and life-long
support" promised in the Military Covenant "to all who have soldiered"
(Ministry of Defence, 2005, p. 5). This difficulty of demobilizing from the
British military and returning to civilian life begins the moment you become
a civilian and veteran, as participants A & B state:

> . . . it's almost like, you know, mind the door on your way out, doesn't hit
> you in the arse type thing, that was how I felt personally when I left the
> forces

> . . . what was it like? . . . it was like getting told, "cheers for your jokes, fuck
> off we don't want anything to do with you."

Despite resettlement courses being available to British military personnel in the process of their discharge, it appears that the closer you get to civilian life, the less effective the support structures from the British military
become, as participant C says:

> I also went on another resettlement course ... something to do with housing
> and how to get a council house, but I don't want a council house, why would
> I need a council house? . . . It was all just a complete waste of time, so I gave
> up on all of that ... when I came out the air force I got off my backside and
> found a load of free courses, which actually had some relevance, like tax.

This thinning of military support services in the process of demobilization
appears to be complete when finally handed back into a civilian world with
civilian services not fully prepared for military veterans, as participant D
says about his disability:

I've got me pension to come because it's medical discharge ... and then, sort of I'll just be handed over to social services and whatever disability services that I'm entitled to, I just work on them ... I'm entitled to disability living allowance ... problem is, coz of the means testing system I'm not entitled to most of the benefits that most of the sort of disability people get nowadays.

Therefore, as a concluding note to this chapter, there is perhaps a clear requirement for a process of DDR to be implemented within the British armed forces to allow for British soldiers to be demobilized gradually whilst being fully equipped to reintegrate back into a complex society of autonomous individuals. Participant A paints this age-old picture of a century of British veterans demobilizing from the armed forces:

At first, the first two months I didn't have a fucking clue what to do because you're conditioned ... to ... follow point A to point Z, through B, C, D ... I suppose being institutionalised into ... some sort of degree after, there's a certain point in your military career where you become an individual to being a number and I was just a fucking number then, you know, I was like a robot.

Notes

1 3 times at risk with a 95% confidence interval of 1.8-6.4 whereby the absence of 1.00 is considered statistically significant (Corbet & Blatchley, 2007: 16, table 4; 12, paragraph 34).
2 Including: (i) a Military Managed Ward (MMW) at the Royal Centre of Defence Medicine (RCDM) at NHS Selly Oak Hospital in Birmingham (ii) 5 Ministry of Defence Hospital Units (MDHU).
3 Including: (i) the Defence Medical Rehabilitation Centre (DMRC) at Headley Court; providing treatment for brain injuries, polytrauma and amputees (ii) 70 Primary Casualty Receiving Facilities (PCRF) (iii) 15 Regional Rehabilitation Units (RRUs) treating musculoskeletal injuries.
4 Including: (i) option of self-referral to Medical Officers (MO) or chain of command during pre-deployment medicals, during operations and post deployment (ii) 15 military Departments of Community Mental Health (DCMH) within the UK providing out-patient mental health care within military Medical Centres.
5 Including: (i) Deployed Rehabilitation Teams to treat and rehabilitate casualties in theatre (ii) Incident Response Teams (IRTs) who save lives and provide vital assessment, treatment and evacuation to hospital facilities in the UK.
6 Including: (i) Post-deployment decompression settings in Cypress and (ii) Trauma Risk Management (TRiM) training military peers and colleagues to identify symptoms of trauma (Langston, 2005; Greenberg Langston & Jones,

2008).
7   *See* http://www.veterans-uk.com/mental_health/announcements.html for more
    information.
8   138 personnel.
9   *See* http://www.combatstress.org.uk/.
10 2220 cases.
11 55 British veterans.
12 261 British veterans.

References

Allport, A. 2009. *Demobbed: Coming Home after the Second World War.* London.
    Yale University Press.
Barker, P. 1992. *Regeneration.* London. Penguin Books.
Black, C. 2005. *7–7: The London Bombings: What Went Wrong?* London. Gibson
    Square Books.
Castells, M. 2000. *The Rise of the Network Society.* 2nd ed. Oxford. Blackwell
    Publishers.
Combat Stress. 2009a. 'Combat Stress.' In: *Proceedings from a Combat Stress
    Presentation, Audley Court, March 2009.*
Combat Stress. 2009b. 'From war zone to Wythenshawe: a post traumatic jour-
    ney.' In: *Proceedings from the Combat Stress Annual Conference, Manchester,
    November 2009.*
Corbet, C. and Blatchley, N. 2007. *UK Armed Forces Psychiatric Morbidity:
    Assessment of Presenting Complaints at MOD DCMHs and Association
    with Deployment on Recent Operations in the Iraq/Afghanistan Theatres of
    Operation January-March 2007.* <http://www.dasa.mod.uk/applications/
    newWeb/www/apps/publications/pubViewFile.php?content=1320&date=2007-
    04-01&type=pdf&PublishTime=00:00:01> – accessed 28 May 2010.
Croall, H. 1998. *Crime and Society in Britain.* London. Pearson Education.
Defence Analytical Services Agency. 2009. *Op Telic Casualty and Fatality Tables:
    Number of Op Telic UK Military and Civilian Casualties 1 January 2003 to 31
    July 2009.* <http://www.mod.uk/NR/rdonlyres/7E86BD05-D4FF-4677-97AA-
    CCFBDCFE4E34/0/optelic_31jul09.pdf> - accessed 28 May 2010.
Defence Analytical Services Agency. 2010. *Op Herrick Casualty and Fatality
    Tables: Number of Op Herrick UK Military and Civilian Casualties 7
    October 2001 to 28 February 2010.* <http://www.mod.uk/DefenceInternet/
    AboutDefence/CorporatePublications/DoctrineOperationsandDiplomacyPublic
    ations/OperationsInAfghanistan/OpHerrickCasualtyAndFatalityTables.htm>
Defence Medical Services. 2007. *Defence Health Programme 2007–2011.* <http:
    //www.mod.uk/NR/rdonlyres/D22E4428-A586-4327-B885-953D8FDBDF4A/
    0/dhp20072011.pdf> – accessed 28 May 2010.
Fear, N. and Williamson, S. (2003) *Suicide and Open Verdict Deaths among
    Males in the UK Regular Armed Forces: Comparison with the UK Civilian
    Population and the US Military.* London: Defence Analytical Service Agency.
    http://www.dasa.mod.uk/applications/newWeb/www/index.php?page=48&pu

bType=2&thiscontent=1310&PublishTime=00:00:01&date=2003-07-14&dis-
Text=1984-2002&from=listing&topDate=2003-07-14 Furedi, F. 2005. *The Politics of Fear.* London. Continuum.
Gee, D. 2007. *Informed Choice? Armed Forces Recruitment Practice in the United Kingdom.* http://www.informedchoice.org.uk/informedchoice/informedchoicefull.pdf – accessed 28 May 2010.
Greenberg, N., Langston, V. and Jones, N. 2008. 'Trauma risk management (Trim) in the UK armed forces', *JR Army Med Corps,*154 (2): 124–127.
Hotopf, M., et al. 2006. 'The health of UK military personnel who deployed to the 2003 Iraq War: a cohort study', *The Lancet,* 367: 1731–1741.
House of Commons Defence Committee. 2008. *Medical Care for the Armed Forces: Seventh Report of Session 2007–08.* London. The Stationery Office Limited. http://www.parliament.the-stationery-office.com/pa/cm200708/cmselect/cmdfence/327/327.pdf – accessed 28 May 2010.
Iversen, A, C., and Greenberg, N. 2009. 'Mental health of regular and reserve military veterans', *Advances in Psychiatric Treatment,* 15: 100–106.
Iversen, A., et al. 2005. '"Goodbye and good luck": the mental health needs and treatment experiences of British ex-service personnel', *British Journal of Psychiatry,* 186: 480–486.
Johnsen, S., Jones, A., and Rugg, J. 2008. *The Experiences of Homeless Ex-Service Personnel in London.* The University of York: Centre for Housing Policy. http://www.veterans-aid.net/pdf/yorkstudy.pdf – accessed 27 May 2010.
Jones, M., et al. 2006. 'The burden of psychological symptoms in UK armed forces', *Occupational Medicine,* 56: 322–328.
Judd, T., Goodchild, S., and Johnson, A. 2007. 'Blair is called to account over abandoned troops', *The Independent,* 11th March: 2.
Kapur, N., et al. 2009. 'Suicide after leaving the UK armed forces – a cohort study,' *PLoS Medicine,* 6 (3): 0001–0009.
Keegan, J., and Holmes, R. 1985. *Soldiers: A History of Men in Battle.* London. Guild Publishing.
Langston, V. 2005. 'Putting the psychological aspects of trauma management into an organisational context: a standardised approach', *Counselling at Work.* http://www.counsellingatwork.org.uk/journal_pdf/acw_summer05_h.pdf – accessed 28 May 2010.
Lumley, T., and Templeton, T. 2002. '9/11 in numbers', *The Observer* 18 August. http://www.guardian.co.uk/world/2002/aug/18/usa.terrorism – accessed 28 May 2010.
McCartney, H. B. 2005. *Citizen Soldiers: The Liverpool Territorials in the First World War.* Cambridge. Cambridge University Press.
MacNair, R. M. 2005. *Perpetration-induced Traumatic Stress: The Psychological Consequences of Killing.* Westport, CN. Praeger.
Martin, G. 2003. *Understanding Terrorism: Challenges, Perspectives and Issues.* London. SAGE.
Ministry of Defence. (2003a) *Strategy for Veterans.* http://www.veterans-uk.com/pdfs/vets_programme/vetstrategy.pdf – accessed 28 May 2010.
Ministry of Defence. (2003b) *The Criminal Injuries Compensation (Overseas) Scheme 2003: Guidance on the exclusion of compensation payments when the injury or death is the result of war operations or military activity by warring*

factions.   http://www.mod.uk/NR/rdonlyres/8CD1C32C-D040-4352-911F-
D364AB89D2DA/0/cicowarfaction.pdf – accessed 28 May 2010.

Ministry of Defence. 2005. *Soldiering: The Military Covenant ADP Vol. 9.* Ministry
of Defence. 2010. *Defence Fact Sheet: Operations in Afghanistan: British
Forces.* http://www.mod.uk/DefenceInternet/FactSheets/OperationsFactsheets/
OperationsInAfghanistanBritishForces.htm – accessed 28 May 2010.

Napo. 2008. *Ex-Armed Forces Personnel and the Criminal Justice System.* http:
//www.napo.org.uk/templates/asset-relay.cfm?frmAssetFileID=317 – accessed
28 May 2010.

Napo. 2009. *Armed Forces and the Criminal Justice System.* http://www.napo.org.uk/
templates/asset-relay.cfm?frmAssetFileID=319 – accessed 28 May 2010.

Rolston, B. 2007. 'Demobilization and reintegration of ex-combatants: the Irish case
of international perspective', *Social & Legal Studies,* 16 (2): 259–280.

Sareen, J., and Belik, S. L. 2009. 'The need for outreach in preventing suicide in
young veterans', *PLoS Medicine,* 6 (3): 0001–0002.

Schuetz, A. 1945. 'The homecomer', *American Journal of Sociology,* 50(5):
369–375.

Select Committee on Defence. 2008. *Select Committee on Defence: Written
Evidence. Memorandum from the Ministry of Defence.* London. The Stationery
Office.   http://www.parliament.the-stationery-office.com/pa/cm200708/
cmselect/cmdfence/327/327we08.htm – accessed 27 May 2010.

Shaw, M. 1991. *Post-military Society.* Philadelphia. Temple University Press.

Spence, K. 2005. 'World risk society and war against terror', *Political Studies,* 53:
284–302.

United Nations. 2006. *Integrated Disarmament, Demobilization and Reintegration
Standards,   1st   August   2006.* http://www.unddr.org/iddrs/download/full_
iddrs.pdf

Veterans UK. 2008. *Veterans Health – extension of the scope of the Medical
Assessment   Programme   (MAP).*   http://www.veterans-uk.com/map/
announcement.html – accessed 28 May 2010.

Wilson, S. 2007. *Synopsis of Causation: Post-Traumatic Stress Disorder.* Ministry
of Defence: Service Personnel & Veterans Agency. http://www.veterans-
uk.com/pdfs/synopsis/ptsd.pdf – accessed 28 May 2010.

CONTRIBUTORS

Paul Barry works in the Management and Governance in Development Group in the Institute for Development Policy and Management (IDPM) at the University of Manchester, where he is Director of the Masters of Science programme in Management and Implementation of Development Projects. In addition to 19 years' service with the University of Manchester, he has worked extensively as a practitioner in developing countries in the education sector with a focus on education in development, working in public and private sector organizations, on national level assignments in public sector capacity building projects. He has worked in the Middle East and in Latin America in countries including Oman, Qatar, Mexico, Panama, Colombia and Ecuador. His research interests include factors affecting effectiveness of development programmes and projects, including themes relating to organizational behaviour.

Eve Binks completed her PhD in 2007 in social and political psychology, with the University of Liverpool, and is currently a Senior Lecturer in Psychology at Liverpool Hope University. Her research focuses on areas of social and political psychology, specifically on social identities, dissociative experiences as a result of exposure to politically violent events, the role of religion in coping with political violence, and the psychological impact of exposure to political violence.

Neil Ferguson (DPhil, University of Ulster, 1998) is the Director of the Desmond Tutu Centre for War and Peace and Associate Professor of Political Psychology at Liverpool Hope University. He has been a visiting lecturer to Lock Haven University of Pennsylvania and the University of York and a Research Fellow at the University of St Andrews, and lectured at the University of Ulster prior to joining Liverpool Hope University in 1996. His research and writings deal with moral development and a number of topics located within political psychology. Dr. Ferguson is currently the President of the Moral and Social Action Interdisciplinary Colloquium (MOSAIC).

Paddy Greer holds a double doctorate in Biochemistry and Educational Linguistics. He has spent most of his working life in education from primary education to college lecturer. In recent years he has been seconded as a consultant for the Council of Europe, working extensively in the field of participatory democracy in the Balkans. Paddy is now a Gestalt psychotherapist in private practice, having retired from the Dundalk Institute of Technology in the Republic of Ireland. In his spare time he enjoys the visual arts, music, languages and voluntary social work.

John M. Kabia works on the Survivors for Peace Programme at the Tim Parry Johnathan Ball Foundation for Peace in Warrington, UK. After graduating with a PhD in Peace Studies from the University of Bradford in 2006, John served as an Associate Research Fellow at the Africa Centre for Peace and Conflict Studies, University of Bradford, UK. He has written a number of books and book chapters on West African peace and security interventions, including *Humanitarian Intervention and Conflict Resolution in West Africa: From ECOMOG to ECOMIL* (Ashgate, 2009) and *UNAMSIL Peacekeeping and Peace support Operations in Sierra Leone* (with Andreau Sola-Martin, Bradford, 2007).

Ruth Leitch is senior lecturer in the School of Education, Queen's University Belfast, Northern Ireland and former head of the School (2001–2005). She is currently visiting professor at the Universities of Bergen, Norway and Alberta, Canada. Her primary areas of research interest are teacher identity, children's voice, the impact of trauma on children and young people and research methodologies associated with arts-based educational inquiry.

Ross McGarry is a final year PhD student in victimology at Liverpool Hope University's Desmond Tutu Centre for War and Peace Studies. His research, due for completion in October 2010, explores the experiences of British veterans returning from Afghanistan and Iraq in terms of harm and victimization through the use of auto/biographical research and radical victimology. Ross is also a guest lecturer in criminology at Liverpool Hope University, a seminar leader in victimology at the University of Liverpool, a Research Assistant within Greater Manchester Police and a former member of the British Armed Forces (RAF Police).

Beverly Dawn Metcalfe is Senior Lecturer/Reader in Human Resource Management and Development at the Institute for Development Policy and Management, University of Manchester. Her research interests are in global feminism, work and organizations, women's empowerment and development in Islamic states, and the role of women's organizations in contributing to conflict resolution, peace-building and the development process. She has worked with women's NGOs in Saudi Arabia, Iran and Bahrain and assisted women's empowerment development training, as well as undertaking consultancy assignments for the Bahrain Ministry of Labour and the Islamic Government of Iran on HRD and women's development. She is currently Chairwoman of the Gender Track for the *European Academy of Management*. Her book on *Leadership Development in the Middle East* will be published by Edward Elgar in 2011.

Joel Rookwood studied Football Science at undergraduate level, masters' degrees in Notation Analysis and Sport Sociology, and a PhD in Football Fandom. He is a lecturer at Liverpool Hope University, where he is leader of the Sports Development and Football Studies pathways. He has been involved in numerous practical and research-based international development programmes across six continents, and has published several related books and articles. This work has centred on social development and peace promotion, incorporating sport-based initiatives working with the underprivileged, and those who have been the victims of terrorism, disaster, conflict, poverty and persecution.

Stephan Wassong is currently a Full Professor at the German Sport University Cologne, Head of the Institute of Sport History and Academic Director of the Olympic Studies Centre. Previously he was an Associate Professor for Sport Studies at Liverpool Hope University. He gained his PhD (2001) and habilitation (2006) at the German Sport University Cologne. Prof. Wassong has been the Editor-in-Chief of the *Journal of Olympic History*, the official publication of the International Society of Olympic Historians, since 2004 and is currently a member of the IOC's Postgraduate Grant Selection Committee and Past President (2007-2009) of the European Committee for Sport History.

Frank Wood is Professor Emeritus of Neurology at Wake Forest University School of Medicine in Winston-Salem, North Carolina; Honorary Professor of Behavioural Medicine at the Nelson R. Mandela School of Medicine in Durban, South Africa; and Visiting Professor of Neuroscience and Society at Liverpool Hope University. He holds a BA with honours in the Arts and Sciences from Wake Forest University, an MA in Psychology from Wake Forest University, a Master of Divinity with Languages from Southeastern Baptist Theological Seminary, and a PhD in Natural Science Psychology from Duke University.

INDEX

Truth and Reconciliation Commission
104–5, 116
Turner, Victor 122
Tutu, Desmond 104–5

unconscious, the 126–7
unemployment, of veterans 174
United Nations
peacekeeping missions 139–40
and reconstruction 167
Security Council 146
see also Agenda for Peace; Peace
Building Commission
United Nations Development
Programme 25
United States, in Iraq and Afghanistan
13
UNMIL (United Nations Mission in
Liberia) 144–5
USSR, occupation of Afghanistan 18

vicarious traumatization 86
violence
forms 33
psychological impact 85–98
statistics of 1
see also child abuse

war 33–4
see also armed conflict
war on terrorism 166, 167–8
Weingarten, K. 85, 86–7
women
in Afghanistan 26, 28
participation in government 23–4, 28
and peacebuilding 7–29
rights 20
in Rwanda 14, 21–4, 28
World War One 166
World War Two 166

young people 34, 92, 115
see also adolescent mentality; schools

Zautra, A. J. 93
Zeidner, M. 93–4